Books are to be ret~~urned on~~
the la~~st date below~~

D0754919

More than Shakespeare, more than the invention of the railway, more than fair play, it was Empire which made Britain into Great Britain. By the early twentieth century, that Empire covered around a quarter of the earth's surface, and embraced more than a quarter of its inhabitants, a mass of over five hundred million people. From Australian sheep farmers to Kenyan nurses, all lived in an imperial world over which the Union Jack always fluttered, and on which it was commonly said the sun never set. From the pirate-ridden Atlantic and Caribbean of over four centuries ago to the success of the Falklands War, this extraordinary patchwork of territories and peoples was the creation of British ambition, ingenuity and enterprise. Underneath it all lay the enduring attempt of Great Britain to shape the world to its needs, against the odds and in circumstances which it could not always choose or control.

From its maritime origins in exploration, plunder, trade and war to the scuttling of the Raj, the Empire was always shot through with paradox. In India, the Raj was the splendour of elephant processions and the gallantry of tiger shoots, just as Africa was the glory of mission Christianity and agricultural progress. British India was also the agony of famine, massacre and labouring misery, just as Africa was also slavery and land seizures. The Empire was both a triumphal cavalcade of governors and commissioners, and a sceptical tributary of humanitarians who believed in the emancipation of colonial peoples. It was always a challenging blend of greed and morality, intervention and callous neglect, liberal virtue and high-handed autocracy. At times, it was a source of strength and prestige, at times a burden and a dilemma. Untidy, even messy, Great Britain's Empire survived on its contradictions, to go down in history as the largest and greatest European empire of the modern era.

This narrative account seeks to provide a balanced historical understanding of the extraordinary diversity of the British Empire, explaining its realities while avoiding either nostalgia or polemical condemnation. Written by an acclaimed South African historian raised under the discriminatory system of Apartheid (itself a vestige of European colonialism), this is a major new historical narrative of the British Empire from an entirely fresh perspective.

ABOUT THE AUTHOR

Bill Nasson was born and raised in South Africa under the Apartheid regime, itself a vestige of British colonialism. At the end of the 1960s he was excluded on grounds of government racial classification from studying at South Africa's main universities but won a series of prestigious scholarships to study in the UK. He gained his doctorate at the University of Cambridge and returned to South Africa during the final era of white minority rule. In 1997 he became Professor of History at South Africa's premier University of Cape Town. He has held visiting appointments and fellowships at Yale University and the University of Cambridge. His other books include the critically acclaimed *The South African War*.

Praise for BILL NASSON'S *THE SOUTH AFRICAN WAR*

'Ground-breaking… a magnificent, subtle and memorable book'
THE INDEPENDENT
'His vivid narrative gains depth as well as scope from paying as much attention to the Boer as the British side' *TLS*
'Its great virtue lies in its unusual balance and evenhandedness… stylishly written and an excellent book' PROFESSOR ANDREW PORTER, *EHR*
'Impressive… a major contribution' *HISTORY*
'A pleasure to read' *THE SUNDAY INDEPENDENT* (Johannesburg)

BRITANNIA'S EMPIRE

A Short History of the British Empire

BILL NASSON

TEMPUS

For Leah and her Commonwealth

Cover illustrations

Front: Colonel Mordaunt's Cock Match by John Zoffany © Tate, London 2004.

Back: Plucky redcoats were indispensable to the martial cult of Victorian valour, rarely more so than here: greatly outnumbered, a small British garrison at Rorke's Drift mission station held out against a sustained onslaught by Zulu regiments in 1879, forcing attackers to withdraw. Author's collection.

This edition published 2006

Tempus Publishing Limited
The Mill, Brimscombe Port,
Stroud, Gloucestershire, GL5 2QG
www.tempus-publishing.com

© Bill Nasson, 2004, 2006

British Library Cataloguing in Publication Data.
A catalogue record for this book is available from the British Library.

ISBN 0 7524 3808 5

Typesetting and origination by Tempus Publishing Limited
Printed and bound in Great Britain

Contents

Our thoughts move across the seas to the many communities in which our people play their part, in every corner of the world. These are our family ties. That is our life. Without it, we should be no more than some millions of people living on an island off the coast of Europe, in which nobody wants to take any particular interest.

Sir Anthony Eden, Foreign Secretary (1952)

Some farmers would have 'Up the Pope! Down the King' written up, but that was all they really did in those days. I suppose we took being British for granted. You just showed your passport and said 'British', and you expected first-class treatment – which one got!

Derek Watson, on his 1933 posting to Londonderry, Ireland, as a twenty-two-year-old lieutenant in the Leicesters. From Christopher Somerville, *Our War: How the British Commonwealth Fought the Second World War* (Weidenfeld & Nicholson, London, 1998)

Preface

S heep continue to ruminate in the Falkland Islands and a Royal Mail ship still potters between Southampton and St Helena, but to all intents and purposes Britannia's Empire is now a thing of the past. In that famous snorting aside favoured by many Americans, it *is* history. What was once so corpulent and pulsating now provides little more than occasional business for morticians. The death of Queen Elizabeth the Queen Mother in March 2002 was also the passing of a British royal who was once the last empress of India. But by then the flag in Delhi had long ceased fluttering over the jewel in the crown. Or, to take a more present instance, for all the Zimbabwean President's ritual bluster about British designs on recolonising Rhodesia, the authoritarian Robert Mugabe is more likely to end up facing Oxfam than another Field-Marshal Lord Roberts.

For the truth is that the ghost of the British Empire will not be passing into some hearty new body. What remains visible is not serious national power but the lively and often idiosyncratic residue of the language, culture and institutions disseminated around the modern world by a once predominant British influence. Depending on where one lives, these continue to include such essentials of life as Scotch, tweed, football, the ubiquitous Royal Hotel and what some acerbic observers have termed British kitsch, like the Keg and Grouse pub chain in Southern Africa, a region not exactly famous for its clammy moors and royal weekend hunting parties.

Across the North Atlantic, the more chic inhabitants of Washington DC live in Somerset, and some mid-Americans reside on Albemarle Street. Thus does the duke of Albemarle, a lord proprietor of seventeenth-century British Carolina, retain his grand mark on the coniferous chorus-line of American suburbia. In Zambia and Malawi, tobacco and tea farms are still called Inverness or Cornwall, except that they no longer await the inspection tour of a Northern Rhodesian or Nyasaland district officer. Indian city roads are flooded with local versions of Austin-Morris sedans, living dinosaurs and a defensive requiem for a lost British motor industry.

Nor has such traffic been only one way. The paisley pattern on British scarves and ties owes its origin to Indian Kashmiri shawls. Even if what he had on his mind was the bacon, it is no less important that Sir Walter Raleigh brought home the potato. And, through the living entity of English, bungalow, trek, verandah, caddy, kedgeree, veld and countless other words capture the cultural currency of an imperial past. Needless to say, multiplying lists of this sort could be done by virtually anyone properly acquainted with the contemporary English-speaking world.

Naturally, in a small offshore European country which once possessed, over several centuries, what was the largest territorial empire in the history of the world, grand habits of some defining global power may continue to linger, if only as illusions. Given a robust legacy of inflated British influence overseas, including a capacity to partition lands, to set national boundaries and to reshape societies, to say nothing of promoting rectangular brickwork as culturally superior to oval mud and reed, a sense of imperial acquisition to rescue and improve things could hardly not have become a particular feature of British identity. At times, this may still take a certain, if increasingly reticent, pride in the notion of Britannia's Empire as a historic mission. In this sunny view, London's imperialism was largely a well-intentioned impulse to bring to undeveloped peoples in slumbering parts of the world the virtues of good government, civilised standards, ethical service and modern market rationality. As if the ushering in of a liberal parliamentary creed were not enough, India and Africa had fine bridges and railways thrown in as well.

In the mess of contemporary international relations, it is perhaps not altogether surprising to find renewed interest in a progressive British imperial record. Take the pamphleteering Robert Cooper, a foreign policy adviser to the post-1997 Labour Prime Minister, Tony Blair. In a 2002 publication of the London Foreign Policy Centre, Cooper argued that Britain could restore order to a wobbly international system by dusting off the more brusque methods of an earlier, nineteenth-century epoch of Great Power expansion. As he put it, and without blushing, these included the careful marshalling of expeditionary forces, and the wily use of deception and pre-emptive incursions to bring unrulier and more old-fashioned parts of the world to heel. For the anti-Western disorder of the early twenty-first century was no time for repose. If anything, it was to bring opportunity and even imperatives for a creeping colonisation, which were as inviting as they had been in the nineteenth century.

As the true benefit of all empire lay in the bestowing of order and organisation, if need be by calculated force, what was required ideally was a moral brand of acquiescent imperialism, hinging on voluntary acceptance of its orderly gains and tranquil benefits. The only thing needed to complete Cooper's whimsical evocation of British world power is a Protestant Britannia which still rules the waves, its navy running down slave traders in the South Atlantic, pounding the commercial enclaves of coastal China, or safely anchoring at a liberal Cape of Good Hope.

Otherwise, the Foreign Policy Centre view amounts to little other than a summoning up of musty Whitehall imperial instincts to play the errand-boy of a grasping twenty-first-century American-Anglo order. If Great Britain was once able to hold the ring at well beyond its own weight, it is many years since that ceased to be the case, despite the best efforts of the Conservative Prime Minister, Margaret Thatcher, who in the 1980s pledged that Britain would bounce off the ropes to become 'Great' once again. Still, in 1982 that may have done something for the confidence of the late Conservative MP, Alan Clark. On hearing of the Argentinian invasion of the Malvinas he had exclaimed, despairingly, 'we've lost the Falklands... It's all over. We're a Third World Country, no good for anything any more.' Any historical allusion to a Great or a Greater Britain carries a subtext which implies some backward-looking connection to a real or possibly an imagined empire. Indeed, there is even an iconoclastic view that a proper British Empire may not really have existed at all, in the sense that Britain's control of its piecemeal overseas possessions was invariably too makeshift or too diffuse to substantiate the more windy doctrines of imperial power. Conquests were always greater than the resources available to administer these properly, and the long arm of the British was always getting stuck in loose and disorderly places.

After all, even defining the scope of a Britannic Empire is not that straightforward. At one stage, Argentina, never British colonial territory, was more or less as dependent on British capitalism as New Zealand, probably the most enthusiastically British of the settler lands that used to be tinted on those old empire maps. Spanish Buenos Aires even has its starched Anglo-Argentine suburb of Ranelagh, founded in 1913, one of the few spots in Argentina where one can expect to find the Malvinas called the Falklands.

If all such informal pieces are added, the empire turns out to have been even larger than the sum of the formal colonial territories to which the British asserted some proprietorial claim. Approached in this way, the idea of a coherent British Empire looks elusive, its pieces all too hodge-podge to make a comprehensible jigsaw. Equally, there can be little doubt as to the special place of that empire in Britain's historic assertion of a national place in the sun. It filled minds as much as maps, even if its popular place in the British imagination can sometimes be forgotten amidst the preoccupations of a European Union relationship.

Still, it merely needs something or other to turn the husk of world influence into a grain of reference for British society, as nostalgia for past greatness from the more bluff inhabitants of the English Home Counties or as concerned Commonwealth sentiment over human rights. In the 1970s it was British arms sales to apartheid South Africa. In the 1980s it was the Falklands War. More recently, it has been humanitarian outrage over grisly excesses in Sierre Leone, land crisis and political repression in Zimbabwe, and discord over Britain's shifty participation in the American invasion and occupation of Iraq.

These calamitous episodes remind us that Britain only reached its climax as Great Britain because of the scale of its maritime and territorial empire. In any long perspective on that entity, it remains difficult not to succumb to the classic proclamations of a Victorian freak-show compère, 'Amazing Yet True' or 'Ponder This and Marvel'. A small island state, containing at no stage more than about 2 per cent of the world's population, once acquired a sprawling overseas empire which expanded over several centuries, bringing it virtually unparalleled global influence, dominance and wealth. A century ago, its shipping fleet amounted to 40 per cent of total world tonnage and conveyed 50 per cent of the total value of world seaborne trade. This state planted its first durable colony in Virginia, North America, in 1607. In the 1950s it was still at it, annexing a remote island scrap in the North Atlantic as another crown lighthouse dependency. Not until 1997 did it relinquish Hong Kong, a territory wrestled from China in the previous century. Gibraltar remains British, to the continuing irritation of Madrid.

Even in the early decades of the twentieth century, an era generally associated with Britain's decline, on the face of it its empire was anything but diminished. Instead, it appeared to be in its prime, receiving unprecedented amounts of capital from London, encompassing virtually a quarter of the earth's land, embracing more than a quarter of its inhabitants, and bristling with ideas for reform and development.

No less striking was the small number of British islanders who shouldered the whole of the white man's (and white woman's) burden. Around the beginning of the twentieth century Britain had a population of just about 40 million, while its imperial domain teemed with over 500 million people. Formal empire was in part a striking phenomenon of so few people wielding authority over so many for so long. In Uganda, by the end of the 1890s, so few meant about two dozen resident officials governing the administrative affairs of some 3 million East Africans. At this level, there seems no end to such equations. In the early 1940s there were about 1,000 administrative officers in British tropical Africa (south of the Sahara and north of South Africa), which is fewer than the current complement of Scandinavian aid workers in the same region of independent Africa. The solitary agent with his snuff box was the human currency of colonial responsibility.

For part of the modern existence of Britannia's Empire, the only other rising states with the ambition and potential to be rival world powers were Russia and the United States: massive continental entities which looked to supplant British imperial power, but which could not match its penetrating reach into far-off places. By bringing on catastrophic world war, Germany sought to forge a European continental springboard to world power, but managed only to be robbed of those cheap colonial left-overs it had already acquired. As the Japanese Empire had Asian limits, the only other state with truly global interests was France. In fact, by the early twentieth century the French world empire was second only to that of Britain. Yet with less than a tenth of the world's territory to its credit, and with only approximately 100 million people under its sway, it lagged far behind.

The empire that transformed an expansionist Elizabethan Albion into the leading world island was also a peculiarly mangled creation, seemingly pieced together almost accidentally from disparate strips of the globe. In part it was this which led to the famous conceit of J.R. Seeley, in his 1880s *The Expansion of England*, that empire had somehow all been acquired in 'a fit of absence of mind', a casual enterprise assembled on the side while looking the other way. In a way, Seeley was on to something. Unlike the integrated land empire of a rival great power like Russia, Britain's imperial resources were uneven and scattered around the world in colonies and other dependencies lacking in common features or natural unity. This was an empire not glued together by a single language, a single religious system, or a single legal structure. Nor, come to that, was it ever administered with the efficient thoroughness of the English county system, or generally within the mild English liberal tradition of autonomous local bodies. Nor, deep within British society itself, was there ever anything like universal interest in, or excitement over, the distant achievements of empire. As for those colonial holdings, not only were they diverse, but the ways in which they had been scooped up were irregular, lacking any consistent pattern of co-ordinated empire construction. In early seventeenth-century West Africa, probing British interest was not fired by any policy of colonisation. Or, in the case of Canada in the following century, it ended up being taken as a transfer of the treaty spoils of successful war against a European enemy. Then, again, in the nineteenth century, the British began formally to occupy areas which they had previously been content to regard as subject to their influence. The form of British rule or command was also somewhat opaque, from the cheap arrangement of being paramount power over a society to the more costly and complex imposition of direct control, responsibility with costs. Thus, the strategically vital fortress colony of Gibraltar was always screwed down so tightly that even the apes scratched their allegiance to the crown. Perhaps they still do, gibbering at intermittent Anglo-Spanish talk of some British disengagement. On the other hand, by the later nineteenth century virtually all the white settler colonies of Australia were effectively no longer being controlled or ruled by London.

Not altogether surprisingly, more sceptical later nineteenth-century European observers declared British world power to be a sham, its empire a flashy ornament. It was far too maritime, having to sustain tenuous territorial connections from port to port. That left the imperial undertaking all too vulnerable, with the security of its ties entirely dependent upon the Royal Navy sticking to its guns. If that navy were ever to come up short, British power would no longer hold the seas, and empire could very well slip away.

French and German visions of the empire suddenly foundering were blotted partly by the size of the British fleet, which then consisted of at least half of the world's larger warships, with access to the colonial territorial waters of numerous island dependencies. The other decisive factor was that in any event the empire was rarely tethered by force of arms alone. What kept it afloat was a dense screen of ties and interests, resting on an intricate balance of coercion, persuasion, submission, accommodation or concession in relations between Britain and its subordinate societies. In addition to that day-to-day lubrication, defending the empire was rarely very costly when the going was good. For all Victorian Britain's grumbling over the fiscal burdens of colonial defence, at the height of its wealth the costs of defending one of the greatest empires in world history were hardly ever more than around 1–2 per cent of national income.

This book seeks to provide a concise narrative account of Britannia's Empire, from its early origins in the rise of an expansionist England to a post-imperial present in which empire has shrivelled into the Commonwealth, a largely dozy body which today paddles in a great world ocean not of dreadnoughts and Sterling Preference but of the varieties of the English language. Naturally, any volume of this size cannot pretend to cover all there is to cover in a chronological overview of British imperialism. That would require equal attention to every place, to every economic, political, social and institutional structure, and equal attention to the impact of every religious, educational, artistic and intellectual experience of empire upon societies and individuals. There lies a bewildering maze or the plainly impossible.

With that in mind, it goes almost without saying that anyone who tries to write expansively on British imperialism is unable to avoid rubbing up against general questions. Some, obviously, are old and some are newer. Why did England embark upon overseas enterprise? What factor or factors propelled the construction of empire? What were its benefits and returns? Was it ever a burden? How were other societies and cultures altered by the impact of imperialism? Or, conversely, in what ways were the British themselves changed by empire? Should Britain today be held morally accountable for the chequered history of its imperialism?

Such concerns have long been the stock-in-trade of veteran historians of the British Empire, to say nothing of more recent scholars of the workings of race, gender and culture in the imperial experience. So, anyone attempting an overview text cannot avoid an uncomfortable awareness that they are steaming their gunboat through someone else's waters. For whatever Great Britain's Empire may end up being remembered for, it will surely have to include its numerous accomplished historians. To their massive scholarship I am, of course, deeply indebted.

To begin at the beginning, the gradual emergence of Britannia's Empire is the consequence of the commanding growth of England into what Shakespeare called 'an Empery', and the long-distance expansion of the British state, lapping beyond the British Isles into the New World. What lay behind that initial impulse?

I

Prologue

In considering present debate around the meaning of British identity, or over the national consequences of deepening British integration into a single European market, it is as well to remember that there was relatively little in early British history to suggest the massive global orientation which was to come. After all, as a Roman Britannia, England was never more than a minor colony of that empire, its ruling elites assimilated into a European ambience of aristocrats and nobles, and like them addicted to a continental world of basilicas and villas.

Later, as a lesser European medieval kingdom, the British Isles trod water on the fringe of Europe, pulled into its trading, political and cultural networks. Then, the wool trade meant Calais not Adelaide, and the Plantagenets made their pile from the Bordeaux wine trade rather than from the gold shares of the Witwatersrand. When part of a Viking world, Britain's western sea routes were conveying Baltic timber or ascetic monks rather than Malayan rubber or the Hicks Pasha expeditionary force. The Middle Ages again confirmed Britain as European, with its bickering kings pursuing their dynastic ambitions within the shadow line of European interests.

Yet, in another way the British in their island bastion were also stuck on the edge of European life. A decisive barrier here was geography, with a deep sea acting as both a material and psychological barrier against closing with continental Europe. Near yet palpably apart, British communities did not fall naturally into the stock European ways of acting and thinking, nor did they plumb Europe's historical, cultural and even emotional frames of consciousness. However European its location, Britain's maritime nature helped to nurture the growth of an independent, aboriginal sort of offshore identity.

Geography also gave the British the insular advantage of a sturdy barrier provided by the English Channel. Virtually no other European state had so secure and safe a territorial base, sheltered by the sea and not saddled with extended and troublesome borders. There were, of course, occasional panics over this or that hostile threat of seaborne invasion, but Britain remained remarkably impregnable to any enemy crossing. The traditional significance of the Channel as a seaward defence was still present in the 1970s parliamentary debate on the Channel Tunnel project, when some MPs warned the house against breaching the country's main protection from invasion. This included a call from the Member for Plymouth Sutton for a demolition contingency, allowing for a sudden collapsing of the tunnel in the event of a hostile emergency.

This thick margin of security had two strategic consequences. Firstly, unlike major continental powers, Britain was free of the costly burden of raising and maintaining mass standing armies. True, it always had strong forces to commit to the European mainland if required by major wars, and it would continue to participate in these as a matter of course throughout the eighteenth century. But the British never had to contend with the draining land entanglements of a state like the France of Louis XIV. Comparatively, then, Britain was able to funnel a greater proportion of its resources into the pursuit of wealth and power overseas. In a decisive maritime era, a big fleet and the English Channel provided the British with superior 'blue water' security at cheaper cost than anything which could be contrived by their rivals.

Secondly, there was the ship itself, Britain's supreme mode of communication and the means of holding the line against any opposing forces. In the fifteenth and sixteenth centuries the Royal Navy and its servicing dockyards like Chatham were tightly organised under a professional seafaring ethos – they represented a well-financed and technically advanced concern. A state which prospered by the capabilities of its shipping system was also helped by the complementary weakening of opponents like Spain, whose maritime power was in accelerating decline by the earlier seventeenth century.

As an island growing more dependent on imports, Britain needed to construct a beefy seaborne commerce and to protect it from the depredations of war, privateering, or piracy. Here, the production of a good standard ship of the line represented one of the most expressive early forms of British expansion. Private and naval yards turned out sizeable vessels, each crewed by hundreds of sailors. Nominally free-wage labour, sailors were compelled to work out lengthy service, confined under ferocious discipline and earned barely a subsistence wage. The crewing needs of British ships were also sucking in large numbers of men from around the world, to the extent that by the end of the seventeenth century a softening of the Navigation Acts permitted foreign ratings to make up as much as three-quarters of merchant marine hands.

In striking ways, then, the ship environment seemed to prefigure the formation of an imperial British economy. Well before its full industrialisation and nineteenth-century growth into the classic workshop of the world, a fundamental feature of factory and plantation work was already a reality on British vessels – strict labour control and time discipline. Well before the notion of a world empire had any substance, British ships were multi-ethnic, with those below the bridge no longer purely English-speaking.

Another part of the early story of maritime enterprise was the way in which the world economy was forming. By surging across oceans and rolling into wide outlets, conditions favoured states able to develop strong and flexible seapower. Part of an old island civilisation with trading arteries which had evolved around river waterways, estuaries, channels and the pull of neighbouring open seas, British merchant interests were nicely positioned to benefit from the growth of an open, ocean-based world market. For hundreds of years traders had been mariners almost by instinct, getting around the country more easily by water than by land. In the case of early modern England or Wales, the Atlantic and its commerce was a port bow jutting beyond the Irish Sea. While it would take time for serious interest in movement beyond European waters to develop, by the sixteenth century the opportunities were there for the development of a powerful strategy of oceanic imperialism in which Britain could concentrate on new commercial and colonial development to augment its venerable tradition of sea warfare and plundering. Clearly, maritime supremacy and effective overseas expansion required firm state backing. This could only come through the formation of a strong state which was territorially secure, internally integrated, able to assert a shared identity and one that rested on a stable political order which enjoyed general legitimacy. In short, any sustained imperial enterprise had to be fostered by a coherent polity, one which perceived how this could strengthen it.

In this respect the evolution of a Greater British Empire is inseparable from the prior formation of a Greater Britain. That, in turn, is linked to the transformation of England into a unified English state within the boundaries of the British Isles. Over time, this state became the assimilationist, integrating engine which succeeded in imposing its complete domination, through the military conquest of Wales and a pushy unification with Scotland. For proponents of union, the geographical determinism of a British Islander identity was crucial to the growth of a single national entity.

This was achieved through centuries of aggressive internal English expansion, increasing in pace from the Middle Ages onwards, when the Normans and those who followed introduced inhabitants of Wales and Ireland to a bullying internal colonial rule and an arrogant cross-border imperialism. By the sixteenth century these weaker nations had been yanked under the authority of the Tudor English crown. Centralising power, England consolidated its grip upon Wales and Ireland to enforce territorial integrity through complete English control of the British Isles.

The hardening of English royal authority in the wake of the decisive Wars of the Roses and the English Reformation further enhanced the public authority of the dominant state, and strengthened its capacity to enforce laws and regulations throughout its subject territory. Meanwhile, under a Union of the Crowns, English and Scottish thrones were combined in 1603, although Scotland itself remained a separate national entity until the end of the century. That continuing elbow-room was eventually removed by the 1707 Act of Union, which sealed a union of parliaments with Scotland, giving its heartier and more monied classes free trade and full access to a rising English commercial empire.

In the aftermath of union and a wholesale shift of authority south, 'Britain' became the nationalist emblem to depict a new English, Welsh and Scottish fusion. What it amounted to essentially was the English state becoming an imperial Great Britain situated in London, a city on its way to becoming the largest metropolis in the western hemisphere. An earlier idea of English empire having to do with overriding island power and guardianship was being superseded by larger representations of empire as overseas dominion. Put positively, in that enterprise England opened up to Welsh and Scots, who romped in as minor Anglo-Welsh and Anglo-Scottish partners, nourished by the consumerism and trading networks of a swelling merchant capitalist economy. Fast national growth and increasing expansion abroad by the seventeenth century sucked all regional Britons into a unified national market and the same growing world market.

A further factor was the achievement of a remarkable level of general British uniformity. This is not to say that the economic divisions and social fractures that have eroded the national cohesion of many other states were never present in Britain. It is merely to suggest that overarching cultural, religious or other divisions have been far less acute. Just as a thrusting Protestantism rose to overall dominance, so the new British economy and state bound people around English as the standard of communication, even if the throne came to be occupied by some decidedly un-English speakers at times. With an old social circuitry of mutual interaction between divergent British societies, the construction of a common imperial nation could have considerable resonance for many incorporated inhabitants of Wales and Scotland, after the cessation of Anglo-Welsh and Anglo-Scottish border conflicts. Not without reason have some writers seen a connection from the sixteenth century between a domestic English colonialism rolling up its Celtic outskirts and subsequent imperial conquest overseas.

By the end of the seventeenth century the British polity had fashioned a sturdy civil society, established religious toleration, erected a ruthless defence of property and of the rights of oligarchy, and had spawned a heavy web of libertarian traditions and acquisitive mentalities. It had also forged a rapacious governing aristocracy, bent on directing the state towards mercantile objectives behind a political self-image of Protestant Britons, intensely maritime and commercial, and uniquely free by birthright.

The thorny exception to this settled pattern was Ireland. Distanced from the outset, although Henry VIII and his successors all claimed Irish kingship, Ireland was treated as a smash-and-grab colony, its armed conquest wrapped up under the Tudors. Efforts were undertaken to establish settlers on much the same invasive basis as the later rooting of Protestant colonists in the New World. This influx of settlers differentiated by culture and religion further deepened hostile Irish-Anglo divisions. Irish support of the losing Catholics, Charles I and James II, in the English Civil War brought a savage reconquest at the hands of Oliver Cromwell, laying the basis for an oppressive colonial separation. This onslaught brought huge land confiscations and the planting of a Protestant, Anglo-Irish landowning class to squat on a downtrodden Catholic peasantry. Crushed and shut out, Ireland was denied free trade and stifled economically.

Outside of its better-endowed industrial north, the site of a minority concentration of Protestant settlers with power and resources, a lot of green grass did little for Irish development through the seventeenth century and beyond. Set as a colonial backwater of the British Isles, the bulk of its alienated inhabitants remained impoverished, subject to periodic shattering famine, and drained by a rent tribute sucked away annually by a parasitic mainland Britain. Rural pauperisation produced a stream of desperate Irish migration which would, in due course, turn into a flood. For England, experience of colonial conquest and settlement across the Irish Sea provided a rough prototype and early pedigree in imperialism for its coming stab at North America and the Caribbean.

The Scots, Welsh and also migrant Irish stake in colonial enterprise meant that by the time 'Britain' came to be minted early in the eighteenth century there was already a maturing, molecular growth of a commitment to empire as a national interest. In this, the impact of emerging assertions of British will or British power in the world was twofold. It could serve as an adhesive to bind people together in British maritime, commercial and expeditionary activity beyond Europe, and it could lift what it meant to be British beyond warlike prowess to altogether more exalted levels.

The external asset of 'Empire', however uncertain and varied its meaning to many contemporaries, was as glorious as the dashing achievements of snarling Elizabethan sea-dogs in their plunder of Spanish or French treasure ships. Island pride in naval supremacy over cocky foreigners worked to fatten the imaginative stock of Britishness, enabling it to press its historic frontiers further and further beyond that of a modest islander identity.

For all this, an imperial identity could not be taken for granted. It needed to parade an appropriate paternity for the tide to run the right way. Behind the imperialist impulse of a free, modernising Protestant Britain lay an atavistic notion of a proudly independent Albion, delivered of any malignant Romanism in its remote past, and providentially expansionist. The Tudors, in particular, took to this misty version of island history, hauling out imposing genealogies, and looking to their Renaissance schools of illustrators, geographers and other scholars immersed in antiquarian surveys and mythic histories, like William Camden, author of *Britannia*.

Much of this wide-eyed scribbling turned on belief in a land no more resplendent than in its British-Arthurian past. Seeping through in high scholarship, poetry and theatrical performance, pristine visions of a conquering Arthurian state gave rising British imperialism a pronounced intellectual and moral charge. New British ambitions became the redemption of *Morte d'Arthur*, enlisting Protestant energy and chivalry in the service of a lofty maritime empire of free people, charting the open seas for rightful gain. Such literary savants of this imperial national character as Thomas Malory, Edmund Spenser and Philip Sidney were as much part of later sixteenth-century overseas enterprise as Francis Drake or Walter Raleigh. At the heart of worsening Anglo-Spanish relations in the 1580s and an eventual war crisis were their respective ideological affirmations and efforts, in the struggle to secure for Elizabethan England the highest returns in the imperial contest for wealth and territory in the New World. In such work habits, there were few who could have held a candle to one man in particular. This was the exuberant London-Welsh mathematician Dr John Dee, a founder of Trinity College, Cambridge, and a leading scholar for whom the Elizabethan era was synonymous with an unbounded world view.

By common account the individual first credited with floating the term 'Brytish Impire', Dee found an agreeable anchorage as a passionate advocate of its maritime enterprise, egged on by the bustling merchants and voyagers who trailed around in his company, and serving as scientific adviser to the Company of Cathay and the Muscovy Company. Captivated by the earlier rise of Dutch seaborne power, Dee cultivated Low Countries links with spreadeagled cartographers like Mercator and Ortelius, and at home fell in with the seafaring Martin Gilbert and Humphrey Frobisher, confecting maps and treatises to launch the British at the Atlantic. Appropriately, his own compilation of his many volumes ended up under the title *The Perfect Arte of Navigation*. More or less in bed with the Tudors, Dee obtained personal recognition as court philosopher to Elizabeth, and it was he who presented the queen with her Title Royal claim over the North Atlantic, as well as 'Atlantis' – his fancy name for America. Historians of Wales have also long been alert to the quirky significance of Dee's scratchings into the primordial folklore stories of a migrant Welsh Madoc, and their conversion into the fable of a pioneering Welsh discovery and colonisation of America, at least 300 years before Columbus. Bizarre perhaps, but the Madoc myth of a first Christian footprint in uncivilised America was useful enough as British propaganda to be turned on Spain in the closing years of the sixteenth century

So beguiling was John Dee that in 1583 George Peckham, a leading English admirer of his fabulous Welsh fabrications, cited his discoveries as inspiration for a bright scheme to clear England of the pestilence of Catholicism by shipping its adherents across the Atlantic. Such innovative thinking on transporting undesirables to distant parts would, of course, come to be echoed by later imperialists as a handy means of seeing off political dissidents and convicted criminals, and of mopping up pools of the unemployed. Lastly, and no less quixotically, Dee's Madoc entered the lofty register of English discovery inscribed by Richard Hakluyt in his acclaimed 1589 praise-poem to a growing command of the sea, *Principal Navigations, Traffiques and Discoveries of the English Nation*. A century later, the notion that a run of the sea would bring empire and liberty was still being unfurled by such zealots of naval expansion as William Petty, in his *Dominion of the Sea*.

While long-distance trade and colonisation would start transforming Britain's world position throughout the seventeenth century, it was by no means the first European state to test far waters. Expansion was pioneered by rival voyaging societies, striving to make tall stories come true. In the fifteenth century when the lift of English sails was still short, it was Portugal that led the advance towards a new transatlantic world economy. Then, knots of English sailors and adventurers were content at first to join long Portuguese voyages down the west coast of Africa and to parts of Asia and South America, benefiting from an Iberian subsidy of the costs and risks of transoceanic exploration.

By the sixteenth century Spain had also emerged as a powerful Catholic imperial state, with prodigious colonial conquests in both central and South America. By proceeding to swallow up Portugal and its imperial interests during the sixteenth and seventeenth centuries, the Spanish secured, as it were, two bites at the New World cherry. Portugal's older domination of slave-trading circuits between West Africa and colonial Spanish America crumbled, leaving the fate of its West African posts uncertain. By then there was a further imperial intruder with which to contend. Alongside the Iberian outgrowth was Holland, another muscular Protestant maritime power, which rapidly built up a strong commercial presence in south-east Asia. On top of the East Indies spice trade, by the end of the sixteenth century the Dutch were also elbowing the Portuguese off their skinny West African coastal sites.

Inevitably, a British pursuit of world trade and colonisation would bring on commercial and strategic enmities with established European imperial powers which would oppose a frontal challenge. Even with Portugal overhauled by the early seventeenth century, British expansion would be a militant undertaking, involving a fierce tussle for a decisive controlling portion of the resources of the New World. For Britain to emerge victorious eventually, it would be fighting imperialist wars for around 150 years, all driven by consuming commercial imperatives. By fits and starts, British maritime mastery would have to be constructed in the teeth of resistance from major rivals, Catholic Portugal, Spain and France, and a Protestant Netherlands.

Writing in the 1570s, it was John Dee who captured what the British required, a balance between a crusading faith for overseas influence and a practical creed for action. In his call on Elizabeth to claim a northern Atlantic dominion, he argued for a mobilisation of all available British resources, bold planning, and for the creation of a 'Pety Navy Royall' of at least sixty big ships, shored up by taxation.

2

An Emerging English
Empire *c.*1500–1700

Imperial expansion did not have especially purposeful beginnings. Nudged by Henry VII, the itchy Venetian Giovanni Caboto (John Cabot) ventured out from Bristol into the Atlantic to search for a Northwest Passage to Asia in 1497. Leaving aside a peek at a coastal stretch of North America, this foray produced little more than the novel observation that the tides around Labrador ran differently from anything to be encountered off the Severn. On his return, Cabot also found sufficient fish to calm even the most anxious disciple.

By the middle of the sixteenth century, bands of English fishermen amid Portuguese, Spanish and French competitors had lashed down seasonal settlements in the coves of Nova Scotia and Newfoundland. But fishing the Grand Banks of the eastern Atlantic and dabbling in petty trade with American Indians was short of an invasion. At first, the English seemed to be preoccupied more with cod than colonisation.

Cabot was one of a handful of sponsored exploratory seafarers in search principally of a route to Asia, a bustling maritime coterie which included the famously pushy Raleigh and Drake, with their lucrative privateering runs at Spanish cargoes. Yet before the last decades of the sixteenth century only a very tiny English trading minority had any real concern in overseas enterprise. Increasing royal patronage helped to inflate the popular standing of ambitious maritime ventures, but there was generally little excitement from ordinary subjects.

Interest in overseas exploitation grew more palpable with the whiff of direct opportunity. By the 1580s officials and merchant groups had become increasingly aware of what Spain was milking from its New World possessions. As Anglo-Spanish hostilities degenerated into open warfare, an imperial British identity began to stiffen. It was up to an enlightened Protestant Britain to fight for its survival and for its right to dig out its own commercial opportunities in America and Asia, against a detested Habsburg Spain and its despotic Catholic monopoly of the New World. For this mission its Arthurian stamina fused well with the claims of English nationhood and Protestant anti-Catholicism.

Bellicose English voices were strengthened by defeat of the Spanish Armada in 1588 and by the continuation of bold privateering strikes against a limping Spanish fleet. These were boosted further by public adulation of raiders like Drake, turned into Elizabethan folk heroes by putting the Spanish out of business or, more accurately, for helping the English to muscle in on that business. Much like Shakespeare, Drake became an exuberant icon of the

Elizabethan era, although perhaps of a rather different moral sensibility.

Moving against Spain consisted of nibbling away at the Iberian Atlantic world, incisions which the Spanish were increasingly unable to close by the seventeenth century. Taking advantage of a rickety Portugal on the West African seaboard, English naval and commercial pressures there rose in the first half of the century, while a sally into African trade and commercial possession also began to rub up against the Dutch by the 1650s. By the 1660s, scattered trading posts and fortifications were being grabbed from European rivals, although new English merchant interests had to adapt to the African terrain. In places like Sierra Leone and Guinea, the extraction of hides, redwood, gum arabic and gold continued to be conducted through entrenched Afro-Portuguese trading channels.

This first incursion into West African commodities was limited, with even the gold trade of little more than glancing significance to the English treasury. Nor was there serious exploitation of the African slave trade. With some bungled slave-raiding and a few forlorn attempts at inland slaving transactions, England looked unlikely to be emulating those exemplary exponents of black enslavement: Portugal, Spain, Holland and France. Indeed, through much of the seventeenth century West African trade largely excluded any distinctive slaving concern, bar the involvement of a few small chartered companies and individual traders in shipping some batches of slave labourers to Spanish American colonies. At the same time, this general aloofness from African human traffic had little to do with any moral squeamishness. Given the lightness of the English touch in Africa, and a slow settlement advance into the Caribbean, there was not much to encourage a big bite at the slave trade.

If anything, for the first century of interest in African commodity trade, from the first voyages of the 1540s through to around the 1640s, there was not much to suggest an imperial commitment. The penetration of merchant capitalism was shallow and fluctuating, and the gimcrack coastal settlements in what would later go on to become the colonies of the Gold Coast, Sierra Leone and the Gambia scarcely constituted English title. Simply beach-head trading posts with a labour demand to hump goods from one spot to another, there was virtually no development of plantation crop or other capitalist agricultural enterprise. Nor, in this opening phase, was there much scope to dictate actual occupation terms. True, African trade was harnessed to the idea of a bullish, maritime English Empire, claiming firm monopoly trading rights over all European rivals, including the Scots. Such trading exclusivity or protectionism was a bread-and-butter feature of early mercantile imperialism. However, here this assertion never amounted to very much, other than to stoke spluttering trading company conflict with the Dutch in the early 1660s.

In any event it was difficult to make a territorial presence look credible when England was unable to establish any sort of sovereign title to its station settlements. Occupation was invariably dependent on coming to terms with one or other African authority, struck by rental or tribute agreement with royal rulers. English business had also to be wary of treading on the wrong corns in its dealings with surrounding African societies, for isolated posts were vulnerable to being overrun by determined opposing forces, gun batteries notwithstanding. Security was often not helped by these being positioned inconveniently, pointing seawards at anticipated European enemies.

Still, by and large the English did not wage local war to enforce their political authority in West Africa. They were content to clinch accommodation and advantage through the mercenary provision of firearms and finance to one or other African side in internal clashes or by assisting African armies in fighting off other European intruders. Equally, these transient strategic marriages could be unstable. At times, the political balance between English patrons and allied African peoples wavered constantly, as some groups increased their leverage by siphoning resources from trading company officials. Others exploited Anglo-Dutch hostilities to their advantage by playing for favour with one hand, and extending the other in the opposite direction. In all, for much of this earlier African period the impact of England was limited to a shuffling coastal toehold. Even if a handful of traders were purchasing slaves and other commodities hauled through from the interior, there was no wider inclination to nose inland.

It was the invasion of North America which provided the first planned colonial possession. For here, the objective was squarely one of long-term colonisation. Spurred on by the influential advocacy of Drake, Hakluyt and similar figures, proposals emerged for the founding of sturdy plantation settlements as models of improving Protestant enterprise to counter Spanish supremacy in the Americas. This represented a forward dilution of Madrid's New

World domination, by chewing on its less contested imperial periphery.

Following several ill-considered and aborted ventures, a first permanent settlement on the James River in Virginia was established in 1607. This Chesapeake colony may reasonably be seen as the founding expression of an overseas empire of settlement and trade. It also embodied perfectly the prevailing rhetoric of colonisation, spiced with the promise of fat rewards for investors in colonial projects, of prosperous agricultural innovation and of the supply of cheap and desirable imports for English consumption. Created under crown patronage as the first permanent overseas colony apart from Ireland, Virginia exemplified the thick nexus between royal sanction, maritime commerce and the spread of transoceanic empire. Always a pestering presence around the royal household, jostling cliques of semi-capitalist aristocrats, courtiers, merchants, leading shipmasters and middling gentry swarmed in to pick up land grants from the crown, and to gain permission to settle enterprising colonists for plantation farming.

A natural precedent or model for the promotion of America were the earlier sixteenth-century colonising plantation ventures launched in Ireland, aimed at 'civilising' and domesticating a 'barbarous' and headstrong Catholic Gaelic population. In this light, hedged with reliable settlers, new crops and industries, an improving Virginia was seen not only as a spot for investment in dynamic new colonial trade. It was also the first soil of a Protestant English colonisation of the New World, a Canaan awaiting its respectable Christian habitation by the watery Israelites of Elizabeth I. Thus was conquest legitimised.

Promotion of the eastern seaboard of North America did not skimp on promises. Through improvement and diversification, potential settlers and investors were assured of coming fortunes in tobacco, silk, hemp and fruit. The home market could also expect to be in clover, as commodities like sugar and plant oil, usually imported from continental Europe and Asia, would soon be obtainable at much lower cost from English colonial America.

For all these golden age expectations, however, early settlement decades were a time of lurching uncertainty. Colonists had to contend with disease, shortages of essentials, and patches of virtual famine. At the same time, long stretches of depressed export earnings could barely raise enough of a return to cover the running costs of a plantation colony. Beset by soaring losses, factional disputes erupted within ruling authorities in Virginia, and groups of London financiers also started to get cold feet. To add to the headaches of the controlling Virginia Company of London, their New World colonists turned up little by way of gold, silver, or other precious metal. And surrounding American Indian societies did not produce valuable exportable commodities which could be expropriated.

As Virginia was not exactly virgin land, early company settlement was marked by a precarious and tense relationship with indigenous American peoples who laced the Chesapeake region in considerable numbers. For these inhabitants, a European trading post was one thing, for it did not threaten livelihood and security. Establishing a white immigrant colony in which land and crops might be snatched by English hands was another thing altogether.

Still, if wary, American Indians were tolerant at first of a modest English existence on their lands.

For that matter, some of the leading lights of new Atlantic settlement did not necessarily look forward to an orgy of land confiscation either. In that respect, the best face put on early Chesapeake conquest was vague obligation, the task given to moralising English settlers to try to improve the lot of a less fortunate heathen. That meant attempting to establish a paternalist basis for the gradual assimilation of Indian people by an encroaching pale Christian colony. Of benign intent, it would assert its God-given dominion by demonstrating its moral authority and power rather than by unleashing war.

Initially, there was no shortage of intangible ceremonies and rituals to fix rights of command, subordination and obligation. Colonial authorities recommended quaintly that any land for settlement be purchased and not stripped from American Indians. There were also solicitous expectations that Algonquian, Iroquoian and other chiefs would submit themselves as tributary subjects of the English crown, and that their subjects would fall in faithfully as recognised vassals. Through homage, deferential tribal rulers could have an assured if subordinate spot in the new colonial order, and savage or heathen Indian societies could be coaxed along the slow path of civilising Christian reform and assimilation.

Setting around this was a thin crust of positive, even romantic, English sentiment towards American Indian cultures. In the first years, more indulgent colonisers even admired their agricultural enterprise and efficiency, comparing the productivity of corn cultivation favourably with that of English yeoman farming, and there was also praise for indigenous hunting and fishing skills, tool-making capacity and archery technique. Other expedition leaders acknowledged the existence of rudimentary governing structures in a local civilisation which, far from being a uniform mass to be stigmatised as heathens or barbarians, seemed to comprise a rich diversity of tribes, cultures and languages. Moreover, although sacrificial elements made Iroquois and other religions seem dark and Satanic, sympathetic observers detected an intensity of religiosity or spiritual instinct, viewing this as a promising attribute for channelling in an evangelical direction.

To help in settling trading arrangements, colonists also tried to forge cordial exchange relations. These transactions included a clutch of strategic marriage alliances to stabilise links through sociable kinship, the best known of which was the 1614 tie between Pocahontas, daughter of chief Powhatan, and the leading settler, John Rolfe. On this front, there was more. A few educated if feather-brained incomers also fancied that they could pick up local oral traces of Latin, Greek and even Welsh, prompting them to wonder if Indians were not really ancient Europeans who had merely grown fond of feathers. Mysteriously marooned in the primitive Chesapeake, white American Indians were the lost descendants of wandering Trojans, awaiting regeneration as lesser Britons.

Colonial interpreters were reared to advance English commercial needs, to serve as political agents, and to wriggle into tribal communities as carriers of civilising reform, converting villagers to settled, productive habits which would best ensure trading profits and social peace on English terms. One tactic was to despatch able English youths to live amongst native inhabitants and to absorb Algonquian and other tongues. At the same time, some younger villagers were induced to find a place among colonists to learn English and English ways, in some instances even voyaging to England. Predictably, for anyone who ended up there having been coerced or kidnapped, the future was not the cultivation of language and literacy but the degradation of being exhibited as human freaks or curiosities by ruthless London sharpsters.

Business and religious concerns also strove to produce word lists, compilations and translations to expand local interaction and to try to facilitate Christian conversion. On the other hand, colonial authorities were repeatedly dismayed by the perceived moral slackness of poorer, rougher settlers. When the going got hard, some backsliding whites would think nothing of slipping away from a respectable Englishness to throw in their dubious lot with Algonquian neighbours or at other times would fight fiercely over scraps of property, undermining peace and frustrating the orderly basis of a Christian colonisation.

In a brief Anglo–American Indian moment, condescending English claims to enlightened commerce and peaceful exploitation of the earth rested upon settling down in harmony and progress. Colonisation would not bring displacement and a wilful tearing down of native life and cultures but a reshaping of superstitious societies through improving Protestant conversion and English civility. Optimism suggested that savage cultures would fold in the face of a persuasive Christian advance and that of an innovative plantation economy, and that American

Indians would come to appreciate the windfall of a superior commercial order and spiritual realm.

Yet there were always other views. More brusque and altogether more racially or ethnically contemptuous of any American Indian place in the emerging scheme of things, they made a stark balance sheet. The clear colonial value of North America was that of a rapidly exploitable resource to aid the construction of an English-dominated Atlantic economy, an asset sufficiently strong to see off Spain. Native peoples were fated to be wholly marginal in this English-dominated world. They could possibly try clinging on as industrious Protestant converts, or they could forfeit their lands to settlers who would make better commercial use of them and keep their former occupiers subjugated.

Increasingly intrusive and intimidating demands from colonists for land and crops soon created explosive conditions. A series of savage risings and rebellions in the first two decades of the 1600s saw Virginia convulsed by ferocious hostilities. Punitive campaigns by English forces led to the wholesale slaughter of entire villages, with bloody disturbances culminating in a massive, synchronised American Indian uprising in 1622, an unsparing swoop upon the small colony which came quite close to destroying it completely. Prolonged, bitter conflict reinforced contemptuous English depictions of American Indians as incorrigibly barbaric and teeming with un-Christian abominations, squashing any lingering optimism about an assimilationist colonial order. Equally, by the mid-1620s recurrent English alarms over the viability of the Chesapeake had subsided. Despite keeping their nerve and going to the edge again and again, resisting tribes had failed to wrest back their fields and their corn from grasping settlers. English military power had demonstrated its capacity to secure permanent colonial settlement, and to lash out ruthlessly through offensive campaigns, expelling disgruntled American Indians and keeping others on their knees.

With resistance crushed, immigrant arrivals multiplied during the seventeenth century, as a widening plantation economy acquired the sheet anchor crop for the cheap labour which most had come to provide. That staple was tobacco. Introduced from the Caribbean, English-American tobacco offered very low mass-production costs and the catch of a booming European market. In time, even the tightly regulated eighteenth-century French tobacco monopoly could not help but become heavily dependent upon a reliable flow of English imports. Next to tobacco and its whopping profits Cabot's shoals of fish were nothing. This success soon turned the marginal Chesapeake region of Virginia and a neighbouring Maryland, founded in 1634, into a thriving English Atlantic outpost.

The tens of thousands of young male and female colonists who left for the Chesapeake were drawn largely from an underclass of urban and rural labouring poor. Uprooted by the enclosure of common land, they became the fodder of colonial expansion, arriving as indentured servants from southern, central and western England in the hope of finding the bread of a better transatlantic life. This mostly turned out to be an arduous existence as chattel labour in a planter and merchant tobacco economy, working off the cost of a sponsored emigration passage.

Starting in the early seventeenth century, settlers also spread themselves across several other north-eastern outposts, further driving down the foundations of a colonial North America. Aside from a transient Newfoundland, only occupied in fishing seasons, New England Puritan settlements like Plymouth and Massachusetts sprouted into life under the diffuse ideological influence of beliefs in providential emigration and the earthly duties of a godly community of righteous Pilgrims. Quakers also made an entry through Pennsylvania, while the English New World proved to be sufficiently porous to absorb even a Catholic influx.

By the end of the 1600s there were almost a dozen stable coastal colonies. Reaping the advantages of a regular immigration stream and high birth rates, their position was helped further by the soaring mortality of an alienated indigenous population, ravaged by European diseases such as measles and smallpox, and increasingly unable to stem land and food losses to engulfing European interlopers.

Meanwhile, the movement of English capital and the export of people and technology aided the construction of maritime industry and increasingly diversified agriculture, with growth boosted by immense forestry stock, inexhaustible North Atlantic fish reserves and, most crucial of all, by a sheer abundance of good land. By the early 1800s these colonies were flourishing commodity exporters of tobacco, grain, rice, meat, fish and timber through England, with consignments set for southern Europe and the Caribbean. Working like some push-pull pump, colonial export earnings then went on the import of increasing quantities of English manufactures, in a classic mercantile-imperial trading loop.

Within colonial trading society, the poor white rural workers of the Chesapeake had been recreated almost as an offshore English working class, heavily male and more or less chronically disorderly. Here and elsewhere in North America in the later seventeenth century they were augmented by shipments of black slaves, imported both directly from Africa and through the Caribbean. Hobbling in to be yoked to plantations, blacks joined whites in a multiracial labour force.

At the same time, England's settlement prong also had a strategic edge. As the outlying, transatlantic ramparts of English imperialism, the colonies were positioned as a wall of Englishness, facing Spanish territories to the south and the inland French claims of New France and Acadia to the north. The sprawling English claim was also a check upon the Dutch to the east, whose New Netherland venture around the Hudson River was burrowing right through lands which England saw as falling within its area of commercial influence. In the course of spluttering wars between London and Amsterdam, an English fleet plucked New Amsterdam in 1664. Renamed New York, its seizure gave England commanding territorial control of the complete north-east coast.

The assertion of rights there was followed in the 1660s and 1670s by the gradual commercial development of New Jersey and Pennsylvania under the authority of varying chartered proprietors. These proprietary company colonies were characterised by a heavy influx of farming families, notable religious toleration, slave ownership, heterogeneous settler communities, and a profusion of complex and shifting alliances between colonists and local nations like the Mohawk. Mostly maintaining a brooding peace, these at least enabled pre-colonial societies and

English settlers to skirt the worst of the bloodletting and the brutalising trauma which so disfigured relations in Virginia and Maryland.

Equally, this hardly meant that New York and Pennsylvania were blooming places for local Iroquois, Delawares and Susquehanna. The combined effects of white desire for land, colonial population growth, creeping epidemic diseases and alcohol dispersion irretrievably blighted the fortunes of tribal inhabitants. Put starkly, the exposed 1620 Pilgrims of the Plymouth colony would have all but perished but for fraternal aid from, and trade with, coastal villagers. Yet by the end of the century bonds of gratitude had dissolved, and mutual ties of live-and-let-live accommodation had virtually all snapped.

At first sight, the West Indies did not look the sort of place to settle down a new colonial order, a warm spot in which to root dominant English values of landed property, family and independent self-reliance. In the later sixteenth and earlier seventeenth centuries maritime incursions into the Caribbean consisted of piratical armed fleets, as shady merchants responded to tempting opportunities. These focussed on accumulating wealth through rampant raiding and plundering, by financing privateers as hired goons to break up puny Spanish settlements and to grab at weakly defended Spanish trade routes. The prize money returns from prowling war adventurers were good, winked at by a collusive Elizabethan regime content to keep its diplomatic distance from such bloody buccaneering forays.

But even as this 'take the treasure and run' enterprise continued into the seventeenth century, tentative Caribbean settlement and trade schemes began to take shape. Although cock-eyed visions of the West Indies as a fabled El Dorado of gold and silver turned to dust quickly, tobacco or cotton production provided more realistic prospects for the exploitation of individual islands. Here, though, there were hiccoughs. A first bite at the Guiana coasts by English settlement expeditions proved fruitless, and colonisation also stumbled in the lesser Antilles, where organised and resolute resistance by Kalinagos islanders was able to check invasion by lighter military landings.

Still, early faltering seemed only to harden the intent of Caribbean colonising interests to open territories to English commercial settlement. Individual magnates, joint-stock companies and stirring syndicates all began streaming in to fund agricultural settlement under crown patronage, and to drum up interest and support. Not unexpectedly, the portrayal of Caribbean colonisation put a high gloss on efforts as a worthy English mission to supplant an unrefined and despotic Spain. Here was a beckoning tropical region, ready for the improvements of advanced agricultural specialisation and the benefits of harmonious trade through the dedicated efforts of free and reliable men of property. In reality, the quest for control of the West Indies rested mainly on blind greed. Promotion of island settlement was an exceptionally contentious and grubby business, riven by cut-throat feuding between elite groups competing for the plum of crown patronage, and dogged by squabbling sets of gentry financiers and rich nobles, panting after royal warrants to claim the islands.

Throughout the 1620s and 1630s England scooped up several islands, including Barbados, and unrelenting mariner incursions secured the Spanish colony of Jamaica in the 1650s. By virtually any measure, the potential of the wider Caribbean and its tropical assets far exceeded that of any mainland English colony, and by the mid-seventeenth century the islands were sucking in a higher proportion of emigrants and investment capital than anywhere else in the English transatlantic world.

Small aboriginal island populations could be forcibly displaced and instilled with habits of industry and obedience under the lash of English work discipline. But they were too skimpy to make an effective labour force for big commercial agriculture. So, as in America's Chesapeake, early production of export staples of tobacco and cotton became dependent upon a healthy outflow of indentured labour from Britain. Impoverished bonded servants made up around half of all immigration here during the seventeenth century, with even the completely property-less mortgaging their labour to try their luck at a better living in the West Indies. While these white indentured workers provided adequate labour for the raising of tobacco, cotton, cacao, indigo and other products on smaller mixed farms, the supply was short when West Indian cultivation turned sugary. From around the mid-century, enticed by a profitable gap in the rising international sugar market, islands occupied by English planters swung towards large-scale sugar production, spooning out from its booming heartland in Barbados to the string of Leeward Islands like Antigua and Montserrat, and on to Jamaica.

As inflated agricultural prices tipped out smaller farmers, scrabbling tenants and scrawny freeholders, wealthy landowners closed in, creating a towering planter elite or 'plantocracy' which was far better off than colonists anywhere else in the English New World. This group of wealthy men furnished larger sugar islands with an imported overlay of a greater English gentry, dominating black and poorer white colonial society from their lavish hillside mansions and drinking clubs in port towns.

With easy profits from extensive sugar production, labour cost was not necessarily of great account to large planters. The real issue for the English West Indies was where to procure and how to maintain a mass of muscular workers. In this regard, well before the arrival of English planting, the Brazilian Portuguese had learned that the back-breaking harshness and unremitting intensity of plantation work was unlikely to enthuse flocks of free labour. Just like sugar cane fields and tools, agricultural labour would have to be owned and penned in.

Commencing in the 1640s, Barbados, Jamaica and the Leewards turned the West Indies into the cockpit of English colonial slavery as tens of thousands of slaves were deposited on the sugar economy. Exposed to high mortality rates through exhaustion, malnutrition and the punitive cost of attempts at resistance and desertion, the African slave labour force had constantly to be replenished through fresh shipments. West African beliefs that slaves were being carried off by white purchasers to be eaten were not entirely without some meaning.

Heavy attrition and the pressing labour need of sugar producers provided a strong sweetener to English merchant and financial concerns to pull African trade squarely towards slaving. By the 1670s Barbadian demand was already forcing the pace of slave acquisition along an extended western coastal rim. Caged labour exports were also taking sail for the Chesapeake colonies as these, too, began to run short of indentured servants. African slaves were mostly acquired as a disposable human surplus from local wars or raiding activity, commandeered as servile captives by victorious sides and then dumped on the growing export market for unfree labour. English traders usually purchased them from African dealers or from the roaming coastal emissaries of inland chiefs. By the end of the seventeenth century England was routinely shipping many thousands of African slaves and confirming its overseas market dominance over slaving competitors like the Netherlands. It was already well on its way to becoming the leading slave-trading nation of the Western world.

These later decades were marked by gigantic waves of merchant-trader ambition, few curling higher than that of bodies like the Company of Royal Adventurers into Africa, formed in the 1660s by the king's brother, James Duke of York. The Royal Adventurers were not shy to make the running, being granted western African monopoly trading rights for 1,000 years for both gold and slave supplies to the Caribbean. Although it did not turn out to be all smooth sailing for the York enterprise, much effort was taken to promote the early success of its trading station activities along what had become known as the Gold Coast and the Slave Coast. Slaves discharged from Royal Adventurers' ships were thoughtfully branded with the letters DY, while the company advertised by issuing New Guinea coinage struck from pure African gold and imprinted with its symbol, an elephant. On the more picaresque fringe of the London working class the company's gold guinea was reputedly dubbed Old Mr Gory, a sardonic appreciation of the pitiless nature of its origin.

While an emerging empire was finding a cheeky echo in their capital, fixing colonial relations in the West Indies was a more serious irritation for the English governing class. Disgruntled servants, largely youthful and frequently no strangers to trouble, were annoyingly prone to break their indenture terms, to duck service and even to resort to menacing defiance. If anything, sullen slaves were even worse. Lurking in a subterranean, nocturnal world of seemingly impenetrable song, ritual and magic, they appeared to be perpetually conspiratorial, hatching possible rebellion or sabotage, or otherwise scheming to band together in runaway gangs.

From the second half of the seventeenth century the fat planter interests which ran island legislatures clamped down hard with tough slave and servant codes to govern master-servant relations. At their core lay the absolute enforcement of property rights in the social order. Unfree labour was owned as an investment, much like an acre of tropical land or a sugar mill. Thus, while indentured, Irish chattel labour was owned by an English master to almost the same extent as a Slave Coast African might be owned, granted only the paltriest legal claim upon rights of sustenance and protection from extreme personal abuse. Backed by companies of government troops and motley stiff-arm militia contingents, planters cut down any slave who offended against property, threatened a colonist, or failed to submit tamely to command. Scattered slave communities lived under heavy force of statute and of arms, and the maximum exertion of summary powers wielded by vigilant colonists and administrators. Furthermore, viewed by the established Church as insolent and irreclaimable heathens, the wretched conditions of island slaves barely touched English philanthropic sensibilities. By the later 1600s only a handful of Quaker milksops had come to view them as deserving of basic rights of humane treatment and consideration.

Elsewhere, among white indentured servants a large complement of Irish labourers was singled out for a particular turn of the screw. The reasons for this were several: they were viewed with suspicion as unreliable papists; they were suspected of harbouring seditious sentiment which might contaminate neighbouring slaves; and their number included several thousand political prisoners, beaten opponents of Irish land confiscations in the 1650s. For the English state, convenient political access to colonial territory now allowed for the transportation of known troublemakers to distant places of social intolerance where even elementary rights or liberties could be kept suspended without very much fuss.

In all, the experience of Barbados and Jamaica threw a long shadow in the 1660s. With Jamaica's easy seizure seeming to confirm increasing Spanish feebleness, the expansive Carolinas region, located on the south-eastern coast of North America between Virginia and Spanish Florida, looked just the ticket for further American exploitation. Bidding for crown settlement title, a fairly incestuous Atlantic faction of royalist West Indian planters, southern English landed magnates and London swells paraded on as the lords proprietor of Carolina. Ways of clearing his chronic indebtedness usually concentrated the low mind of

Charles II, and in 1663 the paying proprietors received their royal grant to establish what their prospectus described as an immaculate and profitable colonial venture, drawing on the usual attraction of abundant productive land.

The main spur to Carolina development was the Barbadian sugar economy which forced land prices to dizzy heights and more or less squeezed out less remunerative food crops like rice and corn. To its ambitious proprietors the Carolinas presented a congenial alternative to the roaring islands plantation boom, and had the right kind of warm, malarial conditions to make servile African labour feel right at home. Slavery was institutionalised from the beginnings of colonisation and the settlement rapidly developed an intensely hierarchical colonial society.

Predictably, in another settlement founded on land expropriation and commercial agricultural development, there could be no rights for the communal lands through which hunting and foraging peoples customarily roamed. In the spirit of the age which had arrived, the only legitimate tenure was the cash value of fixed ownership, with a disciplined and virtuous cultivation of land for individual gain as the stamp of civilised status. Aboriginal land was swallowed up and by the end of the century the free existence of its ranging inhabitants had all but collapsed as they were weakened or killed off in desperate and futile wars of resistance, or were simply enslaved by rural colonists.

On the other hand, the imported slave population grew speedily in response to agricultural demand, with labourers making up fully half of the colonial population by the early eighteenth century. The free immigrants who flowed in from the 1670s were a mixed bunch of merchants, small planters, farmers and indentured servants, a sizeable proportion of these being drawn across from Barbados. Adding a further link to the English Atlantic migration and trading chain, they made their way in an outpost society, commanded by a tiny upper class of podgy merchants and big monied families which exercised power through locally elected assemblies of freemen. For settlers, both North and South Carolina grew a mantle of openness, sustained a liberal religious toleration and fostered a smallholder ethos of inching self-improvement. Equally, over time, the white Carolinas also developed an intensely Caribbean concentration in their clear-cut social order, breeding conspicuous wealth for large landowners with slaves, and a life of demoralisation and dispossession for poor whites and slaves.

Unlike the obsessive cash crop pursuit of the sugar industry, the Carolinas' economic growth was more modest and also more diverse. Speculators' initial interest in the region was in its potential as a sound base for food production, founded on West Indian island absorption of corn, vegetables and livestock. Production was also turned towards timber export, and light trade with American Indians extracted considerable quantities of buckskin to meet the European appetite for hide. The turn of the century brought further buoyancy through the spread of intensive rice cultivation, and the strategically important supply of ship requirements like pitch and tar for navy and merchant marine stores.

As with other fast and freebooting colonies, many acquisitive Carolinian settlers were commercially ruthless. These unscrupulous individuals distinguished themselves by milking the spoils of government office, colluding in murky trade with Caribbean pirates and filibusters, and profiting from the enslavement of entire American Indian families for the local labour market or for despatch to one or other West Indies plantation. Possibly only the beavers were fortunate, spared from extinction by being too few in number to warrant a serious commercial effort to cash them in entirely as fur.

Movement into Asia was shaped by a quite different set of imperatives and transformations. Well before the sixteenth century, English imports of Asian commodities such as spice crops and cotton had been coming via Portuguese trade, or through Middle East land crossings into the eastern Mediterranean and onwards to the British Isles. As consumer demand grew, hungry mercantile fraternities began to entrench themselves as a direct English maritime presence in Asia. This first congealed around expanded merchant shipping links with Turkey, loading up silks, spices, coffee and other goods which had not been cornered by the Portuguese Indian Ocean trade around the Southern African Cape. By the early 1590s the Turkey trade had knitted itself into the usual mercantile-imperial business vanguard, the pacy chartered company. As a pioneering Levant Company, North London Turkey merchants had both the capital and the venturesome instincts to embark on exploitation of grander commercial opportunities. These leading merchant adventurers then engaged in a burst of combined inland and sea exploration, consolidating overland trade ties with Persia and India, and poking through to promising trade spots like Malacca. But, with a forest of Dutch masts around the Cape sea route and the prospect of the Netherlands pulling away with seaborne Asian trade, Levant efforts fell away.

Nevertheless, the Dutch commercial threat was simply bringing on another powerful English rival. Right at the end of the sixteenth century, the usual avaricious assemblage of monied men, keen on speculation and the flexing of influence, set up the East India Company as a joint-stock enterprise to bid for a monopoly charter for English trade in Asia, a warrant granted in 1600. In stacking its cards, the East India venture needed a long pack. Business risks were high, starting with immense transport distances, tricky sea conditions, vulnerable goods, and a volatile political environment in many Asian societies which could scupper transactions.

Not altogether surprisingly, although it would soon become the most powerful of all English overseas chartered companies, in its early operating years the East India Company was not exactly flush, bringing discouragingly pedestrian returns on capital for London financiers. Short of longer-term investment funding, it was also up against glowering competition from mercantile rivals jealous of its crown privilege, and had to contend with Portuguese and Dutch determination to maintain their established grip on Asian cargoes. Early East India trade was nourished by its close attachment to royal authority and its loud claim to good commercial practice in the national interest, although entrepreneurs had a miserable time trying to get English-manufactured woollens and cloth onto Asian markets.

But the real imperative was Asian extraction, not English export, the purchase of large volumes of spices and pepper from coastal India and from other cultivation areas such as Borneo, Java and the smaller Moluccan Islands. Company concerns also slid quickly beyond the Indonesian archipelago, with its hard-driving agents and dealers entering a dense web of Asian commodity trade, spun around bullion and barter transactions, and shrewd diversification beyond the old basics of pepper and spices. Like the Portuguese who preceded them, English merchants also grasped the advantages to be gained by carrying goods for prosperous Asian traders, diverting surplus English shipping into a profitable internal Asian trade.

Filling out into an open, bustling and gluttonous Asian-trading universe, the East India venture soon extended its trading slate. First to be chalked up was abundant cotton and silk from the western and south-eastern Indian coast, and also the enticement of Persian silk supplies in the Red Sea trade, which could be run through the Persian Gulf. Simultaneously, through its protected port stations on the Indonesian archipelago, the company threaded out into ever more far-flung and sprawling trading grids in the Far East. There, although tightly controlled Chinese ports shut out foreign English vessels, the lucrative reselling of Chinese silk, porcelain and gold through Japan and south-east Asia provided a deft way around this. To bolster its steady progress, the East India Company also formed trading posts or 'factories' for its Chinese trade through Japan, the Malay peninsula and Siam. At the same time, interest in sources of silver as a means of augmenting bullion sharpened the English appetite for extending trade with Japan.

While the pepper and spice crops of the Indonesian archipelago and India remained a principal business, mercantile life here was not always comfortable. In sought-after trading grounds like Java and the Moluccas, English intrusions rattled the Dutch, whose own East India Company tried to uphold a monopoly underwritten by canny trade treaties with island rulers. Opposing rival Dutch efforts to push it back, the East India Company then went on the offensive and launched armed hostilities against its commercial adversary early in the seventeenth century. This campaign was ill-starred and brought the rooted power of the Dutch down on its head. Forced to make peace on disagreeable terms, English merchants remained cramped by continuing Dutch trade restrictions and by the 1620s were obliged to relinquish their stake in the Moluccan spice crop. Nonetheless, they were still able to tack down other parts of local business. The availability of contracted Asian ships to convey goods to English factories pricked the Dutch Moluccas monopoly, a Javanese factory site was maintained until the last years of the seventeenth century, and considerable pepper exports from Sumatra continued. Furthermore, shrinking pepper power by the later 1600s was well compensated for by more trading latitude in China, where earlier merchant ventures had been repeatedly frustrated. A more lax political order was now willing to accommodate European port trading agents and, right at the end of the century, the East India Company set up in Canton, giving it a door into China. By the early eighteenth century, silk and porcelain were being outstripped by shipments of fashionable tea, as English consumption began to rise dramatically.

A sipping social dedication to tea could be seen not only in the way that London's leisured classes took to chatting and flirting in decorous new tea gardens. Evangelicals and stern employers also promoted consumption amongst workers as a sober tipple to keep them steady and alert at work, a commendable alternative to dissolute gin. Thus did distant Manchu China do its bit for the championing of British working-class sobriety. Tea also did three other things. It introduced a flavour of imperial acquisition into everyday domestic life in the British Isles. Secondly, accompanied by Barbadian sugar, its heavy consumption evolved as a distinct trait of British character, a national fondness for sweet tea. Lastly, as it required the boiling of water, its consumption did wonders for urban health by helping to reduce rates of water-borne disease.

Throughout this period, the key objective of the East India Company was the extension of its market reach into thriving trade zones and the securing of English domination within these. Coastal India was one obvious catch, and in the early 1600s company ships tried to squeeze into Surat, the natural west-coast entry port to the flowering region of Gujarat. But obtaining a foothold on Surat was not easy. Any English trading presence required the consent of the powerful controlling Mughal Empire, and there was also a prior Portuguese trading claim with which to deal. Ostentatious diplomatic exchanges with Mughal court officials and aggrandising gifts to grease a hard-nosed Emperor Jahangir eventually confirmed English trade rights. Thereafter, the thorn of Lisbon was pulled by the 1630s when the company and the Portuguese agreed to cease mutually damaging Asian clashes.

While East India agents were now able to sit more comfortably in Surat, few Indians themselves were really sat upon. The power and influence of the Mughal imperial system was imposing, and English commercial activity had to fall in with the rhythms of Gujarat life in its maritime stronghold. In short, the company was tolerated by Mughal India, and through the seventeenth century Surat continued to be run by its haughty officials, an imperious Indian establishment which did not see itself as having to sit on committees with upstart English visitors. Resident company servants had to settle in Surat as a tiny Christian enclave, bunched at the foot of the emperor's ornate castle and politically toothless.

Commercially, though, the East India Company was ravenous. From Surat it strung out a line of subsidiary Gujarat trading settlements, and also swung north to cities like Lahore and to southern ports such as Madras. Cotton cloth and indigo exports were good earners in the early part of the seventeenth century but before long calico proved to be even better, with labouring classes in Europe and its colonies providing a huge market for cheap woven cloth. By the end of the 1600s, with Indian textile production radiating ever wider and with Bengal and other new weaving areas on the rise, Caribbean slaves, Virginia and Carolinas poor whites, and English West Country infantrymen were all buttoning up rough Indian cloth.

As English trading solidified around India its structure became more simplified. Merchantmen carrying bullion headed straight for Indian ports, loaded up with textile cargoes and turned around for the long return crossing. On the face of things, there was increasingly less to be over-watched and simple bulk trade looked to be growing effortlessly, provided that local political conditions remained stable. Political stability, however, was something that could not always be assured.

In the 1660s and 1670s Mughal imperialism was dented severely by insurgent Maratha forces, causing more than a flutter in the stomach of English dealers in Surat. Still, the company was able to stay put in western India, retaining the strong base of Bombay, acquired from Portugal in the 1660s, as sovereign English crown territory, and adding to its other holdings towards the end of that decade. English strength also increased in newer areas like Madras and notably in Bengal, where business fixed on Calcutta. Oozing sites of English commercial enterprise and overseas power, East India settlements formed a strand of distinctively segregated towns containing bodies of prosperous Indian merchants, artisans and labourers, and separate pockets of white agents and passing sailors. Increasingly, they were also becoming strongholds of English military power, stocked with garrisons of regular troops and studded with palisade and other fortifications.

In this period, trade could certainly run amicably enough as an Indian-Anglo business compact, smoothed by the backing authority of stable local rulers. Equally, if a trading environment turned rocky, the rattling of English force, in however small a way, had its fair political value. In later seventeenth-century Madras for instance, it brought in dues and favours from Indian merchants dislodged by rampaging Mughal army campaigns in the locality, and appreciative of a protective English umbrella under which to scuttle. On other occasions, though, the availability of company troop contingents merely encouraged overmighty company spirits to overreach themselves.

Roused by the strutting Sir Joshua Childs, a chairman who viewed himself as a fighting cock tearing through a softening Mughal Empire, the East India Company launched a chancy military offensive against its edgy host in the 1680s. Calculating that Mughal strength was fraying seriously, Childs and his directors tried to secede from Indian overrule by establishing Calcutta, Bombay and Madras as wholly autonomous colonial settlements. Secured and well fortified, these would be sustained by English customs levies on Indian shipping and the systematic taxation of local weavers. Then, able to fleece with the best in India and freed from having to curry favour with its potentates, the East India enterprise would be able to focus squarely on its strategy of collaring the entire Indian textile production.

But this premature grab for power was poorly judged. Expeditionary war for absolute power went badly, and at the end of the 1680s the company had no option but to make peace with the victorious Mughals. Yet it was not all bad news. At Calcutta, renewed trading terms permitted the expansion of fortified settlement, while the company intensified its financing of Indian merchant associates and also stepped up its promotion of piecework in the weaving industry. By the end of the century not only were English commercial rights more grounded, but the East India presence now also had an easy-going licence to make war on non-Christian populations and to enforce its own justice in recognised English settlements. From 1698 that meant the authority to hang offending Indians in Calcutta; Bengal had acquired its Tyburn, much as if it were the county of Middlesex.

By the beginning of the eighteenth century, the East India Company had become the quintessential emblem of English Asian trade. Wreathed in textiles, pepper, spices and tea, as well as coffee, its exports to and through England were already easily up with, or were outpacing, commodities from North America and the West Indies. In addition, as London's most conspicuous overseas commercial enterprise, the company also embodied English mercantile imperialism in its most redoubtable form. By 1700 West Africa's company was a mess, its monopoly a sieve. Other colonising companies, such as several in the Caribbean, had folded, leaving disgruntled packs of smaller financiers and hucksters. In sharp contrast, a sturdy East India Company showed no sign of ever dissolving. A very large London employer, its stock was now good and its investment base looked sufficiently respectable to mop up the savings of prim London widows.

For all this, the intersecting interests of chartered company capitalism and those of the crown were always tense. Company privileges were detested by untold scores of East Indies buccaneers, itching to trade outside its monopoly. There were also periods when company profits dipped and it tended to stagger rather than swagger. Certainly, investors in its stock did not always see handsome gains. Furthermore, the strategic advantages of bedding down with the crown came with an annoying disadvantage. The court had a tendency to be fickle or unreliable.

In this respect, both James I and Charles I quietly distinguished themselves in the old royal game of money and favour. On one hand, the monarchs pocketed large East India fees and loans for their crown monopoly concession. On the other, they watered down company trading privileges through the double-dealing sale of licences to a number of dubious private interlopers. In the 1640s probably the only way to stay the gambling king's signing hand was to bribe him to the tune of tens of thousands of pounds. If anything, it was the stack of gifts and loans around court circles and parliamentary cliques of gentlemen which was so crucial to regular renewal of the East India Company charter. So was the company's convenient ownership of a large chunk of the Bank of England, which happened to own debts on both the king and parliament. This hold mattered when the company was seriously reduced in standing in the 1690s.

Then, despite being outfoxed by a predatory New East India Company, which was awarded a charter over its head as reward for a grubby royal loan, the old Asian enterprise survived by fusing its stock and its skills with the new venture, merging into a United East India Company in the early 1800s. Circulating within the ruling political elite, well-placed East India bribes did much to distribute wealth among the least needy, just as they were coddled by its premium linens and fine silks. Those fastidious English envoys of the early 1600s who proclaimed the Mughals to be variously immoral, decadent or barbaric must evidently have known what they were on about.

By the end of the seventeenth century, with London's commercial influence gushing deep into the Atlantic world and Asia, the energies of the British Isles were increasingly no longer defined by nation, geographical location or ocean. Even if never formally proclaimed as a national doctrine by the crown or by parliament, nor necessarily even pursued with overall consistency, Anglo-British over-seas expansion was becoming a compelling definition of national interest, embracing state personnel and policies. For an advancing imperial power among others which were faltering, it was also providing the British Isles with a strong point of strategic coherence.

At that level, the purpose of English state policy was to assist the enterprise and political efforts of its merchants and settlers in a general struggle for command of the New World. Naturally, that meant a responsibility to ensure that the benefits of commercial growth flowed into some of the right coffers. Any colonial outgrowth, whether Pennsylvania or Jamaica, whether sustained by free labour or by slavery, was a foreign English estate, a productive asset which would add directly to the wealth and prestige of the home country. By the early 1800s politicians and press were already identifying London and its dependent acquisitions as one great imperial country, although those who inhabited it could hardly be seen as a single or unified community. Proponents of a British Empire celebrated it as Protestant and politically free or libertarian. But its colonial subjects included not only white Protestant settlers across the Atlantic but also indentured paupers, deportees, Catholics, Hindus and other non-Christian or black populations. Many of these could not exactly be termed free. Nor could they be termed deferential underlings of the English crown.

Still, whatever the ideological muddle of what is often called the First British Empire, the emergence of an organisational shape was discernible. In addition to the principle that once a colony had been acquired it was expected to pay for itself financially, settlements and trade claims were roundly taxed and were subject to tight trading controls. Where conditions were appropriate, they served also to soak up surplus labour in Britain, opening an emigration channel for a growing landless and unemployed population. This was not the only imperial use for induced emigration, as we have seen. Morose rural rebels from flattened Highland chiefdoms or Cork malcontents, inflamed by the loss of ancestral lands, could now be exiled cheaply as dissidents. That expedient took care of punishment, while at the same time depositing troublesome groups on colonial labour markets helped to meet North American and West Indian hunger for cheap labour.

From the 1650s onwards, the domestic operation of various imperial activities became more systematic in the aftermath of the Civil War. During the brief tenure of the English republic, Oliver Cromwell passed potent Navigation Acts, creating a single, unified national trade monopoly for all merchant interests. Henceforward all trade was to be conveyed by British ships and all colonies were placed under the regulating authority of state councils, commissions and committees. On paper at least the state had the statutory imperial authority it needed.

Aggressive encouragement of mercantilist expansion was kept on course after the Restoration. Charles II bolstered crown licensing of all imperial commerce, with its burgeoning spoils system of chartered companies maintaining an English transport and import monopoly of trade goods. In the Atlantic world, the use of ships based in English ports was declared mandatory, and new overseas settlements were assured of exclusive access to English markets and commodities. Lastly, a 1696 Laws of Trade, governing economic returns from overseas empire to crown and nation, led to the formation of a Board of Trade to police the terms of colonial commercial expansion.

Although never watertight, the system of chartered monopolies and the close identification of empire with the state was a snug arrangement. Maritime commerce bloated the crown through customs duties and excise duties, ensuring that for a royal state which lived that sort of life, there was always an ample war chest into which to dip. Protectionism also aided the turnover of immense sums of wealth to grease the wheels of patronage and bribery, as the future of great merchant and financial interests depended heavily upon political as well as military favours, not least those bestowed by a grasping crown. And those were always paid for at a high rate.

By the end of this early period, the growth of English deep-water shipping capacity had become especially marked. With wealth being sucked into major ports like Bristol and London, urban growth stimulated by local capital derived from the India and Atlantic slave trades made them conspicuously mercantile-imperial in character, with flourishing docks and warehouses pulling ever more people into the servicing of foreign trades. In this manner, the life of whole swathes of English working society was gradually transformed by the needs of an imperial-merchant capitalism, and not only in employment. By the 1700s port life was exuding a cosmopolitan outer rim, as African and American-African sailors and ex-slaves, many spilling from ships in London's West India docks, fell in with nomadic bunches of Irish weavers, Welsh tinkers and other tramping workers. London may have produced no sugar cane nor Bristol tobacco leaf, but to see a Black Henry, Black Tom or Black Lucy around their docklands was to have glimpsed the plantation of Afro-Caribbean experience.

At the same time, colonial labour had other perceived associations. For some later seventeenth-century exponents of workhouse rigour for the urban poor, there was optimism that this might inculcate the kind of desirable control and discipline which some English observers claimed to be encountering on West Indian plantations. Francis Bacon, who in the 1620s had already called for a disciplinary Holy War upon the disorderly poor, would no doubt have been encouraged.

Like its European imperial rivals, England insisted that its own traders have the benefit of exclusive national supplies of valuable imports. The tools to these lay only partially in shifting alliances or truces with competitors, or in subsidies, bribes and minor aggression to overawe rivals. They lay frequently in war, either for random plunder or to dash flanking commercial challenges. Never famous for shrinking from the test of war, the English state had its war-making capacity renovated by the outward-looking Cromwell and Charles II. Under Cromwell, around three-quarters of state revenue went to the navy, which had its eye not only on the defence of home waters but on a sweeping offensive against plump targets such as Spanish possessions in the New World.

Expeditionary strikes on the basis of naval supremacy were an effective way of getting at imperial rivals by hurting their trade. Indeed, through most of this period the naval fleet was little more than a roving looter. Naval power was so enmeshed with the private trading self-interest of merchants, shipowners and shipmasters that a large chunk of its operations was the blatant pursuit of war for profit, exulting in what could be hauled away from rival Europeans. And as for England's territorial gains, the navy had its own measure of their value. This was strategic, as resupply base stations from which to raid across ever greater distances. Becoming ever more dispersed, the gains of empire had to be won and secured overwhelmingly on the ocean.

Concentration on the prosecution of war at sea with larger and better-armed vessels did not mean any relative neglect of army resources. On land, Charles II developed a standing army of almost 100,000 soldiers by the 1690s. Over time, their active service would come to mean distant foreign service. The fronts of various commercial struggles with Spain, Holland and France, starting in the 1650s and lapping over into the early 1800s, were now not merely the theatres of an old Europe of Gaul or Hispania, or even Ireland. Struggles for one or other kind of national ascendancy were scouring North America, the Caribbean, Africa and India. Rather more than a Channel crossing, continental warfare had come to encompass plenty of continents, far-off areas with which England had previously enjoyed no intersecting history. By 1700, army garrison posts mortgaged to merchants and traders were already very remote. Military movements, like those of trade and migration, were becoming more and more global in orientation.

Steadily improving fiscal and organisational capability for military mobilisation was the natural other side of the seventeenth-century coin of imperial trade, plunder and settlement. For the systematic expansion of armed expeditionary forces in the post-Elizabethan era became a vital cog in the machinery of effective crown dominion, a cushioning against internal risings by trampled slaves, enraged Iroquois villagers or intervention by other European powers.

To suggest that many colonial gains were secure, and that trade and shipping power was growing comfortably at the beginning of the eighteenth century are generalisations which make the formation and nature of the early empire sound simple. It was not. In Ireland, for example, the need to pin down an obdurate peasantry was central to colonial settlement. The drive for American territories was different, spurred by notions of agricultural potential and habitable land. This was a venture to transplant productive English society into a free New World, to create self-sufficiency and to generate profit, more than to pull pre-colonial peoples into trading desirable commodities.

At the same time, imperial movement did not slip into colonial settlement habits everywhere. In places with substantial, resilient and well-organised societies which produced valuable goods, weaker English groups were largely content to tack on a trading company position, restricting themselves to exchange relations. Thus, posts in West Africa or South Asia mattered as no more than a service to merchant trading interests.

Official regulation of possessions was a no less varied part of the picture. Far trading posts and forts were run in the protective ways that private company interests, such as the East India concern, liked to run them. It was in any event futile for the English state to pretend that it could provide continuous armed protection from hostile Gambia Africans or Gujarat Indians, in addition to lunging European raiders. In the case of trade and settlement chartered companies, crown jurisdiction and rights were delegated or licensed to one or other English agency which, in some American colonies, ended up forming a loyally affiliated colonial government. Elsewhere on the imperial spectrum royal authority sometimes also meant direct crown rule of a colonial settlement, as with Jamaica and its military Governor-General in the 1660s.

In yet other instances, the basis of royal charter settlement was by proprietary grant, which handed over all manner of authoritative rights to groups of influential men or even to an individual favoured by the crown, like the well-connected William Penn, whose biggest step up turned out to be Pennsylvania. These governing arrangements were as variable as the life of companies and colonies, some of which folded or merged, added or shed assets. Imperial England had no singular system of trade and settlement, more a baggy set of ruling cultures which was constitutionally part precedent and part improvisation.

For all that, by the end of the 1600s a discernible pattern was being laid down by two strong forces. Colonists occupying aboriginal lands were supposed to be engaged in building virtuous new settlements, rooted in a loose measure of kindred liberty and a natural claim upon a new age of English self-determination overseas. Notwithstanding their assent to crown title and colonial tribute to the monarchy, free white settlers asserted rights of common assembly and entitlement to representative government of a sort, based upon the dominance of male association. The acclaimed rights of freeborn Englishmen were exercised with some vigour beyond their country of origin. Anything but listless, colonies developed political systems consisting of legislatures dominated by wealthy and powerful planter and other social elites, and governors appointed by the crown.

Secondly, if unevenly, the English state was also increasing its governing authority from the centre, through giving governors greater muscle to deal with colonial legislatures and through the imposition of more exacting royal customs and excise systems. By the end of the seventeenth century the state had a good measure of the extent to which colonies were productive holdings to be exploited. Even if overseas ledger returns did not always glitter, by 1700 surging long-distance trade was accounting for around one-fifth of all overseas commerce.

London may have been unable or ill-prepared to direct imperial affairs in a properly co-ordinated manner, but it could ensure that the dividends of overseas growth would benefit not only companies and individual sponsors of colonial development, but would be a windfall for England as a whole. That meant opportunities for restless, ambitious and careerist members of English society to try for the rewards not merely of trade, pillage and land acquisition, but also of enriching advancement through new imperial office, title, sinecures and prizes.

At the end of this century, around 350,000 British people had undertaken a major transoceanic implantation of their society, to say nothing of the tens of thousands of migrants from Ireland to North America and the West Indies. In the Caribbean, most of the required digging was done by slaves, whose numbers had reached about 115,000 by 1700. For many white settlers, an Anglo-British identity in new homeland surroundings was maintained by institutions and community norms, as well as by the transmitted power of migrant memory, custom and tradition. Much was shared with domestic subjects of the king, including political ideas, patterns of consumption and business networks. Although immense distance and prolonged isolation could not but change cultural identities and weaken links to metropolitan society and the crown, there were at the same time family and other social ties which remained binding. At the very least, there was also the simple business of keeping their end up, as identity-conscious and status-conscious immigrants generally tended to do.

But life in South Carolina, in Barbados or in New Jersey was hardly life on any known English model. In many fundamental ways, it was not even slightly so. The prickly realities of racial differentiation, the thumping domination of slaves by free men, and the bloody purges of New England Pequot communities by growling Puritans and their cunning Naragansett allies, were just some of the experiences which made an English future in the colonies so radically different a historical experience. Matters were never so extreme back in Britain, even for the most desperate Staffordshire poachers.

For their part, displaced, unstuck or shovelled across a changed environment, overseas native populations adjusted to the coming of colonial rhythms, sometimes adopting and absorbing English trade goods and agricultural implements, sometimes accepting mission Christianity and its efforts at reconstructing livelihoods, and sometimes just battling for independent survival and opportunity in the midst of unforeseen change. By the 1700s, they too were on greatly altered foundations, linked by diffuse new identities born of conflict, defeat, resistance, or collaboration with the forces of a hungry English imperialism. In some other powerful quarters, however, England's claims to authority were still contested, a picture to which we turn next.

3

Wars and Continuing Expansion *c.*1700–1800

England finally became Britain early in the eighteenth century, with empire as an accumulating accompaniment. Many of its colonial prizes in the West Indies and in North America seemed no longer things to be fought over. Britain had taken them. In Europe, British maritime power was able to dominate its southern carrying trade, and to police Mediterranean commerce through its watchful Gibraltar base. London was nailing down its position as the leading capital and commodity market, hub of shipping and port servicing skills, and exchange centre for a truly Byzantine commissioning network of credit, insurance and trade brokerage activity. Manufacturing for the colonial export trade was accelerating and growing more diverse, while across the Atlantic a thickening base of plantation staples and slave cargoes was lifting national wealth at the expense of European competitors. At the controlling heights of the political order, an oligarchic and commercially-minded landed elite was hitting it off with an ascending patrician class of merchants, bankers, financiers and prosperous businessmen. Depicted as gentlemanly capitalists by some leading historians, their monied priorities and expanding stake in overseas trading companies and in great metropolitan investment and insurance houses was deepening the imperial bias of the British economy. There was also another positive effect on the credit of commercial empire. The seemingly endless seventeenth-century maritime wrestling with the Netherlands had now been eased by the 1688 accession of Mary II and her Dutch consort, William of Orange. With a Protestant succession sealed by the Glorious Revolution, it appeared that toleration, liberty and constitutionalism would be released to further stimulate the health of an amphibious merchant empire.

Yet the galloping development of British power during the previous century had still not been free of some considerable competition. In general, it was the usual chafing story of European rivals not yet exhausting themselves. Britain's share of slaving and other African coastal trade was flourishing, but its commercial posts were not the only ones on the continent. At its southern tip, things were already settled by the Dutch who had founded a viable Southern African colony in the 1650s. Elsewhere, too, through earlier conquest, central and southern North America were saddled with Spanish and Portuguese colonies.

In south-east Asia, Dutch trading interests continued to make a good deal of the running, while the Philippines was in the lap of Spain. India had ripe company pickings, but there the British were still up against several trading competitors with their own privileges. In other words, global British power had to be set against the position of other European states. It was by no means entirely self-evident that trading enclaves and colonial settlements would become large imperial domains.

Nonetheless, conditions for achieving such a conversion were forming. Domestically, rapid political stabilisation under William and Mary provided congenial conditions for mariners, plunderers and other coastal Protestants on the make. Customs and excise revenue grew ever more inflated as maritime commerce and industry pulled away through the later 1600s, creating large reserves of taxable wealth upon which to pile up the foundations of an efficient system of public finance. While many contemporary observers were jittery about European challengers, the depth of British fiscal credit furnished a crucial edge in meeting the demands of war expenditure through additional emergency taxes and war loans. What this boiled down to was a telling national advantage in organising for war against major imperialist foes. Much pointed to it being flexed in the coming century.

By the 1700s the problem for British imperialism was not only a Catholic Spain, an empire commonly derided by British Protestants as despotic, ruthlessly oppressive and infected by primitive superstition. There was also the rival empire of Catholic France. English America had already been harried by French raiders from Canada in the 1680s and 1690s and, even though hostilities ended without territorial loss, the threat from Louis XIV had not been shaken off. The French had also had a go at invading Jamaica, thinking that with only a light deployment of crown expeditionary forces in the Caribbean, their chance may have come. Meanwhile, along the southern fringes of English American settlement, colonists had been locked in running clashes with Spanish opponents during the 1680s.

The bleeding impact of these and other attacks certainly went to the heads of the French, who in the early eighteenth century tried for some larger prizes by hitting the Spanish Empire as well. Britain duly despatched naval forces to the Caribbean where they fought hard against a French fleet but were unable to check some destructive French and Spanish raiding of the petty British Bahamas and more trivial Leeward Islands colonies. British sea control was emphatic but not yet absolute.

If these moves against the British may have amounted to showing off, in North America the French again raised the tension significantly around the turn of the century. By bolting down their recently acquired settlement of Louisiana and attempting to pull it into a front with Canada, France was building a strategic situation that threatened to bottle up British colonial activity, restricting it to the east. By the early 1700s this had set the stage for a war between British maritime and land forces, allied Franco-Spanish opponents, and collaborating American Indian warriors who flitted between imperial sides. In a laborious struggle of teetering offensives and counter-offensives, running from Massachusetts, New York and New France in the north to South Carolina and Spanish Florida, virtually everyone became trapped. But, with French Acadia in the bag as Nova Scotia by 1710 and with their enemies' position weakening, Britain ended up least trapped of all.

War was concluded in 1713 by the Treaty of Utrecht on gloomy terms for French ambitions in this stretch of the New World. France lost its half of St Kitts, while Acadia, Newfoundland and the massive Hudson Bay territories were also transferred to Britain, drawing with them an endless spread of profitable fur stocks and vast cod fisheries. On top of these gains, Britain landed exclusive rights to supply slaves, as well as other commodities, to Spanish American colonies.

As French meddling became less of a worry to London, by the 1730s it was the turn of Spain to be menacing. Apprehension over the security of South Carolina was due not only to French restiveness to the east in Louisiana, and to intermittent American Indian raiding to try to recover losses, but to heavy breathing from Spanish Florida. Here, Britain's northwards establishment of a Georgia commercial colony was potential dynamite under rocky Anglo-Spanish relations.

Not unexpectedly, Madrid saw this as a forward movement to frustrate Spanish expansion north of Florida, and something to which it could not nod. Although Britain had its anti-war critics, fearful of a disruption of good commercial ties with peninsular Spain, there were more flinty forces urging on a wide war against the Spanish-American Empire. Britain, or more particularly, its aggressive West Indian merchant trading faction, was looking to profit considerably from the market gains of Madrid's collection of American viceroyalties.

By the end of the 1730s an Anglo-Spanish colonial war was underway, with rather mixed early results for London. Although its territorial line was held, British intentions to

nab Panama and Cuba and to push into Spanish Florida all
foundered. Meanwhile, France was in no mood to countenance a British assault upon the Spanish Empire. In 1744
it dropped any trifling pretence of restraint and came out
in war against Britain. The British colonial troops who
were now thrown at a fortified Canada barely dented it,
while repeated raiding by the French and their Iroquois
allies was unable to crack the northern frontier defences of
British colonies. With each exhausting operation both sides
became stuck, and slid inexorably towards stalemate.

By the mid-1740s there was jumpiness elsewhere. British
and French East India Companies had at first tried to buy
Indian neutrality by accepting respective trade spheres,
but there was to be no peaceable commercial way out of
the crisis. In the Bay of Bengal an attacking French fleet
proved unstoppable, defeating local British naval power,
taking the trading prize of Madras and later beating back
a reinforcing squadron.

Confident British ministers and politicians, including
William Pitt, had clearly failed to foresee the difficulties
of breaking into deep, upland Spanish colonies. All the
same, the virtual deadlock which ended the war was not
all cloudy for Britain. Its disruptive maritime blockade of
French commerce had squeezed their position in Canada,
and in India Royal Navy supremacy had been re-imposed
by the end of hostilities. And, while the 1748 Peace of Aix-
la-Chapelle obliged Britain to return Louisbourg, which it
had seized from the French on the St Lawrence, it regained
Madras which was worth rather more.

Both sides were haunted by the knowledge that peace
was more like a truce, which would only hold for as long as

they behaved themselves. This was destined not to be long, for Britain was committed to the defeat of French ambitions. It had in its sights a chain of lesser West Indian islands and continental settlements, whose heavy dependence on subsidies and imported goods made them vulnerable to being throttled by naval power. But French offensive intentions firstly sent hostilities in a quite different direction. Facing a tide of cheaper commodities that threatened to undermine their trading relationship with American Indians to the west, in 1749 the French stormed through Ohio to drive out British commerce and impose their sovereignty. A British counter-offensive several years later ended in grief, with regular regiments shattered by tough American Indian fighters allied to the French, who spat on their corpses for not having measured up to manhood.

After again putting pressure on Louisbourg, Britain's forces were also obliged to back down on their St Lawrence area of activity. They were more effective in pushing aside the French in Nova Scotia, not only turfing out enemy forces but ruthlessly expelling French Acadian inhabitants, thereby securing the territory completely. For the most part, however, in what is often depicted as a trackless wilderness war, British regular and colonial troops with American Indian levies were on the back foot against French infantry and Canadian militia reinforced by thick fighting alliances with loyal bands of Iroquois and other irregular combatants.

Along with its conduct of imperial war in North America, France was also playing its cards in India. In 1750, Jean-Francois Dupleix, its governor-general at Pondicherry, gambled on swallowing the troubled Mughal localities of

Hyderabad and Carnatic, both rocked by internal rivalries and succession disputes. The notion of putting compliant French nominees in control, propped up by French troops, looked appealing. But such intervention in domestic Indian affairs was another of those instances of the remedy proving worse than the disease. For the British East India interest was now impelled to take action, by turning out company forces against its worming enemy in the Carnatic and Hyderabad. Conditions were combustible.

The spark came in 1754, with the despatch to India of naval and army reinforcements under a bright and scheming company soldier, Robert Clive, a man perpetually on the lookout for a large political opportunity to show how well he could get things done. One soon fell into his lap. Since the earlier 1700s, Bengal authorities had been growing increasingly alarmed at the spread of East India Company influence and no less irritated by its flat unwillingness to shoulder a larger share of state dues. Never passive, the company was now becoming dangerously presumptuous. To tame the disdainful British, Siraj-ud-Daula, the Nawab of Bengal, overran their Calcutta settlement in 1756. The following year, an expeditionary force under Clive regained Calcutta and then swept on to take the French Bengal claim of Chandernagore. But, as a shrewd and manipulative company man with strong forces at his disposal, Clive himself looked beyond merely restoring the British position. He and a trusty clique of East India cronies plotted to steady Bengal affairs in ways that would secure far more favourable terms for company business, and bring in substantial individual spoils for a hard core of conniving East India officials.

With Siraj-ud-Daula an untrustworthy political encumbrance to be shaken off, Clive and his following took up with a plotting rival, Mir Jafar, who had the necessary long purse to interest the British in his promise as an alternative Nawab. After the pocketing of plum bribes, the company army overthrew Siraj-ud-Daula at Plassey in 1757. Under Clive, the British had become eager mercenaries in the violent service of Indian political intrigue, not forgetting, of course, to take a very large cut for themselves.

Through infiltration they were now bidding aggressively for more decisive power by inserting their leverage into an increasingly fraught and distended Mughal political order. By the 1760s the British were fairly firmly in the saddle as the virtual rulers of Bengal, deeply involved in the tailoring of Nawab succession, nosing down tax revenues to finance their garrisons, and raising cheap Indian *sepoy* infantry to bolster the new order against European incursions and Mughal or Maratha assaults.

As the cancerous British agent within the body of Indian courtly power, away to the south the company could not but stand firm with pretenders to the Nawab of Arcot or the Nizam of Hyderabad, who were up against French-sponsored rivals. Its own quest for power had to be attuned to the terms and needs of Indian politics. Lured by generous grants of territory into backing Muhammad Ali as Nawab of Arcot, British forces at Madras toppled the French at Wandiwash and Pondicherry by 1760. Committed to shoring up the open-handed Muhammad Ali as Nawab and ally, the company became thoroughly ensnared in Carnatic politics.

To meet his obligations to the British army and to ensure his survival, the Nawab slipped easily into the habit of extending his influence among his East India protectors, borrowing from them, distributing largesse in return for their political favours, and drawing on the campaigning efforts of their arms to enlarge his territory and augment his resources. Muhammad Ali drifted on under the wolf-ish protection of the company, advancing its fortunes and increasing his control over the south-eastern Carnatic lands. His avarice was matched only by his gullibility, for his state was unlikely to hold out for long. Another British opportunity, it was fated to be nabbed as a further East India Company prize.

By the mid-1760s, the company had acquired significant political influence and effective control over varied patches of Indian territory, including parts of the south and the south-east, Bengal, and the territories of the Wazir of Oudh, which had also fallen into its lap on the basis of heavy garrison protection. A trading interest had turned into sub-stantial territorial power, with the ostentatious company figure of Robert Clive turning into an effective regional Indian ruler in 1765, once he had gained the ruling author-ity of *diwani* of the civil government of Bengal from the Mughal court. For Britain, South Asia was now sprouting a major new crop of political and military imperatives.

As they spread their tentacles through Bengal and beyond, plundering company agents, along with Indian trading partners and underlings, honed in on trading networks, either placing these under their paws or speculat-ing voraciously in various stock ventures. But the longer-term security and profitability of the East India Company required a more predictable financial environment than that provided by its gouging servants, army officers and civil officials, whose opportunistic feeding frenzy resembled nothing so much as a shoal of piranha at breakfast.

The critical issue was authority over tax revenue to fund a growing trade system and to finance the large company armies which safeguarded British territorial gains and commercial assets. Having accumulated regional power by inserting themselves into the Indian political order and exploiting its flux, the British again used Indian systems as the means of establishing control over the new company provinces. Success lay in the company renovating the basis of its interest and power, weaving its influence into the political imagination of Indian society. The East India concern would be posing not so much as a London commercial operation but as an integral Indian ruling power, with the kind of mock Mughal identity adopted by Clive, a dab hand at mingling and making alliances with restless members of the Indian aristocracy. In this interpenetration, the British were more than content to ape the society over which they were slowly extending their dominion.

The fiscal foundation of Indian states was tax revenue extracted from huge numbers of rural cultivators. To meet its own high taxation needs, this system was essentially absorbed and implemented by the company. Accordingly, funding empire in India differed completely from the approach in British settler colonies, where finance was usually voted on as grants by elected male assemblies or raised through customs duties. Battening on a dense Indian peasantry, the company confiscated at least one-third of their produce as taxation and imposed stiff trade duties. This levy was channelled through a complicated rigmarole of rights of collection and tribute, with landed rural elites, known in Bengal as *zamindars*, still taking their customary slice of peasant property. As the British fell into step with a collaborating local gentry, they entered a long phase of intricate involvement in Indian rural tenure rights and in the workings of judicial authority over land rights and tax submissions. Inevitably, British administration of Indian law would become fraught with daily disputes and other difficulties. But it was this rural control over the profits of taxation and justice which gave the East India Company its power.

Even as Britain was tapping down its national interest in India during the 1750s and 1760s, there remained unfinished business with the French in North America. Following defeat or the resentment of being fought to a standstill, the British redoubled their efforts, massively enlarging their naval and infantry forces for a renewed campaign to bring conclusive victory. Intended to flatten the French through sheer superior weight, these forces were mobilised efficiently under the hard-nosed Jeffrey Amherst, a general who had the required aggressive drive. Fencing in British America to ward off the French-Canadian threat was not enough. Canada was to be overrun and the French tipped out of the region entirely.

Towards the end of the 1750s, the bleeding French were battered back into New France and its Quebec stronghold where, in 1759, the death in battle of General James Wolfe during a victorious British assault from the St Lawrence provided an iconographic legacy of peerless sacrifice by an imperial warrior hero. In the following year France lost Montreal, its final remaining slice of any worth, and with it went New France. It was just about all over for the colonial French in North America. In this bleak situation, Paris opted for hard-headed practicality. For all the fuss made over the cultural affinity and imperial belonging embodied by its white French-speaking North Americans, France was quite willing to trade off its Canadian immigrants to the British Empire. The St Lawrence Valley was far less lucrative for the French than their Caribbean plantation holdings, and the economy of those slave islands would continue to be fought for more fiercely. Sugar and its sweetness counted more than the thickness of blood.

Through the Indian and North American gains of the costly Seven Years' War, ended by the 1763 Peace of Paris, Britain did not neglect the potential of its seapower in strangling the wider French position. In a curving grand strategy, well-provisioned Royal Navy squadrons maintained an unrelenting blockade of enemy trade in both the Atlantic and the Mediterranean, a strong and vigilant presence which also hampered the despatch of French army reserves to North America, India and the Caribbean. At the end of the 1750s the British also mounted a heavy amphibious onslaught on the French Caribbean, seizing the profitable sugar islands of Martinique and Guadeloupe, and also scooping up Tobago, Grenada, St Vincent and Dominica.

This was not the end of French losses in this phase of British bellicosity. In West Africa, the easy fall of Senegal and Goree gave Britain control of the most important French slave-trading stations. And, when Spain looked to be cutting in through a fighting co-ordination with France, its Caribbean and Philippine colonies received much the same treatment. After declaring war on Spain in 1762, the British captured Manila in the Philippines, as well as Havana in Cuba, where an enormous store of bullion proved a brighter prize than cigars.

Even after the return under the 1763 peace settlement terms of a number of French and Spanish colonial territories, British imperialism had largely eliminated French influence in India, had a mostly uncontested grip on much of continental North America, and had extended its control in both the Caribbean and along coastal West Africa. With influence over lands and sources of national profit on this scale, what need had a flush Britain of European regions like Silesia or Lorraine, relatively lacklustre prizes over which its continental neighbours were squabbling so rancorously?

Equally, none of this is to imply that its empire was free of looming problems and knotty challenges of governance and authority in a global order being glued together by colonial trade and settler expansionism. Won at any cost, the Seven Years' War had been horrendously expensive, and for all the gain from escalating levels of overseas trade, by the 1760s the British national debt had still risen steeply. Inevitably, the sagging legacy of war finance meant some domestic strain for the Pitt regime. Further on, down but not yet out, an aggrieved France and Spain licked their wounds, hankering for any chance to reverse British gains. Nor, for those American Indian belligerents involved in hostilities as tactical allies of the French or the British, had it been a war to be fought and then forgotten.

Although superlative Indian bushcraft skills and powers of endurance had helped British forces to clinch out-right victory, that also meant they had now forfeited their precious balancing position between Anglo-French imperialisms. For Britain, Indian claims were now an irrelevance. Not altogether surprisingly, after the end of the war spurned warriors around the Great Lakes area rounded upon British positions in a widespread assault which became known as the Pontiac Rising or Rebellion. For an exasperated General Amherst, the ideal solution to the problem of tribal disaffection was cheap biological warfare, by praying for a way to be found of spreading smallpox.

Meanwhile, continuing British advances in India were being checked in the south by the Mysore polity, and to the north and west by the bulky Maratha confederacy. These regional rivals were not overawed by the company's pugnacity and had no intention of seeing the British supplant the fragmenting Mughal aristocracy as top dog. All the while, the company itself continued to demonstrate its costly impulsiveness, with its leading servants continuing to provoke armed hostilities with surrounding Indian powers through and beyond the 1760s. Although, on the face of it, a private capitalist enterprise, the East India venture did not fail to give a lead in defining national interest as the prime protection of its trade and territorial security. On the back of trained and increasingly massive *sepoy* armies, and reinforcing regular regiments and naval squadrons, Britain was being sucked ever further into India, committing major funding and other resources to look after its profitable stake. Whatever the fluctuating operational difficulties and war-related financial crises of the sub-imperial East India Company, by now empire in India could not be permitted to fail.

In North America, however, it was to do just that. For decades, Britain's mainland colonies with their elected assemblies, basically English governing structures and popular sense of being the domain of free crown subjects had been fostering a consciousness of local autonomy and of the elementary rights of self-government. The growth of these prerogatives among colonists opened up grounds for dispute over the terms or demands of the imperial relationship, such as London's wish to see North America remaining a protected market for British goods and not becoming a competing manufacturer. Still, provided British governor-generals did not bully unduly and avoided excessive meddling in colonial economic arrangements, the imperial relationship remained calm and stable.

The Seven Years' War ended such easy-going latitude as sharply differing views over its implications merged into a wider conflict over imperial defence and colonial autonomy. For local settlers, Britain's territories had been saved from France by the resolute will of local militia patriotisms, an indispensable and fiery combat element which had augmented the strength of regular British forces. Born to arms, in the field hardy colonial men were of equal or almost equal stature to trained metropolitan Britons.

The war experience had been nothing of the kind for British commanders. Settler militiamen were generally regarded with contempt as unreliable irregulars, undisciplined and incapable of combining effectively to confront the enemy. As if that were not bad enough, the level of colonial co-operation had been annoyingly low, with some colonies even trying to duck their royal responsibilities for requisitioning men and supplies for the imperial war effort. Far from contributing much to victory, flabby American colonists had been bailed out by the prowess of British regular forces. As winning the war had been all their own doing, the implication was clear enough. Defence could no longer be entrusted to colonial garrisons.

These perceptions set the stage for harder imperial pressure in the handling of American possessions. The war crisis had shown that the North American territories could be a burden as well as an asset, and to deal with this the organisation of imperial structures had to become more efficient, and the authority of imperial institutions had to be buttressed. One consequence in the later 1760s was the insistence by a great majority of London parliamentarians that as imperial representatives they had the right to exert their legislative authority anywhere in a Greater Britain. The House of Commons was the house of Great Britain, representing the interests of all British subjects, however distant their residence.

A second development was London's assumption of direct responsibility for colonial security, by garrisoning a large peacetime British army in North America as a defence against any renewed troubles with the French or Spanish. Thirdly, Britain resolved to fund part of the costs of the new standing army through imposing parliamentary taxation on the colonies after 1764. Demand for this was uncompromising and strident. The regular army had to be properly maintained by parliamentary taxation, as this was the foundation of political control over the military. Passing on a share of the burden to colonists in America also made political sense by sparing the pockets of British taxpayers. Ultimately, too, if North American settlers were laying claim to the benefits of being British and free, it did not seem so unreasonable that they be taxed as such.

The intended solution to the frustrations of North American imperial defence became the stationing of a permanent British military establishment and the levying of a local cost. But a scheme to bolster Atlantic empire and enhance imperial revenue had the opposite effect, for it provoked a major crisis in colonial relations. Its fatal arrogance lay, above all, in a complete disregard of the question of colonial consent to new duties on American commerce and to taxation measures like the 1765 Stamp Act which hit the costs of a range of basic printed documents, including newspapers and playing cards. These levies were introduced in peremptory fashion, with not even a show of official consultation or entertaining of objections.

Resistance from the colonies was immediate and blunt. Although there were other anti-British grievances, including a post-war depression worsened by cuts in British spending in colonial ports, the main outcry was over parliamentary taxation. For the colonies, the issue was more than one of economic hardship being aggravated by London taxes. It was fundamentally constitutional. Theirs was an argument for a continuation of the usual contribution to imperial defence, as a royal levy on sums raised by their own legislatures. Against this, British parliamentary taxation was denounced as unacceptably autocratic. American spokesmen asserted that as the charters of colonial governments embodied the Magna Carta and the Bill of Rights, colonial subjects shared the hallowed rights of free Englishmen to be taxed only with their own consent or that of their elected representatives. Westminster taxation was a clear denial of the rights of free colonists to have control of their own property. This was tyranny or despotism being attained by the back door, for once freemen had relinquished rights of control over personal property they would be reduced to slaves. This quickly became the popular idiom of colonial resistance as settlers constructed their conflict with Britain as a struggle for liberty over tyranny, freedom over slavery, and a stand of righteous buckskin patriotism against a corrupt and arbitrary authoritarianism.

Diplomacy functioned for a time, as lukewarm conciliatory initiatives had their run at a peaceful resolution of conflict. In the early 1770s the Prime Minister, Lord North, floated a grudging concession in the hope of enticing less militant colonies to agree to terms, thereby splitting the united anti-British front that had emerged in America. But none were inclined to split. On the British side likewise, for that matter, few influential imperialists were willing to countenance any serious concessions to upstart backwoodsmen who, for all their political claims, were still colonial subjects along with American Indians and conquered French Canadians. By 1775 the crisis had run away with both parties and war broke out. The empire was about to be stretched and to be found seriously short.

Among seemingly countless judgements on why this lengthy, see-sawing confrontation turned out badly for Britain, there are two which still stand out. Both relate to the severe problems faced by imperial strategy. One was the scale of a land war fought at the enormous distance of some 3,000 miles from a home base. Even though the British were prepared to commit heavy resources to North America, eventually drafting in well over 50,000 troops, putting down a concerted rebellion in largely self-sufficient settler societies was a tall order. Maritime superiority helped for a time, but the impact of blockading was far from decisive. In any event, Britain had its own long-distance supply headaches with which to contend.

Winning the war entailed mounting an offensive to conquer and hold down the complete eastern lands of North America, a huge expanse with around 3 million people. This was in itself a tall order. To add to the challenge of subduing such extensive and poorly mapped territory, Britain had severe communication problems in directing its war effort, and was also hampered by serious internal divisions and dissension within army and navy command. To take one instance, those who led forces supplied by the East India Company were almost driven to drink by the meddling of its Madras council, which interfered incessantly in the running of field operations. It is no less notable that the quality of American forces was patchy, that equipment shortages diluted their military potential and that the pull of fierce state loyalties or local communalism diminished the cohesion of a national American war effort. Yet, whether as defensive weekend militiamen or as more disciplined continental army troops, the weight of colonial land forces was overwhelmingly superior, with perhaps as many as 200,000 men having served in some kind of military capacity. Aside from a numerical disadvantage, the British also faced other large obstacles. Settler societies were so loosely dispersed that the taking of their larger towns or cities did little to break off action or to induce them to back down. In the insecure countryside, British generals such as Henry Clinton, Charles Cornwallis and William Howe grasped that imperial will and authority could only prevail when territory was overrun and firmly occupied. Yet, almost always, that was only the half of it. Once regular garrisons were withdrawn for further campaigning and defence was left in the slithery hands of colonial loyalists, rebel power seeped back to reassert itself.

The second problem for the British was their diplomatic isolation or, more precisely, their lack of any continental ally to deal with French or other European opportunists looking to exploit their worsening American entanglement. Had Britain had a major European ally, its American campaign might well have turned out like all its other big imperial wars, in victory. As it was, with an antagonistic France, Spain and the Netherlands all entering the American War between 1778 and 1780, the overstretched British cause now confronted an expanded list of enemies against which additional sea and other resources would have to be committed.

The entry of other imperial belligerents ruled out any tame Anglo-American ending to the crisis by turning colonial hostilities into an international war. American confrontation spilled over into the Caribbean, India and even along the West African coast, where British and French scrapped over control of supplies of slaves. European continental intervention was also critical to scuppering the British imperial effort in North America. With Britain unable to seal coastal waters and running increasingly into the sand by the end of the 1770s, French naval intervention on the Chesapeake in 1781 led to the surrender of a large army under Cornwallis at Yorktown. This crushing capitulation had heavy political repercussions for domestic British war opinion and morale. With the will to fight on for America largely broken, the independence conflict was coming to an end.

By 1782 Britain's costly campaign had exhausted itself, and its war in North America to stamp out colonial rebellion was abandoned. Having got out of hand on other fronts, fighting there continued until virtual stalemate forced an Anglo-French compromise, with peace terms signed finally in Paris in 1783. All the same, if the general outcome of the American debacle was mixed for the British, it was even more so for two of their imperial opponents. Dutch intervention had been disastrously ineffectual, and in consequence had seriously eroded their commercial strength and colonial position. While Spain had made a crucial financial and naval contribution to the American independence struggle, its own war aims of recovering prime Caribbean territory like Jamaica, and vital Mediterranean strongpoints like Gibraltar, held by the British since 1704, were frustrated. France, on the other hand, looked to be a real beneficiary of the American conflict. Britain had been defeated in war and had lost thirteen – or most – of its North American colonies, widely viewed as a fruitful kernel of its empire. Meanwhile, the French had achieved territorial gains in the West Indies and also in West Africa. Furthermore, the creation of an independent United States saw Britain's world position wobble, while from 1784 France's Caribbean trading position improved as its islands began to import cheap supplies from the new United States.

Nevertheless, the 1776 disaster and the disappearance of around a dozen American colonies was not quite the end of empire. Great Britain's first post-colonial crisis was perhaps more one of ideology than anything else. Despite the loss of a few islands like St Lucia, it had comfortably retained its most valuable West Indian colonies. In India, despite a determined French push to displace British interests, company resistance had been stiff and Paris was obliged to settle on a restoration of its pre-war trading stations. Moreover, as a financially more robust power than its main opponent, Britain was more easily able to avoid internal calamity brought on by the colossal costs of the prolonged American fighting. In point of fact, the burdensome economic disruptions of the later 1770s and early 1780s were fairly short-lived. Not only was transatlantic trade left virtually unscathed, the United States remained a key commercial partner and, on the back of a post-war boom which restored trading relations, by the later 1780s it was absorbing over a fifth of all British exports.

Meanwhile, to its west, the war proved favourable for a British Canada. It was now able to strengthen its English-speaking core through the absorption of an incoming stream of up to 100,000 American loyalist refugees who voted with their feet, shoring up a more dutiful kind of settler Protestantism and nudging colonists towards a safe representative legislature by the 1790s.

Elsewhere, Indian trading operations increased their momentum and, with a virtual doubling of British merchant shipping between 1782 and 1788, the annual value of Asian exports was soaring into several million pounds by the 1790s. Caribbean profitability also recovered, in spite of having been punctured by the depredations of war and ruinous tropical storms. Property, not least slaves, had been devastated, with some 15,000 labourers perishing from food shortages as supplies from North America were slashed. But, by the later 1780s, not only had the productive capacity of sugar islands like Jamaica been restored; their export levels were already overtaking those of the earlier 1770s.

Recovery was fuelled by the immense consumer demand of an industrialising Britain which, in the later eighteenth century, saw sugar changing from a mostly genteel, upper-class indulgence to a working-class food staple. Empire was coming to mean not only land and foodstuffs. It also represented the coupling together of a labour regime under which British plantation slaves would be supplying the energy needs of rising armies of British factory workers. Per capita consumption, which had been rising steadily from some 4lbs in 1700, began to soar in the later 1700s, reaching about 18lbs a year towards the end of the century. As the pillar of the West Indies slave economy, the renewal and expansion of staple crop production brought back good times for slaving merchants and shippers, a sweetness flowing from the bitter.

Fattened by its prime trades in sugar, slaves and South Asian textiles, Britain was not about to slacken its effort to assert control over a commanding portion of world labour. Nor, for that matter, were its more crazed, rumour-driven investors and dogged mariners losing any of their famous taste for the fruits of expeditionary enterprise. A doomed eighteenth-century search for the elusive Northwest Passage continued, flogged on into the 1790s by the irrepressible navigator, George Vancouver, who put in an epic three-year voyage in an astonishing test of determination and endurance. For all that, it has to be said that it did not take too much to achieve eighteenth-century civic immortality. In 1792 Vancouver sailed into a deep-water bay for several hours, an act sufficient to get it named after him.

Rarely can an age which so fancied itself as the embodiment of good sense, reason, enlightened rationality and sober scientific inquiry have looked more deluded and confused. On one side, there lay a suspension of sensible judgement as the faster kinds of London investor and coffee house speculator and glib-sounding expedition organisers, including parliamentarians, poured funds into elaborate shows of navigation, lured by the promise of rich rewards awaiting those who could crack open legendary prizes like the Northwest Passage. While these chancy expeditions may have done their bit to add to British chart knowledge of the wider world, a good few came to grief. This was hardly surprising. More gullible mariners and their braggart backers were under the spell of what can only be called a scoundrel science, built upon sham maps, fabricated ancient accounts of successful voyages and pseudo-surveys of sea-routes by ingenious navigators of earlier millennia. It was imperial enterprise of the most dubious kind, shaped by a mercurial universe of wild ambition and consuming greed, and a bumbling belief in the sillier forms of astronomy and other mock-scientific interpretation of the contours of the new world.

On the enlightenment side there lay belief in a more judicious and exacting universe of imperial knowledge, a widening comprehension of the nature of the world which had been accompanying British maritime and commercial expansion since the later sixteenth and seventeenth centuries. Animated by the notion of scientific rationality, it was wedded to systematic hydrological surveys, intensive mapping, the application of mathematics and astronomy to navigation, natural history inventories of new territories, and studies of indigenous languages and cultures.

Established Orientalists of the 1780s and 1790s, like Sir William Jones, were constantly on the brink of stupendous research discoveries, such as the notion that Sanskrit was closely related to Celtic languages. On that basis, were the spoils of South Asia then not obviously a part of the Celtic Dawn? If the resources of empire were to be efficiently exploited and properly defended, colonial projects had to be informed by wide, systematic learning. And cultivation of knowledge had not only to accompany but also to precede any traffic in goods, capital and people. As empire had a small base, it had to be indomitable in all of its commandeering efforts, whether of materials or of its versions of superior knowledge.

This was a world peopled in particular by professional maritime men of serious repute, embodied most famously by Captain James Cook, whose successive South Seas expeditionary voyages of the later eighteenth century charted many thousands of miles of coastline previously unexplored by Europeans, and mapped the basic outline of the Pacific and its inhabitants. His seaborne scientific and surveying initiatives in the service of acquisitive British interests proved potent in this period, sharpening expertise in the fields of meteorology, astronomy, hydrology, oceanography, medicine and linguistics, taking fossil and specimen collection to manic levels, and constructing packed inventories of the natural world and of the economic, social and cultural order of Polynesian islanders and other Pacific inhabitants. Ever mindful of the mythological heroes of English folklore, on one of his Pacific explorations the captain of *Endeavour* was accompanied by ships named *Ralegh* and *Drake*. Whether charting the strategic significance of the Alaskan peninsula or insulating his crews against scurvy on strenuous voyages which could last for several years, Cook and his clique of salty explorers could not have claimed a more virile pedigree in imperial exploration as they helped to mould a select and powerful aristocracy of imperial intellect.

Their refinement of progress was seen as emerging naturally from what Britain had now grown to become, a proud empire of reason, rational order and the improvement of knowledge. Increasing the national stock of scientific knowledge of overseas plant species, animals, geological specimens and even antiquities could not but aid trade and colonisation by identifying potential new commodities for extraction and land for exploitation. By the 1790s, such pursuits as botany, astronomy, geometry and cartography, and the increasingly numerous learned societies which sustained them, were being moulded largely around the intricate needs of imperial expansion, be these the use of botanical gardens for experiments in plant transfer or new colonial crop cultivation, or the methodical development of trigonometry to enhance long-distance navigation.

Similarly, the proper defence of imperial boundaries and the optimum exploitation of its human and natural resources required ever more exact skills in ground survey-ing and mapping, in various other forms of measurement and calculation, in the assiduous construction of invento-ries, and in the population census undertakings so crucial to the effective imposition of taxation and the levying of military service obligations. Enthusiasm, even passion, for the accumulation of scientific expertise and intellectual knowledge gripped influential sectors of British society, coursing through the ranks of chartered company mer-chants and officials, animating clubby bodies of leisured gentlemen with misty interests in the faraway and exotic, stimulating patronage and sponsorship of travellers and collectors, and turning those key managerial levers of the imperial state, the Admiralty, the Board of Trade and the War Office.

The self-styled virtuous pursuit of imperial knowledge along with commerce came rapidly to encompass more than botanical inventories and the devising of new meth-ods of animal husbandry for colonial ventures. Checking cloth cargoes in Calcutta and looking for tigers may have been a rich enough life for British India, but these were not its only pursuits. From the latter half of the seventeenth century, the East India establishment had already begun to explore ways of plumbing South Asian civilisation, embarking on the study of Hindu law and tradition, languages like Bengali and Sanskrit, indigenous Asian arts, and landscape.

Here, as elsewhere, land which was falling under British control and responsibility was no longer merely land. It had become an improvable landscape, with spaces to be measured, an architectural line to be recorded, and a teeming mix of subjects to be annexed, chivvied and cajoled into place as the newest bastard children of an imperial Britain. Inevitably, in their growing refinement of knowledge of the colonial sphere, many British scientific professionals, collectors, surveyors and explorers were mixed in with, and heavily dependent upon, skilled local informants and native assistants. On every continent touched by Britain there were established forms of medical, botanical, geographical and other indigenous knowledge, as well as elaborate traditions of astronomy, natural history and marine intelligence which, in regions like the Pacific, were very old indeed. For educated gentlemen who devoted their lives to calibrating the depth of the North American wilderness or scooping up South Asian insects, knowledge was assimilated through intimate quarrying of local cultural expertise. In a way, one historical mind infused with a magic King Arthur set out to transcribe another, infused with the chants of a South Seas medicine man.

Shrewd insights into distant societies furnished by Bengali givers and interpreters of law, Tongan soothsayers or Guinean remembrance poets were smartly transmuted into a distinctively British creation, something uniquely superior and expert in its grasp of the wider world. At the same time, as roving Britons mixed with other social systems, mostly as inquisitors but sometimes also as captives (of disgruntled Delaware warriors, South Seas 'nymphs', or Indian princes), in turn these civilisations learned about them. In such complicated transactions, sometimes friendly, sometimes hostile, sometimes rewarding, sometimes baffling, it is not always clear who was using whom.

Whatever the continuing annoyance of France and its sophisticated use of scientific intelligence and maritime surveying in the development of trading posts and colonies, few British observers doubted that the talent and discipline behind their imperial impulse was by now set to carry all. After all, it was not merely that learning was enlisted in the cause of patriotic and commercial aspirations, or to back religious and philosophical motives in fulfilling a Christian duty to tame and cultivate a naked wilderness. Britain's pundits provided superior knowledge, too, in a seemingly unlimited Enlightenment faith in the scientific power and rational purpose of spreading imperial responsibilities and obligations. It would be wrong to think of this being in any way sentimental – quite the reverse. Naturally pre-eminent through its miraculous marriage of rationality and humanity, a progressive British civilisation of the later eighteenth century had all but limitless confidence in its ability to improve what it saw as lesser human orders.

After all, every day its science and philosophy was uncovering a malleable universe for those who had the tools to get to the heart of things, who understood the principles of development and who were culturally contemptuous of anything seen as myth or illusion. This was coupled with a lofty sense of guardianship over the New World. As the most efficient agents of human improvement, it fell to the British, uniquely scientific and saintly, to leave their domestic islands to improve societies not favoured by Christian providence. Just as the natural universe could be plotted with accuracy, so could its uncivilised peoples. Starting with the unlettered and superstitious Irish, others could be weighed up and assessed, and placed on the path of rational progress.

This seemed a grand enough prerogative of imperial expansion, augmenting the more grasping enterprise of conquest and gain with a feeling of patriotic pride in missionary achievement and in the discharge of civilising obligations to turn other peoples into useful, logically managed societies. Far from subjugation, Britannia's Empire represented rehabilitation, a magnanimous moral chore for its citizens overseas, whose self-imposed duty it was to put backbone into neglected societies of barbarians and primitives. For numerous imperialist intellectuals, it was this which legitimised continuing British colonisation, giving no more thought to the consent of the Iroquois of British Canada than earlier to the independent rights of the Irish.

The natural destiny of a scientific, sober and efficient Britain was to preside over peoples who were deficient in the attributes of a modernising civilisation. Accordingly, the challenge was to bring advanced principles of a rational market economy and systematic social organisation to those stagnating at the bottom of the evolutionary pile. In due course, many who had been wandering or loafing about their far shores in unreason would come to know the moral benefits of reason and a productive temperament. This was the usual outlook of leading writers and commentators – under British enlightenment, assorted pagans in the wilderness would be freed from the shackles of ignorance and unscientific superstitions, and raised in human as well as monetary value.

At the same time, not all eighteenth-century commentators were so self-consciously smug about their culture. Some in Asia and North America produced books and other records which carried glowing, utopian accounts of nobler, simpler ways of savage life, or portrayed rich landed worlds with art, literature and an abundance of servants at least equal, if not superior, to anything European. Equally, whatever their differences in perceptions of contrasting civilisations, mellow and romantic as much as hard-nosed views were constructions in racial imagination and exercises in imperial illusion.

In all of this, a reflective concern with the *idea* of empire did not lessen its reliance on the sword when it came to business. In 1790, Britain stared down Spain in a clash over fur-trading rights along the north-west Pacific coast. Some, like the dreamy Scot, Alexander Mackenzie, of the Canadian fur trade, contemplated the creation of a great British fur enclave stretching across the continent from ocean to ocean, and curving out into the China trade around Canton, where there was a fortune to be made from bear and otter skins.

Shortly before this, in 1788, the British established a Pacific convict settlement at Botany Bay on the coast of New South Wales. A substitute for the American colonies which had previously been the favoured spot for transported felons, the Botany Bay site enabled London magistrates to sustain their severity, consigning prisoners to punishing isolation and servitude. Among the very first men shipped off were several former slaves, whose free existence as light-fingered Londoners proved pitifully short. Not every black docker could box commercially to put sufficient meat on the table. The sugar web of the imperial economy had already developed a settled pattern, with hundreds of slaves from places like Virginia and Barbados setting up in London, Bristol and Portsmouth, while thousands of individuals were leaving Britain, making for a West Indian economy built on the backs of blacks who were flooding in through the slave trade at an annual rate of 40,000 by the 1780s.

In Australia, uneasy relations between the early settlement of convicts and guards and neighbouring Aborigines of the Sydney area soon turned ugly. For light-stepping communities sustained through close integration with the natural resources of a bald land, it was bad enough having to accommodate indifferent intruders who sought to transform the environment to their Western ends through construction, enclosure, and the enforcing of notions of individual proprietorship and trespass. Circumstances turned more ruthless in 1789, when an outbreak of smallpox gutted much of the local Aboriginal population. Unlike guns or gates, this was a menace from which inhabitants could not back away.

With Spain and, in particular, France still both snooping about the Pacific region, British agents and empire-building adventurers remained on the lookout for openings through which to establish a strong mercantilist presence in this outlying oceanic domain. Around the turn of the century, the navigator Matthew Flinders set out to survey the coastline of what was becoming Australia while, just a few decades earlier, the mesmerising lure of navigation, science and trade took Cook's first discovery expedition not only to the east coast of Australia, but also to the Torres Strait and the islands of New Zealand. In nabbing land for the crown, Cook had been urged to do so only with the assent of its native inhabitants. But if he was happy to pretend at a skimpy show of Maori approval in 1770 for his terms of possession, he was usually not one to take pretence very seriously. For instance, later that year he annexed eastern Australia out of the blue, on the basis that it was there to be taken. It would take more than the 1773 slaughter by Maoris of one of his New Zealand beaching crews to make Cook waver in his quest for acquisitions.

His expeditionary efforts in the South Pacific extended almost all over, taking British flags and posts to remote spots including Tahiti, Easter Island, Tonga and the New Hebrides, with his inordinate seafaring persistence at one point carrying him close to the South Pole. But at the end of the 1770s, Cook overreached himself once too often. Looping around Hawaii on the northern edge of Polynesia, he chose a disastrously bad time for his ships to make land, a moment which breached rules of behaviour under sacred seasonal rhythms of island tradition. For Cook, there was a price to pay for so glaring a transgression of hallowed local custom. He was killed by aggrieved islanders at Kealakekua Bay in 1779.

British – as well as other European – perceptions of the Pacific Islands and the personable cultures of their peoples had been rosy from the start. The region was seemingly an earthly utopia or fertile paradise, free of cruelty, brutality and war, wreathed in fraternal fellowship, governed by soft and easy ways of life, and steeped in the virtues of lavish hospitality for visitors. Contact was kept harmonious by mutually sustaining trade, and by the availability of summery women for casual sexual encounters with European sailors.

This bucolic idyll was soon sullied by a steady peppering of violent incidents, above all, the killing of Cook, and other emerging tensions over the arrival of diseases, alcohol and firearms. Islanders became worried by the overmighty British rolling their maritime power through their territories, while increasingly suspicious imperial observers were horrified by the detection of practices such as human sacrifice and cannibalism. For some, this shattered all picturesque optimism about the island inhabitants of the Pacific, who now evolved into an inherently duplicitous, cunning and brutal lesser breed, lost souls whose incomprehensible nature made it unlikely that they could ever fuse with the forces of progress and development.

Despite this, there was still much to be said for ensuring that exploration of the South Pacific was followed by the usual exploitation of commercial imperialism. In the 1780s, the ill-fated Captain William Bligh raised sails for Tahiti to stock up with breadfruit plants for the sugar colonies of the British Caribbean. This expedition was linked to an ambitious cultivation scheme intended to provide a cheap and plentiful food supply for plantation slaves. By the end of the following decade, traders, whalers and fur sealers were fanning out to secure bases for mercantile operations, and missionaries were filtering into places like Tonga and Tahiti, enhancing the British commitment to an empire of holy perfection, as well as muskets and cannon. The London Missionary Society would soon have the evil of infanticide in its ethical sights, and would also be rounding on rum-soaked sea traders for corrupting island communities through the spreading of venereal disease and the barter of alcohol and firearms for local produce.

Another part of this flurry was the movement of British settlement beyond Botany Bay, with the establishment by the later 1790s of over 2,000 colonists in arable and pastoral farming in New South Wales. With ample woodland and water, good soil and exploitable marine resources, incoming free settlers and others had all that was needed. Officials behind the developing of settlement were unperturbed by the presence of the Aboriginal population, declaring them to be so puny that they would swiftly turn tail and leave lands to much stronger colonists.

Like North America earlier, a white Australia would be rooted in abundant land and the advantage of rich ocean resources, with the additional attraction of the hard labour of incoming waves of convicts, and a fairly marginal native population of under a million people who could be turfed off their lands. As the Botany Bay clashes had shown, Aboriginal submission and withdrawal could not be taken for granted, but in the face of strong force there was every confidence that their resistance would crumble.

Settlement ground was also being sought for lesser or more refined purposes around the same time. A Sierra Leone scheme emerged from a bubble of British initiatives which arose in the 1780s to extend trade or colonisation interests along more promising patches of the West African coast. While commercial exploitation of the area was to be promoted in the usual way, by the chartering of a dedicated Sierre Leone Company, this time there was a further dimension. In 1787, a pioneer Sierra Leone family settlement was established for over 400 freed slaves and black

British Loyalists who had fled North America, with the objective of forming a free and upright labouring community, leading a steady and useful life at the plough. Although sanctimonious aspirations had little chance of being realised in exceptionally impoverished and trying settlement conditions, Sierra Leone hobbled along towards recognition as a British colony at the beginning of the 1800s. Its Freetown base would come to form the main West African anchorage for the Royal Navy in its stalking operations to squash the slave trade of other countries. But that lay ahead. Of more immediate significance was the place of Sierre Leone in British humanitarian, philosophical and other critical discussion of the increasingly prickly issues of slavery and the slave trade.

By the mid-eighteenth century, philanthropic anti-slavery feeling, associated first and foremost with abolitionist sentiment in Quaker communities on both sides of the Atlantic, had become an increasingly noisy campaign against both the institution and the trade, and was already beginning to influence sympathisers beyond a small if shrill constituency of concerned Friends. The crisis of the American War of Independence took the slave abolition question off the boil for a time, but it kept simmering.

Soon mixing in with Quakers in the same stirring of humanitarian moral improvement, Methodism and its growing following began to channel its ideological energies into the abolition movement. By the 1780s, reformist agitation from sections of the press had widened and had become increasingly bitter. Such agitation came not only from various Nonconformists and radicals, philosophers, and other intellectuals. Those who lined up behind abolition included buzzing politicians like the Yorkshire MP, William Wilberforce, and the newer and more crusading kind of laissez-faire capitalist, committed to competitive labour markets and to getting rid of antiquated protected labour practices. Under mounting pressure, disconcerted planters and slave traders rallied to the defence of their slaving empire through well-organised and politically influential bodies like the West India Committee.

For prominent religious opponents of the black slave trade and, later, slave-holding itself, enslavement of Africans represented an un-Christian wickedness or abomination. In every way, the nature of slavery was an outrage, maintained by pitiless planters who squeezed every last ounce of labour from their pitiful workers, with no regard for the most elementary principles of humanity, such as mercy and justice. It even followed that for its sin in remaining a slaving nation and people, Britain would be courting divine retribution for clinging to so immoral an economic and social practice.

The campaigning case of prominent abolitionists like Wilberforce – far and away the most famous individual embodiment of the anti-slavery cause – was that ending the trade would make more tolerable that which was intolerable. If plantation labour could no longer be replenished, callous owners would inevitably have to become more mindful of their welfare. Here, in pressing its anti-slaving case, the humanitarian lobby was clearly careful not to be seen to be trampling too hard upon rights to property. Abolitionists of this era were, after all, Quakers, Methodists and Baptists of a fairly worldly type. Some of their radical opponents were no less worldly, attacking Abolitionists for getting their charitable priorities mixed up. Instead of taking up the plight of the British poor they had become obsessed with the bondage of Africans, who were a different order of being. Only libertarian Dissenters and a tiny minority of radicals favoured wholesale abolition and equality for blacks.

At the same time, rising denunciation of the West Indies slave trade did not imply any falling off of British interest in West Africa. As the preachy Sierra Leone development illustrated, a renewed involvement would probably have been inconceivable without intensifying concern over the issue of slavery and the slave trade. For many Abolitionists, it was up to Britain once again to become destiny's child and to encourage West Africa to develop in a healthier direction. Instead of the sordid business of slaving transactions, African societies needed to be encouraged to retain their labour, and to diversify into more palatable kinds of profitable home production. Through a diversification of local trade, commercial relations with the British would be both stabilised and expanded peacefully. And, through an enlightened transition, the reprehensible slave trade would eventually be squeezed out by peaceful commerce.

As public discussion over the survival or disappearance of slaving raged on in the 1790s, the Caribbean end of things experienced a serious fright. Hit by the corrosive impact of the French Revolution, the French West Indian colony of Saint-Dominique exploded into slave insurrection. Within a short time, a ferocious war erupted which would sweep away local slavery and precipitate the collapse of a booming colonial economy. Topping post-1789 edginess across the French Caribbean, the Haitian Revolution curdled British blood, and immediately infected all debate on the questions of abolition and emancipation.

For liberal reformers, the bitter Haitian harvest was a sobering example of what lay in store if nothing was done to check the continuing degradation of slave life. On the other hand, slave-holders and their parliamentary political allies drew a quite different conclusion. The conflagration illustrated the terrible danger of any indulgence, the chilling consequences of slaves falling under the influence of irresponsible talk of rights and liberties, and getting ideas above their station. With potentially vengeful and blood-thirsty instincts seen to be lurking within all plantation workers, conditions were brittle. Panic over the possible impact of the French calamity upon the slaves of Jamaica and other British islands made for a nightmarish picture in the early 1790s. Sure enough, from there alarming reports of impudence among labourers were soon reaching the Colonial Office. For jittery island planters and other whites, rebellion in Haiti was a recipe for wider disaster. Alarmed by the apparent leakiness of the West Indies sugar pool and egged on by the cries of French royalist planters, who prudently offered to switch allegiance to the British crown in return for being rescued, London despatched an invading army in 1793 to put a lid on the Haitian revolution. With affairs evidently getting desperate for Paris and its faltering Caribbean trade, Britain now banked on a romping occupation of the French West Indies colonies.

Heavy campaigns over the next several years could not avoid stepping on several banana skins, with a straining war effort costing some £10 million and around 100,000 army and navy casualties. Despite this extended operation, all islands seized from France could not be held, although British forces did capture Demerara and Trinidad from its Spanish and Dutch allies. Meanwhile, the French made other difficulties by stirring up anti-British animosity among Francophone colonists on islands like Grenada, and encouraging restiveness among the Caribs of St Vincent. Amidst falling sugar production, there was further aggravation when the free Maroon community of Jamaica, descended from runaway slaves, came out in rebellion, an eruption accompanied by scattered revolts in half-a-dozen other British islands. In 1796, London had to despatch its largest ever expeditionary contingent to batter rebels into submission and restore the position of its West India merchants and planters.

The wars of the 1790s were undoubtedly hard going, but a combination of military victories and new territorial acquisitions ended up boosting the strength of British slavery and the slave trade. Now revitalised, the continuing economic strength of the British West Indies rested upon swollen slave populations which dwarfed those of any European rival, with island conditions for new labour exploitation looking as promising as ever. It is small wonder that things were not exactly rosy for the abolitionist cause. For the march of events had created a paradox. Even as its articulate anti-slaving movement was gaining in momentum and popular support in the closing years of the eighteenth century, so Britain's slave system seemed to be more successful and impregnable than ever.

To territorial stabilisation in the Caribbean on the eve of the nineteenth century must be added a pronounced swing of the imperial pendulum towards Asia. Having notched up impressive revenue gains from successive decades of gnawing away at the larder of an infirm Mughal Empire, the highly manipulative East India Company continued to enhance its wealth and to stabilise its political authority. Under Warren Hastings, the wily British governor of the 1770s and 1780s, Bengal became a plum catch, with its roughly 20 million subjects and annual tax extraction of around £3 million, furnishing easy finance for a large British Indian army to serve imperial needs in the wider region. Well in with a close circle of no less parasitic Indian aristocrats who appreciated his keen admiration of South Asian art and culture, Hastings ruled as a vainglorious nawab, playing politics by ear and aping the manner of lax despotism that had characterised the rule of preceding Bengal nobles.

Around the same time, however, the spreading political hand of the East India Company in ruling and taxing Indians became a matter of dispute. While, in theory at least, official British policy was to limit Indian territorial expansion, in effect there was little to curb the continuous growth of company occupancy and influence. For London observers and critics, the crux was not just that of an uneasy balance between the pursuit of mercantile interests and the accumulation of political influence to wield state power. It was also – even more so, perhaps – the question of settling what the British purpose in India ought to be. Hastings had no interest in trying to transform Indian society, and favoured the retention of many customary land, taxation and legal practices under British overrule.

Ranged against that was a layer of reformist sensibility, including strident evangelicals, which saw British influence differently. For their part, absolute free traders attacked the corrupt and monopolistic identity of the East India Company, while British Enlightenment radicals denounced its cavalier conduct and bandit rule, declaring its Indian Empire to be too wasteful of British lives in various wars, and damning it as immoral for its exultation in plunder. Other sectors of opinion saw India as unimproved land needing to be improved, which meant the company planting more than its bribes and tax collectors. What was required was company patronage for missionaries to Christianise India, and for the ambitious transposing by administrators of proper British models of law, civil government and land rights into an Asian context.

Amidst a growing furore over the messier aspects of company operations in western and southern India, in 1784 the Pitt administration passed an India Act, with the objective of handing the crown greater control over the affairs of British India, and more influence in the shaping of East India Company policies. The company was now being brought into line with British needs, which were moving steadily beyond a simple mercantile concern with the export of Indian commodities and stable political conditions. Britain's industrialisation in the later eighteenth century required Indian markets for its emerging products and, no less crucially, the squashing of competition from Indian industries through prohibitive duties to exclude Indian manufactures. The East India concern faced widespread and persistent parliamentary pressure to service these market imperatives, and to embark upon land reform and the establishment of an organised civil service.

Amidst all this, the affable and learned Warren Hastings, with his enthusiasm for Hinduism and patronage of the Anglo-Indian Asiatic Society of Bengal, had rather a hard time of it. Facing sulphurous attacks in the House of Commons for bribery, despotism and flagrant disregard of company policy, Hastings was recalled to London and impeached by parliament in 1788. Petitions in his defence from Indian religious leaders underlining his easy-going acquiescence in Bengali ways of culture and governance would not have cut much ice with impassioned opponents. For evangelical Christians and other fundamentalist antagonists, Hastings was all that was obnoxious about the company in India – chronically corrupt, prone to gross misappropriations of power and too loose in the licence afforded to goings-on in the temples of Benares. The remedy was to impose dutiful and reforming governance based on a notion of moral rectitude and scrupulous honesty. For critics, the administration of British India simply had to become more British.

As for Hastings, a lengthy trial ended eventually in his acquittal on all charges in 1795 and retirement on an East India Company pension. By the time that he had been put out to pasture, company direction had already changed tack. Under the governorship of Charles Cornwallis, a precise-minded Suffolk landowner and veteran of the American wars, Bengal property rights and land taxation were reorganised under a Permanent Settlement proclamation of 1793. More fluid practices in which land was owned by Mughal emperors or the crown, or some combination thereof, and farmed out on flexible terms to landowners were to be replaced by a fixed system in which land was settled permanently upon the *zamindars*, establishing a Bengal gentry with exclusive proprietary rights of ownership.

In this transformation, the rights and claims of peasant cultivators to land went the way of those of the dispossessed English commoners of an earlier era. Permanent Settlement was prompted not only by the desire for easier and more efficient revenue collection, and by the need to curb the abuse and diversion of tax remittances. As in Cornwallis's own Suffolk, it was assumed that larger men of landed property and influence could be counted on to assist in the wider preservation of peace and civil order. Further administrative reforms and legislative measures buttressed the Britishness of the company presence.

All over India, British racial attitudes began to harden in a climate changing towards greater exclusivity, helped by the arrival of increasing numbers of English wives and accompanying social and sexual constraints upon the conduct of British residents. The need to strengthen social distance required exemplary conduct, something which precluded tolerance of intermarriage or taking up with Indian mistresses. Newly heightened intolerance and prejudice was directed not merely at Indians, now defined as benighted and licentious heathens dwelling in darkness, and requiring conversion and guidance towards the path of Civilisation. Mixed Anglo-Indian communities also felt the pinch of racial arrogance and disdain towards non-Europeans, and the squeeze of a harsh new legislative regime to cut their rights and prospects. Under Cornwallis in the 1790s, East India Company servants were banned from wearing anything other than European dress, company army officers and tax collectors who had fallen into Indianised ways were barred from participating in Hindu festivals, and anyone with an Indian parent was denied employment in the company's civil, marine or military branches. Curry was now frowned off the table at English parties in Calcutta, replaced by hostess rituals of imported salmon and cheese, and pyjamas became a garment solely for sleeping in. By the end of the eighteenth century, British India was becoming more than a lucrative trading operation, turning on the ebb and flow of commercial and social intercourse. With the arrival of Richard Wellesley in 1798 as governor-general of Bengal and titular head of the Supreme Government of India, there was a renewed thrust towards the extension of British rule on virtually any and every pretext, and to secure the public revenue and administration for an authoritarian imperial regime. The Raj was being brought into being, lodging India squarely at the heart of British imperial ambitions.

At the end of this period, authority in India and control of other possessions had achieved a certain coherence, in the sense that Britain now represented a territorial British Empire to be governed, financed and defended as a national responsibility. Commercial effort and strategic doctrine continued to focus on the sea, prosecuting war against European rivals in the New World to pocket yet more overseas territory. In the French Revolutionary and Napoleonic Wars (the last of the great colonial wars of this era) Britain, aided by its European allies, throttled France. Telling success in hostilities between 1793 and 1815 signalled the end of the French threat to British commercial and strategic interests, and to its bid for world imperial hegemony.

In addition to stepping up Australian and Canadian settlement, and to bagging the bulk of the spoils of the West Indies after its wrestling with France, Britain continued to push on remorselessly with other new conquests overseas. In the late eighteenth and early nineteenth centuries, its enemies were allowed little breathing space in the Indian Ocean. Territories of strategic importance on its coastal rim like the Cape of Good Hope or Cape Colony were confiscated from the decaying Dutch as a substantial Indian sea-route base. The security provided by Cape naval power screened not just the approach to India itself but also Australasia, as well as the fishing waters of the South Seas, in which nearly all the big nets were British. Harbour and provisioning needs also brought on the occupation of the trading posts of Mauritius and the Seychelles, nabbed from France and retained as British colonies under the Treaty of Paris peace settlement, and the seizure from the Dutch of Ceylon with its valuable port of Trincomalee.

Elsewhere, too, Britain was in a position to gain bases for further regional expansion and to stamp its command of the seas from island outposts. In the South Atlantic, St Helena, which had been annexed by the East India Company in 1651, began a fleeting flirtation with coffee and quinine production, while the navy and Royal Marine garrisons had turned the strategic anchorages of Ascension Island and Tristan da Cunha into rocky frigates by the early years of the nineteenth century. With the Mediterranean a growing market for manufactured goods and a supply basin for raw materials, in addition to being a crucial corridor eastwards to India through the Levant route and to interests in Egypt and Turkey, British naval power also began to straddle its islands more firmly. By the end of Anglo-French hostilities, Britain had sealed its capture and occupation of a new ring of naval bases, from Malta and the Ionian Islands through to Corfu. This virtually turned the central Mediterranean into a floating empire of the Royal Navy.

From the 1760s, strategic influence and trading rights in south-east Asia were also being enhanced at the expense of the Dutch. With their stake in India secure, the British could scarcely resist the commercial lure of the China trade, filling a commodity route spanning Madras and Canton. Although imperial Chinese reluctance to grant more favourable concessions to barbaric nations like the British continued to frustrate merchants, millions of pounds of tea were being imported by the 1790s, a highly profitable trade for the East India Company and a staple source of government excise revenue. Moving forward in the Malay peninsula, Britain netted coastal Penang as a strategic base on the China route in the 1780s, with Malacca in the Straits of Sumatra falling to it a decade later, followed by the acquisition of Singapore in the early decades of the nineteenth century. For all that the growth of Penang soon began to stutter, these outlet stations drew south-east Asia into the commercial web of British India, helping to knit together the company's India trade with Chinese export markets and with its crossings to Europe.

With the prick of naval power and army force from India, British imperial strength and eminence in the region also mushroomed out from these colonial frontier enclaves. Of course, in the pursuit of their objectives it was not all plain sailing. While the Dutch could no longer block expansion, there was local resistance to be stamped on, incessant squabbling and trafficking with the rulers of kingdoms and sultanates, and the use of both the sword and the pen to settle the overriding question of British suzerainty. Here, London's tactical civility resided in a fondness for wordy and shifty negotiated treaties and agreements behind which to advance its acquisitive cause. In 1786, the sultan of Kedah may have grasped what he was conceding when he handed over Penang under agreement to the ample trader, Francis Light, in return for British protection against his Asian enemies. But he had only grasped the half of it.

For the sultan and others like him who were losing out or now finding it necessary for their survival to fulfil some bargain with stalking British power, the writing was on the wall and ready to be read. The steady creep of British responsibility had what it saw as the corrupting excesses and stagnation of Asian societies in its sights, ending the easy run of what traders and officials liked to term Oriental misrule. This was a springtime of confidence based on the civilising responsibilities of a free and superior people who stood for liberty, absolute security of property and an energetic drive towards capitalist economic improvement. According to much imperialist opinion, the unparalleled virtue of British world expansion lay in its expression of orderly constitutionalism, of a peace grounded in respect for lawful authority and of an adherence to freedom or liberty.

Naturally, as in so many other colonial matters, the meaning and implication of British liberty was a slippery affair. Immigrant communities which upheld a British identity overseas and were impervious to the seductions of republicanism were healthy extensions of a free and contentedly conservative Britain. Places settled by white emigrant stock, like Canada, could look to their colonial gain of elected assemblies and to becoming rather more democratic in tone than their crusty Mother Country. Other whites in British enclaves, as in India, were privileged crown citizens.

The position of those who had been variously conquered, subjugated or annexed, like Bengali peasants or the Khoi pastoralists of the Cape Colony, was altogether a different matter. There, another sort of empire was being allowed for, one uncontaminated by the growth of representative government and local self-rule. With its members still stuck in some evolutionary infancy, their fate was the benefit of being governed by autocratic British power, a mentor in incorruptibility and superior custodianship. Adam Smith, the Scottish philosopher and liberal economist, would have done well to weep at the magnitude of what was emerging. In his influential 1776 work, *The Wealth of Nations*, an apprehensive Smith had sounded a warning or two about the burdening creation of a great empire by what he called a deluded nation of shopkeepers.

4

The British Sun in Orbit
c.1800–1914

The eighteenth century closed with Britain's protectionist and crown-dominated imperial trading economy still rooted very much in the old monopolistic system of the Navigation Acts. All trade between London and its colonies was protected to sustain a national lead through the advantage of possession of exclusive colonial markets and sources of raw materials. Had Britain's naval strength not come to assure the protection of its increasingly extensive and diverse colonial trade interests by the early nineteenth century, then rival states such as France would have continued to bear down on British colonies to drain British trade.

As we have seen, aside from the loss of the American colonies, Britain had done well in the heaving trade wars of the eighteenth century, a position buttressed by the decisive naval superiority it acquired in the Revolutionary and Napoleonic Wars of 1793–1815. This picture was sealed by the Navigation Acts, that thick fist of controls designed to keep all colonial trade in British ships, to enforce the primary use of British ports and also to inhibit the development of manufacturing in colonies. The purpose of this thick rampart of mercantilism was to benefit British trade by hauling in cheap colonial commodities, and by fixing a stable outlet for British manufactured goods.

Still, by the turn of the new century a raging debate was underway about the best policy or strategy to ensure continuing British domination of the world economy. This turned on its direction as a commercial trading nation. From the late 1700s onwards, there were growing attacks on mercantilist protectionism by pushy traders and associated commercial interests which argued for a transition to free-trade imperialism. Articulate support came from figures like that acerbic zealot of the free market, Adam Smith, who linked a vigorous advocacy of free trade to criticism of an empire of vested monopoly needs.

For Smith, its advantages and profitability were questionable. Squabbling with rivals over colonies had become a national headache and dependencies were not only costly to keep but intolerably expensive when wars had to be fought to grab or to retain them. British colonial expenditure could only be justified in support of a commercial policy of open world trade. The great issue, simply put, was not about British aspirations to world power or about whether or not to hold on to an empire, but about the basis on which to function. In policy terms, it was a question of managing an empire of protected trade based on colonies or upon a global free trade of international relationships in which Britain would remain predominant. All those who had begun to clamour for free trade from the 1780s had been doing so on the assumption that it represented the cheapest strategy to secure continuing British domination of the world economy.

By the early nineteenth century, this substantial shift in imperial thinking was being pushed by new forces. Over two centuries of wealth and strength built up through a welded system of colonies and protected commerce, the plunder of India, and a voraciously hungry trade in slaves and sugar, was now being augmented – and overtaken – by the impact of modern industrial capitalism. While economic historians may continue to debate the precise extent to which the development of British industrialisation was fuelled by capital accumulated from the slave trade and its sugar plantations, or from the stripping of Gujarat and Bengal, one cannot overlook the degree to which British industrial civilisation was the product of an imperial formation, sucking in the endowment of world export enterprise. Early nineteenth-century English entrepreneurs such as Josiah John Guest, who brought heavy industry to Wales, did so largely on capital which came from the West Indian slave trade and from the pickings of empire in India. In time also, with the rise of steamships, theirs would be the bunkers keeping the Royal Navy full ahead in the South Atlantic, just as their copper and tin mines in the meanwhile were geared to the growth of Caribbean plantation production.

A great leap in industrialisation through the period of the Napoleonic Wars changed Britain's international trading position. By 1815, British domination no longer rested only on its major colonies, its protected trade and its naval supremacy, but also on its world industrial leadership and the superior productivity of its clanking industries. Now, passionate free traders could no longer be dismissed by protectionists for living in some fool's export paradise. Britain's virtual monopoly of early industrialisation, and the abnormal lead in productivity and technological innovation which its industries had established, meant that British goods would have a clear-cut competitive price and quality advantage in conditions of open trade.

For all the rancour of parliamentary and other free-trade disputes, the switch to free trade, commencing in the 1820s and culminating in a free-trading British Empire by the 1850s, was accomplished with remarkable ease. Essentially, the momentum had become irresistible, as the forces of commerce and expansion overseas combined with the needs of rapid industrialisation at home to override and isolate protectionist agricultural interests. For a new and expanding urban working class, free trade promised imports of cheaper food. More importantly, in the absence of an adequate home market, the early industrial economy was dependent for its growth on an intensification of international trade. Britain needed a world market for its exports and, secure in the confidence of its productive power, was willing in return to open up both its own market and those of its colonies to other states. By the mid-nineteenth century, free trade had become a great marvel of the natural world to a figure like Richard Cobden, as open international commerce became transfigured into a strong moral creed, bringing on civilising peace and reclaiming the uncivilised. An enlightened, industrialising Britain was the shining sun of this orbiting system of complementary, free-trade interchange. Its massive imports of food and raw materials would lift income in dependent economies, stimulate economic development and growth in infrastructure and communications, and extend markets for British manufactured goods, as well as for advanced City business supplies such as banking, insurance and capital, and services such as shipping.

In practical terms, the nineteenth-century move to free trade seemed a natural enough extension of traditional British habits of maximising commercial advantage through highly ambitious levels of expansion. With a firm footing in key spots around the world, and with a strong navy and merchant marine able to ride the high seas and restrict rival trading powers to the shallows, Britain after 1815 was on the way to unparalleled dominance and wealth. Equally significant was the emerging character of its commercial hegemony and international position. Through its effective monopoly of industrialisation and settled colonial relationships, Britain was positioned to develop its international trade to quite exceptional levels.

As the world's first industrial nation, its industry could expand into what amounted to virgin territory, pocketed in earlier years and kept captive for trade by the Royal Navy. Another characteristic of the classic free-trade era was that Britain's share of trade and investment in its own colonies continued to be of elephantine dimensions. Imports of cotton manufactures of the 1820s or railway stock of the 1840s were British, whatever their cost, because trade ties were so squarely British, with English and a common imperial currency in place to ease commercial exchange.

Thirdly, the heavy reliance of the British economy on foreign trade began to assume an almost emblematic quality. What determined the rhythms of its life was an internationalism of exchange, in which Britain exchanged its own manufactures, capital and financial services for primary products – raw materials and food – from all quarters of the globe. It did well out of this international division of labour. Through successive decades, overseas markets for British products and overseas outlets for British capital for the financing of colonial governments, railways, plantations, mines and the like came to play a gravitational role in the economy. Just as British finance was making the most of its good living from servicing the world at large, so mos production was for export. By 1830, over half the value of the cotton goods' output was being exported, while a decade later overseas markets were swallowing some 40 per cent of all iron and steel production. A very large portion of the profits was simply totted up and returned abroad again as capital investment. In short, as global economic entanglements grew abnormally large, so profitable foreign markets ran the national show.

A fifth factor, and perhaps most crucial of all, was the overall implication of all this for the British imperial state itself. In its much earlier, mercantile era, Britain's profitable trading expansion into the world economy had rested on an insular position of relative self-sufficiency. For all the importance of its seaborne commerce, that insularity had worked to its advantage, enabling it to weather isolation and crisis in its wars against France, and to prevail in the struggle for trade and colonies. A protectionist Britain had had no absolute dependence on the flows of world trade. Free trade, in a sense, broke the ancient spell of a sheltered protectionism, as London abandoned self-sufficiency. Supremely confident in its naval strength, its colonial possessions and creeping imperial influence, and in its lengthening industrial and technological lead, this seemed a light price to pay in preserving Britain's power in the world economy.

Yet, in the final analysis, the future and survival of imperial Britain had now become tethered to the international system. To be sure, other countries were becoming dependent upon the British as the staple trading nation for their products. But bullish Britain was also growing dependent upon foreign trade for its prosperity and being. Inevitably, it became the first powerful industrial state to grow reliant on its world trading arteries for the regular flow of supplies of food and raw materials necessary to sustain its position. Not only were key industries, like textiles, hamstrung without raw material supplies from overseas, but also, by the middle of the century, Britain was no longer able to feed itself from its own agricultural output. Thanks to the price blessings of free trade, the British population was able to sink its teeth into nourishing foodstuffs which stimulated its growth. However, that growth was soon far in excess of any size that could be maintained adequately by home food production.

In the more immediate future, such considerations did not matter much. For the underlying precariousness of Britain's powerful world position was well disguised by the seductions of further snaking imperial opportunity. Such expansion of influence through the early decades of the nineteenth century did not necessarily entail the fixing of formal colonial borders and the imposition of controlling authority. Countries could be outside the formal imperial network and remain technically independent, yet still be tugged into a British sphere of influence. In Latin America, for instance, London was cautious of the unpredictable outcomes and potentially costly consequences of getting itself ensnared in colonisation of a sprawling region notorious for its levels of turbulence and insecurity, and where its maritime police would have had some difficulty in menacing rebels and bandits in Bolivia or Paraguay. Instead, the British took full advantage of the nationalist independence wars of the 1810s and 1820s which toppled Spain's lumbering empire in the Americas. British agents, naval officers, army advisers, mercenaries and freebooters bedded down alongside insurgent Latin American nationalists, egging on their anti-colonial struggles with passion and venom. The British government then duly managed to swallow its monarchical, conservative instincts in favour of a swift recognition of newly independent republics.

Reward came in the spread of an 'informal empire' of far-reaching and successful commercial penetration and gain. Battening on to trade privileges and access to strategic ports such as Valparaiso and Montevideo, British goods, government loans and direct investment, especially in mining, flooded into Latin America as the cream of the City parlours now added Chilean, Venezuelan and Peruvian stocks to their daily dabbling. At various times, Britain acted as a major market for Chilean copper and nitrates, for Peruvian guano, and for Argentinian beef, wool and cereals, while its Latin American trading partners swallowed large volumes of Lancashire textile exports.

Although British capitalism certainly had its Latino dog days in the 1820s and 1830s, any serious listlessness or loss did not apply to Argentina. With a stable political system and a secure and burgeoning commercial life, it made the right kind of intensive trading partner, attracting an ever larger share of London's Latin American investment through the nineteenth century as its banking and insurance sectors, railways, slaughterhouses and other profitable assets ended up under British control. Although never roped in as a colony, Argentina became tied so closely to London's trade and investment interests that, in a sense, by the later decades of the century it was as much British colonial as Canada and Australia.

In this region, commercial and financial domination was enough. This was not North America or Australia, to be annexed, carved up and settled. British migration to South America was never more than a trickle and tended to be expatriate in character. But it was not without cultural and social influence. Skilled Cornish migrant miners introduced Mexicans to the culinary rewards of putting meat and carrots inside pastry, seamen and railway workers carried football to Uruguay and Venezuela, and merchants and brokers found their elite Argentinian clients to be more than partial towards polo, flannels, English nannies and an Anglicised schooling. When it came to cementing business ties and understanding mutual self-interest, there was nothing quite as helpful as converting the collaborationist commercial elite of Buenos Aires to British ways. In an age of tightly controlled mercantile family business, no less helpful was the family tie. While many British expatriates remained stiffly aloof from their host society, clinging together in a tribalism of high teas, clubs and Protestant churches, some traded in their stale Britishness, marrying into the local middle class to become naturalised Anglo-Argentine citizens.

Elsewhere in Latin America, the requirements for capitalist development – peace, institutional order, and an imposed respect for the principles of property and contract – were not always conspicuously present. Chronic political instability, bumpy commercial conditions, endemic banditry, peasant restiveness and a huge hinterland of impoverished labour with no interest in consuming imported manufactures were all a curse to the British in the post-1820s decades. The commercial oligarchs of Buenos Aires may have been able to acquire the gentlemanly ethos necessary to share in what the British were pursuing as progress. But the roving *gaucho* of the Pampas was as exasperating as the shifty natives of Lima.

By the 1840s, British officials were declaring it their national interest to improve trade conditions through the promotion of order, and the imposition of more professional social discipline upon the disorderly classes and feckless labour of Latin America, in alliance with friendly states. Most of the British involved in local affairs were contemptuous of Latin Americans, painting them as idle, slovenly, beset by graft and corruption, in the grip of a bloated priesthood of medieval Catholicism and all too sun-blotched. One of the issues in the 1820s which bothered the discerning Foreign Secretary, George Canning, was that British recognition of independent Latin American statehood might oblige George IV to receive what he termed a coconut-coloured minister.

Britons' distaste for some of the things that empire was causing them to rub up against, even when its grasp was informal, was also finding an echo at home in the earlier years of the nineteenth century. For prominent libertarians, reformers and radicals of various hues who stood for a pristine, John Bull English identity, empire had an increasingly insidious side. The venomous William Cobbett, for one, turned on the plunder and gambling associated with East India enterprise and was equally indignant at the amoral fortunes amassed by ruthless West Indian planters. His loathing extended to the City, depicted as an alien den of greed and usury, beyond rational control. Nor was Cobbett enamoured of some other comings and goings associated with his imperial country. The decks of its Royal Navy were being adulterated by too many foreign hands, to say nothing of the dubious nature of the trade it was protecting. For the wholesome wheat, oatmeal and barley diet of the honest labouring classes of Lancashire and Yorkshire was being spoiled by unsavoury colonial imports of tobacco, sugar, tea and coffee. To add to the culinary and other alien corruptions of empire in English life, there was also the disagreeable sight of black men not only freely walking the streets, but being fraternised with by white Englishwomen. No anti-slavery reformer, Cobbett was especially bitter over female petitioning of parliament in the 1830s for the complete abolition of slavery in all British colonies. What seems to have repelled him was the inclination of almost 300,000 local women to take up the rights of muscular black men.

It was probably just as well that William Cobbett's touchy masculinity did not determine the final outcome of the humanitarian anti-slavery reform movement in Britain, one of the most popular and dynamic public causes of the later decades of his life. As we noted earlier, a great paradox of the early nineteenth century is that the shipping and plantation interests of the slave trade and of slavery itself looked to be as substantial as ever, even as abolitionist agitation from the 1780s onwards was making rapid and vigorous parliamentary progress among reformers and humanitarians of all parties. In general, by the early 1800s slavery was no longer viewed as defensible on the familiar moral or ethical grounds of justice and humanity. For reforming evangelicals and other radical abolitionists who pressed the anti-slavery cause with imperial ministers and colonial officials, a continuation of slavery had become a blot on British claims to a superior and progressive empire of humanitarian trusteeship. But the moral clamour of British humanitarian anti-slavery sentiment alone was not enough to push through abolition.

Abolitionist reformers now had other powerful arguments. The wretched conditions and overall backwardness of slave systems in the Caribbean colonies was intensifying slave discontent, with disaffection and outbreaks of revolt in some places like Demerara in the 1820s raising the possibility of open rebellion. What had happened to the French and their colonial authority in Haiti threw a long shadow which would not recede. And, while the sugar trade certainly remained buoyant, its relative value to overall British colonial trade looked to be declining.

Furthermore, free-labour production was being embraced for its superior efficiency and flexibility. A growing number of newer industrial capitalists were critical of slavery for restricting the mobility and freedom of labour, and for bottling up capital in fixed monopoly ownership. What the market required ideally was emancipated labourers in an unregulated economy, at liberty to sell their bodies for wage-earning subsistence. As slavery became costly, as well as immoral, it was the turn of free labour to service healthier and more prosperous enterprise. By so doing they would also be affirming the humanitarian ethos of British imperialism.

Lastly, the pressures, arguments and evidence marshalled by the broader abolitionist campaign did not fail to neglect the prospect of Africa itself. Britain's future lay not merely in reformed West Indian plantation colonies, but in a more serious crack at the African continent. There, the deep distortion of years of Atlantic slaving had either curtailed or smothered other forms of commerce and industry. An end to the horror of the slave trade would remedy a grim situation, allowing legitimate free commerce to transform the region into a peaceful and industrious British asset. The official creation of the Sierre Leone sanctuary for freed slaves was but the start of more salubrious, reformed Afro-British trade relations.

Abolition succeeded in a drawn-out process long on rhetoric, deals, threats, evasion and obstruction. Abolition Acts in 1806 and 1807 firstly banned British involvement in the Atlantic slave trade. Thereafter, a liberalising London put other countries under pressure to fall in step by signing anti-slave trade treaties. Curtailing and ultimately successfully suppressing the slave trade was a highly aggressive and imperialistic activity, entailing political intervention in states with plantation economies, such as Brazil, and putting out the Royal Navy to intercept vessels engaged in slave trafficking. As a self-appointed maritime police force its West African squadron was charged with keeping the seas open only to legitimate commerce, which meant being kept busy regularly capturing slavers.

With the great bulk of their own slave trade abolished fairly quickly, the wider British campaign against this traffic was promoted as being in the interest of national economic expansion. For a figure like Lord Palmerston in the 1840s, the use of gunboats to enforce slave trade treaties was a blow against ignorant competitors who were still peddling slave-grown produce, and a lesson to people like the Brazilians that it was time to clasp the civilising benefits of free commerce. When the Atlantic trade had dwindled, there seemed little cause to continue holding off the inevitable completion of emancipation. In 1833, slavery in British colonies was abolished entirely. Where a slave labour system had been inherited, as in the previously Dutch Cape Colony, British political power ended the existence of a slave society. Slaves were emancipated from 1834, subject to obligatory periods of apprenticeship to their erstwhile owners, with all labour freed completely by 1840. Owners were compensated for their loss of property from a British government fund raised from home taxation. This was dutiful charity to the possessing classes in a time of loss.

Abolition and emancipation did not quite usher in the age of rights and benevolence to which many radical British humanitarians had been looking in their campaign for improved standards of colonial practice and government welfare responsibility for freed slaves and other indigenous peoples. Despite years of forceful diplomatic intervention and intensive naval involvement in slave trade suppression, evasion of the British ban on trade continued and slaving remained an exasperating problem for the pursuit of legitimate commerce. For one thing, even when African slaves were no longer being exported overseas, the penetration of new forms of British commerce stimulated demand for agricultural production within West Africa. This tended to increase the seizure and holding of cheap slaves by local societies with a healthy slaving heritage. The scrapping of slavery also brought another deception. After the 1830s the supply of free labour was neither sufficiently ample nor particularly efficient in meeting the needs of continuing commercial expansion. Wages and work terms offered by estates and farms were not such as to bring freed slaves stampeding back to the gates.

Confronted with intractable production difficulties in various parts of the empire, the British returned to an old colonial standby, the system of indentured labour which had previously brought poor English and Irish workers to North American and West Indian colonies. Once more, indenture exchanged a period of contract labour for transport, wages, housing and food. From the 1840s, recruitment of emancipated Africans and Indian 'coolie' labour for agricultural employment in Caribbean colonies and in the newer British Indian Ocean sugar bases of Natal and Mauritius increased steadily. Later in the century, South Asians shipped off as Pacific island labour in places like Fiji were augmented by an influx of impoverished Chinese 'coolie' migrants, who sweated out their contracts in Caribbean plantation and construction work. In all, close to 1.5 million people indentured themselves to labour in British colonies between the 1830s and the early decades of the twentieth century. This movement created ethnically diverse colonial societies, acutely sensitive to community divisions, regulated by customary segregation, and dominated by small white elites which held political and economic power. As for the experience of those tropical workers recruited and employed by the indentured labour trade of spreading plantation economies, there was no shortage of abuse and malpractice, ranging from kidnapping to misrepresentation at recruitment of work terms and living conditions.

Arguably, for some freed Africans, apprenticeship and emigration was also not entirely unlike a new system of oppressive bondage. Throughout the first half of the century, those liberated from slave ships boarded by the Royal Navy represented prizes captured for the benefit of British dependent territories. Only rarely given the choice of freedom on landing after capture, tens of thousands of freed slaves were instead conveyed to the nearest suitable British station to be apprenticed to employers for periods of up to fourteen years in territories such as Mauritius, Jamaica and Trinidad. In the ideology of the imperial government, this represented a valuable bout of apprenticeship or training for ex-slaves, equipping them with skills which would sustain them for an emancipated life. In addition, in the view of its Colonial Office, distributing such Africans in settlement colonies with more civilised populations would also help to wean them from perceived savage habits and barbaric customs. In practice, the British policy of diversion and ensnarement looked to be rigged in favour of securing a supply of cheap African labour.

The British territorial presence within Africa itself remained slight for more than the first half of the century, although it was not completely idle in the far south. There, following its conquest of the Cape Colony, Britain consolidated control, advancing colonial boundaries and expelling Africans from the lands that they had been occupying and farming. In decades of brutal land wars from the early 1800s in which resisting Xhosa chiefdoms put up a prolonged fight for their territory and independence, British leadership forged alliances with African peoples like the Mfengu to exploit divisions within southern Nguni society. Conquered land was divided into farms for settlers and eastern territory that remained in African hands became reserves under a colonial administration which brought magistrates, tax collectors, labour recruiters and traders to close in on the old order of rural life.

To strengthen their position the British brought in several thousand immigrants as early as 1820 to occupy newly conquered lands, and took steps to Anglicise the Cape by imposing a British identity through such measures as the establishment of English-medium schooling that taught British history and culture, the importation of a Scottish Calvinist priesthood to service the Dutch community, and judicial reform. The British came to flourish in a temperate climate, not to assimilate. The result was a division of white-settler identity into British and Dutch or Boer colonial populations.

While Britain dominated external trade in wool and lesser agricultural commodities, by the 1850s colonists had gained political control of the large Cape Colony with the setting up of representative government. Although black inhabitants were effectively excluded from the governing political community, the Cape nevertheless contained a measure of positive significance for earlier nineteenth-century patronising British liberalism. For several decades its political and social order followed a policy of gradual assimilation. Rather than racial identity, an individual's level of attainment in the mark of Western 'civilisation' was the formal test of incorporation. In this view, even if all human beings were potentially equal whatever their skin colour, all cultures were emphatically not so. In order to have at least a lick of the cherry, Cape Africans would have to ditch their culture, their religion, and their communal heritage of economic and political customs.

Known as the Cape liberal tradition, this multi-racial colonial order embodied principles of legal equality and common citizenship rights, including franchise rights for a tiny minority of acculturated Xhosa men who fulfilled educational and other qualifications, such as literacy and income or individual property ownership. It was a moral framework which pleased more politically activist missionaries like those of the humanitarian London Missionary Society who campaigned hard against the brutal racial attitudes of white settlers, and were appalled by their excessive greed for African land and labour. All the same, these developments and the acquisition of a further coastal colony in Natal in the 1840s should not be taken to imply too much for British interests at this stage. South Africa's prospects were fairly meagre and failed to pull in substantial numbers of emigrant settlers. What mattered most was colonial stability, strategic command of the Cape sea-route, and keeping a lid on the fluctuating costs and liabilities of formal control of the coasts and waters of this region.

As for African Empire elsewhere, the British were barely wriggling their few coastal toes. In West Africa, merchant settlements were few, costs were high, revenue was lean and wasting diseases kept European graveyards busy. Scientific and mercantile interest in exploration of the interior was hamstrung by forbidding environmental and geographical obstacles, and imperial authorities were lukewarm about any public support of inland movement. If anything, an inert Britain seemed to be balancing repeatedly on the edge of withdrawal from the Atlantic side. Across on the East African coast, the scene looked no less fitful and untidy. From the 1840s, the British secured a treaty nod from the Sultan of Zanzibar to tack on a consular and naval presence for the purposes of countering the slave trade, keeping a beady eye on any French trawling of the Indian Ocean, and protecting a small circuit of British Indian traders. With nothing much to draw it forward and little to co-ordinate, early Victorian Britain hung on here with little more than one eye open.

At the same time, if explorers and missionaries in this earlier era were still having to kick their heels, this could not be said of all African trading interests. As the industrial needs of Britain grew larger, so commercial enterprise fastened on West Africa as the source of new products, such as wild rubber, beeswax and vegetable oils. Derived from palm, palm kernel and nuts, the export of oils from West Africa to Britain had commenced well before the nine-teenth century. Now, stimulated by accelerating British demand for oil to be used in soap, candles and as an indus-trial lubricant, palm oil produced by African cultivators became an important trade staple from the 1820s.

In turn, an industrialising Britain greatly boosted West African shipments of its manufactured goods, which in addition to cloth included arms and alcoholic drink. As their price declined, so the consumption of Africans increased. For advocates of the accepted dogma of legitimate commerce and its civilising free-trade intercourse, it all looked to be going the right way for the British and their coastal African trading partners.

Ambitions for a wider British world in these years were considerably more forceful in some other regions. Again, as in Latin America, the lure of domination carried Britain beyond the boundaries of colonial empire. Not surprisingly, from the earlier decades of the century China saw the increasingly obsessive British use of free trade as a lever to prise open doors to expanding commercial influence. Indeed, in more ways than one, the China Seas loomed large in British hopes of grand mercantile conquest and empire in the Far East. What this populous society and massive market promised was fabulous commercial gain, and a field ripe for modern British philanthropic, educational and medical improvement, be it the saving of local heathens by Christian missions or the saving of expatriate Europeans from the dreaded judicial hand of the independent Chinese authorities.

At one end of British perceptions, imperial China was far up the scale of Oriental stagnation and decadence, needing to be opened up to the vigour of outside commerce and modernisation for its own good. At the other, the Chinese represented an alarming yellow peril, a stubbornly suspicious civilisation to be derided yet also feared. Still, the hope was there that through their good offices,

Britain's diplomats, traders and missionaries would in time show China how it could be respectable and yellow but not perilous.

The persistent reluctance of the Chinese to open their economy to those viewed as inferior foreign barbarians and devils, like the British, was extremely frustrating for free traders with their modest demands for a liberal trading regime, rights of full access to major commercial centres, recognition of residence rights, privileged personal status and treatment, and other guarantees. Commercial wrangling between cheeky British merchants and the Chinese government prompted fierce British government intervention between the 1830s and 1860s. Here, Britain called up its naval power in the traditional gunboat manner to force China to accept the penetration of its capital and the circulation of its goods and influence. Between 1839 and 1842, and 1856 to 1860, the so-called Opium Wars were fought along the China coast, handily provoked by the offending Chinese who had the nerve to imprison British merchants for not handing over illicit cargoes to be destroyed by their customs. These were, of course, opium shipments, an import that had been specifically banned by China. For the British, it was persecution in violation of international laws governing the extraterritorial sovereignty of foreign merchants.

Always confident that it could more than hold its own at sea, Britain was glad of a pretext upon which it could bombard and subdue Chinese coastal opposition to its encroachments. The Opium Wars ended in treaties which diluted China's sovereignty by obliging it to grant increased access for Western trade, and to accept the right of the Royal Navy on the China Station to patrol emerging treaty settlements which bound the Chinese to what was called an acceptable standard of civilisation in the conduct of beneficial free trade. What this roughly translated into was no harming of British interests. The gains of these conflicts were followed by the later seizure of Hong Kong and Kowloon, along with the securing of other outer headlands from which to aim European market capitalism at the Chinese economy.

Continuous pressure from Britain extracted a string of treaty ports, concessions and protective privileges for foreigners which made life tolerable for its merchants, advisors, administrators, engineers and other citizens in what for Europeans was often a difficult and turbulent environment. It was sufficiently tolerable to ensure that by the second half of the century, control of most of China's foreign trade was in British hands, without the territorial costs and risks of accompanying colonial responsibilities.

All that said, the scale of that trade made up only a small proportion of Britain's total world trade. In the 1840s and 1850s, Palmerston and Lord Elgin, the wide-eyed British envoy to China, called for champagne all round to celebrate what the Chinese market would do for the fortunes of British manufacturers. After all, British trade was rising steadily from about £4 million in 1830 to almost £15 million by the end of the 1850s. But hopes of an imminent cornucopia were somewhat inflated. Chinese merchant networks were resilient in the face of competition, and the poor purchasing power of Dongchuan peasants made it hard to clothe them in Manchester shirts. China could be slit open, but not as deeply as British ambitions anticipated.

The British also eased down on the Ottomans. Interest in this empire focused on the strategic and economic importance of Turkey and Egypt to their own imperial arteries. Given Turkey's strategic positioning for holding the prized route to India, London was committed to propping it up, coming to its defence in hostilities with Egypt in the 1830s and taking the same step against Russia two decades later during the Crimean War. A constant British refrain was that if Turkey were allowed to weaken or to fold, their position would also be shaken. To preserve a friendly Turkish independence, the British calculated on reforming and strengthening its Ottoman administration and rejuvenating its economy through another dose of free-trade treaties.

After the 1830s, Turkey's economy was prised open for British financial loans, investment and goods. Ottoman trade with Britain was rising sharply by the middle of the century, mainly swopping cotton and wheat for textile goods. The establishment in London of an Imperial Ottoman Bank in the 1860s, issuing Ottoman currency, also helped to set the tone of Anglo-Turkish relations. As the City financed governments, as well as plantations and mines, an indebted Ottoman government found itself ending up at the mercy of its market sentiment. Yet here again, as in China, Britain's reach largely exceeded its grasp. Although its trade and investment grew significantly, hearty hopes of completely regenerating Turkey through unfettered trade were not realised.

Deliberate bureaucratic inertia and resistance from local manufacturing interests and trades were a constant check upon British progress. The bankruptcy of the Ottoman government by the 1870s was also a salutary reminder of the fine balance of burden and benefit under a British paramountcy over Constantinople which was skin deep. And, by the end of the century, the Whitehall spectre of a drooping Turkish state was becoming a major strategic concern. As the bearer of British interests in its part of the world, it filled a vacuum and could not be cut loose.

Similar strategic and economic preoccupations were shown in the case of strapped Egypt, a place for which the City was acting as a ledger clerk as its rulers mortgaged revenues to British and French bondholders to service mounting debts. Its importance rose sharply after the opening of the Suez Canal in 1869, a development which turned London's stake there into one of national interest, as more than three-quarters of its shipping traffic was British. This cleared the way for Benjamin Disraeli's government to give British interests in Egypt a more decisive shove. By the 1870s, Egypt was tottering under the weight of several decades of Western indebtedness and commercial exploitation, a crisis which was of no advantage to Britain. It was, more precisely, the reverse, for the brittleness and insecurity of a failing Egypt was bad news for British interests.

The Canal, in particular, was made potentially vulnerable. In 1875, Disraeli bailed out the ruined Khedive Ismail of Egypt by purchasing his last remaining decent asset, a major shareholding in the Suez Canal Company. This bonded him as a Downing Street debtor, and also captured a thick slice of the Suez Canal interest. It is perhaps not too much to observe that on this rare occasion, Britain could indeed say that its word was its bond. Its declared official aim in acquiring a say in Suez Canal affairs was to check any further spread of French interest in Egypt. But there was more. As the British drifted in further on the basis of their international anchorage around Suez, they now had fixed property in Egypt which would have to be kept safe. The political advantage of that more regular foothold was that if the protection of those resources ever brought on war, intervention could be legitimised on the grounds that it was being undertaken in defence of Britain's legal assets. Sure enough, when things were made too hot by Arab nationalists later in the century, the Royal Navy was at hand to shell Alexandria early in the 1880s, followed by the despatch of Sir Garnet Wolseley's army to mow down any remaining opponents who had failed to get the message.

Egypt did not show William Gladstone at his best. The Liberal Prime Minister who liked to think of empire rhetorically as a moral cause, best led by British justice and enlightenment, found himself invading it in 1882. After all, vital interest counted for more than his or any other great name. The personal price of that name cropped up again two years later, when Britain sent out General Charles Gordon to evacuate an Egyptian force besieged in Khartoum by Sudanese Islamic Mahdists. One of Victorian Christianity's more wilful and unstable zealots, Gordon decided to perform a tactical miracle by staying on to be the saviour of the whole city. In so deciding, he revealed that he had lost more than just his bearings.

Gladstone eventually yielded to public alarm over the plight of his rash commander and cast off an expeditionary force to relieve a beleaguered Khartoum. But it arrived too late for the headstrong Gordon, who perished in what quickly became a mythical episode of unflinching imperial valour and Christian martyrdom. Although the general's fate was all his own doing, Gladstone came out badly, his administration denounced widely for having squandered the life of a sacrificial Christian hero.

What British informal influence over Egypt required was not manly leaps of faith by its more opportunist warriors. For a region through which they envisaged being able to secure overland communication with India and the East, they required the opening of a liberal, free-trade economy in which British enterprise would be able to block the threat of French influence. Ideally, they also required a collaborating, pro-British government which was stable enough to safeguard their interests. For a country which the British found messy, the easier first requirement in some ways took care of the second. By the time of the actual 1882 invasion, Britain had battened on Egypt's foreign trade. By the 1880s, it was absorbing more than three-quarters of Egypt's exports, and delivering almost half of its imports. No less significantly, with the City shovelling out big loans to finance the vaulting ambitions and pressing needs of Egyptian rulers, at some stage the chickens were bound to come home to roost. When they did, by holding the lion's share of the regime's public debt Britain became intimately involved in outside European control of Egyptian finances. By the end of the century, the British had a circling control of Egypt's fortunes and destiny.

Britain's touch in enlarging its influence through informal empire in preference to the pricey annexation of territory proved its magic in places where it worked particularly well, as in much of south-east Asia. In Siam, colonial free-trade pressures induced treaty concessions permitting British subjects to acquire territory and to reside in the Bangkok area, as well as the stationing of a British Consul. He exercised the usual power to keep them safe, wealthy and free, that of extraterritorial jurisdiction over their lives. By the 1850s, Mongkut of Siam had had enough of his state being beaten over the head by insistent British commercial demands and yielded to imperial influence. By accommodating pressures for reform and modernisation, the kingdom was able to remain technically independent. But that independence became deeply compromised by British leverage in Siamese foreign affairs, and by their domination of key trading sectors of the economy, including shipping and banking.

Agents, businessmen, advisors and officials also busied themselves consolidating British paramountcy on the Malayan peninsula, and in the other regional territories of Burma and northern Borneo. Burma had the misfortune to be located inconveniently close to British India, and could not escape the hot breath of its colonial commercial avarice and strategic concerns. After decades of dribbling territory and commercial concessions to British merchant interests in Rangoon, by the 1880s the Burmese side of Anglo-Burmese relations had grown both weary and wary. It was annoying enough having to ward off peevish and increasingly confrontational complaints from British merchants about unsatisfactory commercial privileges. There was the added annoyance of a great diplomatic hue and cry over the customary imposition upon the British resident to remove his shoes when in the presence of the king, a mundane enough ritual of deference. It was

certainly nothing to match the degrading British humiliation inflicted on beaten Xhosa chiefs of the 1850s in the
crown dependency of British Kaffraria, who were forced
by the Cape Colony's overmighty governor, Sir Harry
Smith, to kiss his boot as he was astride his horse, and to
address him as the greatest chief, *'inkosi enkhulu'*.

British worries ran beyond Burma's commercial
potential and that of upholding their prestige. Faced with
competing Franco-Burmese business dealings, they were
equally anxious about France worming its way in to secure
a bridgehead right on the very borders of British India.
When Burmese Mandalay refused to grant Britain control
of its foreign affairs, a breach was inevitable. For a third
time British forces invaded and occupied the country, stationing a powerful troop and police establishment to crush
resistance and impose order. With Lower Burma already in
their pocket since the 1860s, Upper Burma was annexed in
1886. All of it was then governed as a province of British
India, with a local colonial state exercising its authority
through a new bureaucracy of government departments
for such things as public works and agriculture, a judicial
system and police. India was convenient as a place from
which to copy local village and district administration. It
was also convenient as the garrison of the Indian army,
available to pacify any Burmese who continued to be restive.

Again, the urging of a free-trade market fanned the
Burmese colonial economy, which saw widespread exploitation of rice and timber resources and exceptionally cosy
relations between government departments and capitalists. Indian and Chinese merchants and other immigrants

swarmed in to grab their slice of an immensely profitable trading environment, shouldering aside a weak Burmese middle class and reducing peasants to miserable poverty. Naturally enough, British snouts were the largest in the trough. The European rice trade and the biggest rice mills were safely British, as was most company activity in timber.

Buoyed by their free-trade imperialism, British interests were itchy elsewhere in this area. The opening of the Suez Canal cemented the strategic importance of the Malacca Straits as a pipeline to East Asian trade, giving Britain a further incentive to spread out its shipping interests and to deepen its investment in its nineteenth-century acquisitions of Singapore and Hong Kong. For several decades, Singapore had been creaming off the benefits of increasing British trade with China. By the 1850s, its pivotal strategic role in holding the Eastern sea passage for the British was lifted further by the construction of major dock facilities and coaling services for steamships.

Meanwhile, the sea lanes, and a good deal else besides, were being cleared elsewhere in south-east Asia. Labuan, off the Borneo coast, was pegged down in the 1840s. In Borneo the cavalier and conniving freebooter, James Brooke, had set his heart on personal position and influence. Behaving well, he helped the sultan of Brunei to crush a rebellion, for which he was rewarded with the custodianship of Sarawak on the mainland. Granted the opening to create a territorial aristocracy, Brooke made the most of his little imperial windfall, ruling virtually independently. He and his governing descendants carved out a conspicuous existence as British rajahs, fostering

1 *Above left:* An ambitious colonial explorer who never tired of the Atlantic: Sir Humphrey Gilbert, sixteenth-century seafarer, soldier, writer and Christian stoic.

2 *Above right:* The *Golden Hind* in which Sir Francis Drake completed an unplanned circumnavigation of the world at the end of the 1570s, revealing the formidable oceanic reach of English plunder.

3 *Below right:* Sir Walter Raleigh ponders imperial honour, the glory of conquest and the destruction of Spain.

4 *Below left:* Captain John Smith, leader of the North American island colony, Roanoke, established by Walter Raleigh in the 1580s to try to beguile Elizabeth I into providing support from state coffers. Raleigh's real object was possession of a potential base from which to raid Spanish shipping in the Caribbean.

5 *Above left*: 'A Hieroglyphic of Britain' from John Dee's 1577 *Arte of Navigation*. In this allegorical engraving, light streams down upon Elizabeth I at the helm of a European imperial ship, heading towards a safe rock of Victory to establish a semi-mystical, British-Protestant imperial world order. Tragically for this celestial Tudor romantic, Dee ended his days in that least mystical of English places, Manchester.

6 *Above right*: The rewards of indomitable seamanship: scene on the Northeast Passage over Europe to fabled Asian markets, 1594.

7 A royal with a nose for seaborne expeditions. Rather more lavish with the provision of guns than investment finance, the queen did not always provide comfortable arrangements for scheming private adventurers: portrait of Elizabeth I.

8 *Left*: Headquarters of the trading riches of the 'East': the old East India House, Leadenhall Street (1648–1726) in the City of London, a formidable repository of specialised trade skills and merchant enterprise planning.

9 *The Ark Royal* of Queen Elizabeth's navy in the 1580s, typical of sixteenth-century English ship design in its swiftness, manoeuvrability and very heavy armament. Elizabethan men-of-war had little spare cargo capacity, something which Spanish opponents attributed to English seamen eating far too much.

10 A massive merchant port by the mid-eighteenth century, London was the major bridge to everything connected to the empire, from finance to colonial trade to government administration: London Bridge, *c.*1750.

11 *Above left*: A lion monopoly with a voracious appetite for commercial fortune: original arms of the East India Company, 1600.

12 *Above right*: When West African sea trade was still in animal hides rather than human bodies: arms of the sixteenth-century African Company, 1588.

13 *Below:* Far Eastern tea when it was the 'China drink' rather than the habitual daily cuppa: early advertisement for tea, the 'China drink', in the London newspaper *Mercurius Politicus*, 1658.

14 *Bottom:* Promoting the king's shilling far east of Dover: silver coin of the East India Company, 1675.

THIt Excellent, and by all Phyſitians approved, *China* Drink, called by the *Chineans*, *Teha*, by other Nations *Tay.alia Tee*, is ſold at the *Suitaneſs-head*, a Qophee-houſe in Sweerings Rents by the R'oyal Exchangé, *London*,.

15 Henry Hudson, veteran seventeenth-century English sea captain, found Canada, and the colder the better, risky but irresistible: here he is about to test some chilly waters.

16 From the sixteenth century, ever more expansive maps projecting the land and sea distribution of a navigable world became an increasingly important tool of imperial commerce and colonisation ventures: map of the world, 1771.

17 *Above left*: Gilbey's caricature of a disaffected and bloody-minded Irish chieftain at Wexford in the 1790s. A 1798 secessionist rebellion against the Protestant governing elite at a jittery time of war with revolutionary France was stamped down by an imperial army of nearly 100,000 soldiers under Lord Cornwallis, determined that Sligo would not become another Yorktown.

18 *Above right*: In its pacification of upstart Catholics in the wars of the 1640s, Oliver Cromwell's army was not short of bloodlust: atrocities carried out by English forces in Ireland, 1641.

19 English soldiers swing through Ireland, 'that barbarous land', no Gaelic on their lips or bog in their breeches. The deployment of large expeditionary forces there was a major cost for the Elizabethan state.

20 *Above*: The detested pennies
and shillings that started it all:
royal stamps for the American
colonies, 1760s.

21 *Above right*: Those rebellious
American colonists broke more
than just George III's heart.

22 *Right*: An early indication
of terms for the later Anglo-
American alliance: Lord
Cornwallis with nothing left
to lay down but his sword after
defeat at Yorktown, Virginia, 1781.

23 *Below*: English medal awarded
to Indian chiefs for loyal service
in the imperial war effort.

24 Colonel Robert Clive does his bit alongside East India Company troops to batter Mughal Bengal in the 1750s, soon netting it as a valuable commercial prize for the British. Not one to be left behind in the scramble, the adventurous Clive amassed an enormous personal fortune before he left India.

25 An eighteenth-century, country-house world in the heat of the East: Company officials and their families resident in pleasant parts of towns like Calcutta and Bombay yielded little in matching the swagger of the Indian gentry. Expatriates spilled out onto imposing greens and parklands in public displays of wealth and authority, turning these into a customary part of the Anglo-Indian scene, here displayed at Bombay Green, 1767.

26 In 1799 Colonel Arthur Wellesley (the future duke of Wellington) restored the ancient rights and liberties of Hindu people by disposing of an implacable foe, Tipu Sultan, the legendary ruler of Mysore. A stiff opponent of East India Company expansion, the state of Mysore fought several eighteenth-century wars of resistance, with 'Tipoo' being demonised by the British as a cruel, satanic tyrant. His character even made it onto the London popular stage as a classic Oriental ogre.

27 Mughal emperor Shah Alam casts an expert eye over some of Robert Clive's more persuasive assets: the sovereign reviews East India Company troops in Bengal, 1760s.

28 Imperial glory and a grave for General James Wolfe in North America: in his victorious 1759 assault on Quebec, the stronghold of New France, Wolfe perished on the cliffs of the St Lawrence.

29 The sentimental pieties of European imperial fighting: Admiral Mazareddo surrenders the Spanish fleet to Admiral Nelson at Cape St Vincent in the late 1790s, with conspicuous good grace.

30 Heroes of the lawns of India: East India Company militiamen parading in Calcutta, 1802.

31 Napoleon making it difficult to rule the waves: battle engagement between a French fleet and East India Company vessels, 1804.

32 On one of his encounters with the Maori along the coasts of New Zealand in 1770, Captain James Cook explains the value of market relations and the benefits of a Westminster connection with the Pacific islands.

33 In the Pacific, Captain James Cook finds peace, fraternity and flowery artistry of an almost classical kind. On all of his later eighteenth-century voyages he was accompanied by artists and illustrators who portrayed a pure realm of native nobility, a benign world of nature.

34 In a land often depicted as well tamed and highly agreeable for European settlement in the nineteenth century, some free white colonists found that Australian Aboriginals were not all melting away.

35 Disembarking from *The Investigator* in the early years of the nineteenth century, maritime explorer Matthew Flinders decides upon Australia as a land title, and invites its Aboriginals to open bidding on an attractive ship's cask.

36 The value of the bayonet in pressing home commercial advantage: rollicking local caricatures mocking British soldiers and sailors on the China coast in the 1840s, invading to clear trading ground for ambitious eastern firms like Jardine Matheson.

37 A 'foreign devil' pecking at the Chinese economy: Chinese caricature of an English sailor in the 1839–42 Opium War.

38 *Above left*: A Mandarin very reluctant to appease Lord Elgin, unaccustomed as he was to receiving stray British 'barbarians' fluttering aggressive trade treaties: Prince Kung, relative of the emperor and leading Chinese statesman of the 1850s and 1860s.

39 *Above right*: A diplomat who shared Lord Palmerston's partiality to gunboats in dealing with those frustrating Chinese: Lord Elgin, British high commissioner and envoy to China.

40 He fell in with Sir Stamford Raffles, ceded Singapore to Britain, received a leg up from the East India Company in his contested bid for dynastic power and was proud of the baubles bestowed on him by the English throne: Sultan Hussein of Johore, a nineteenth-century Malayan ruler.

41 Victims of the battle for peaceful commerce: Chinese fort at Taku on the approach to Peking, captured in 1858 by British forces of an Anglo-French expedition despatched to enforce liberal foreign trade treaties upon the Chinese Empire.

42 Nothing like the tropics for those who had had enough of drab Victorian rituals: depiction of 'Miss Bird' at a Malayan wedding ceremony in the 1870s.

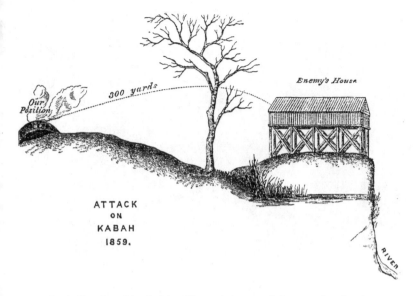

300 yards

Our Position

Enemy's House

ATTACK
ON
KABAH
1859.

RIVER

43 James Brooke, white Rajah of Sarawak (1843–68), keeps a clear line in his campaign to clear northern Borneo of headhunters and other dangerous predators.

44 George Orwell's *Burmese Days* (1934) declared that under colonial rule 'the official holds the Burman down while the businessman goes through his pockets'. Leisurely representatives of the British presence, teak and rice trade concessions securely in their pockets.

45 The gentility of free-trade imperialism in later nineteenth-century Latin America: British merchant families indulge the Anglo-Uruguayan relationship by turning Montevideo into Brighton.

46 Assured that Queen Victoria would now be keeping a maternal eye on them, Pacific islanders of New Guinea are egged on to applaud the British annexation of their territory in the 1880s.

47 Theirs was expected to be a future of Christian schooling, agricultural service and rural employment: New Zealand Maori still getting by without canals, postage stamps and bottled disinfectant.

48 *Above left*: The ultimate in crown flattery from a nineteenth-century prime minister who knew exactly what it took: Benjamin Disraeli elevates Queen Victoria to empress of India, 1876.

49 *Above right*: By the end of the nineteenth century, British preference for the 'China drink' had been supplanted by a national thirst for Indian and Ceylon tea as the daily char: for Lipton's, Ceylon was its gold mine.

50 The Asian cat which survived slaughter by a visiting nineteenth-century British royal: handed to the prince of Wales as an Indian army regimental gift, a caged panther ponders an uncertain future.

51 A sturdy tent to secure the lonely British body in Africa against anything bar dysentery, malaria, food-poisoning and blisters.

52 *Above:* Maori chief of the late nineteenth century in 'his Robe of State', pictured during the New Zealand governor's tour of its Hot Lakes. With Maori fortunes at a low ebb by the 1890s after the loss of land and control, what their chieftainship retained was dignity of a distinctly doleful kind.

53 *Above right:* Plucky redcoats were indispensable to the martial cult of Victorian valour, rarely more so than here: greatly outnumbered, a small British garrison at Rorke's Drift mission station held out against a sustained onslaught by Zulu regiments in 1879, forcing attackers to withdraw. Despite, or perhaps because of, their fighting power, the Zulu came off well in the imperial imagination, respected as a fearsome but manly warrior society.

54 *Right:* British official ready to dispense justice, enforce treaty obligations and keep an eye on customs revenues: as always, the flag had not only to be sold but also underwritten by local agents.

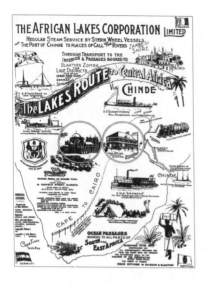

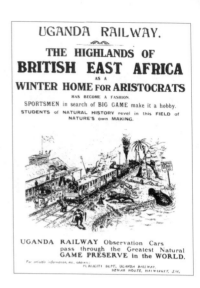

55 *Above left*: The rosy African empire of water, energy, machinery, communications, technology and porters. Early twentieth-century advertisement.

56 *Above right*: Late nineteenth-century 'railway imperialism' in tropical Africa saw the laying down of the Uganda railway from 1895, designed to develop colonial infrastructure by linking the East African hinterland to the port of Mombasa. It also went on to be a service to the Edwardian shooting aristocracy, enabling big hunters to adorn their country houses with stuffed lions or elephant tusks.

57 Something to bring a gleam to the eye of any district officer, even the most juvenile of colonial Africans absorbing those essential qualities of English cricket: honesty and fair play to the other side.

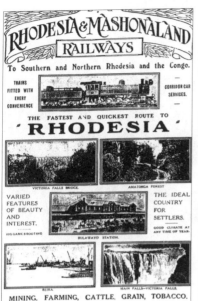

58 *Left*: Provision for white settlers, speculators and syndicates to move through Southern Africa at an optimistic pace: Rhodesia and Mashonaland Railways supplies the pretty side of colonialism.

59 *Below:* Late Victorian colonial preference: if British agriculture needed protection, so did the British liver. A popular pint for those imperial subjects addicted to sandals and vegetarianism.

60 *Below left*: The heavy-handed Cecil John Rhodes at the height of his power, full of vanity and remorseless taste for conquest in the early 1890s. Here, swatting aside a Portuguese hindrance, he is on his way to occupying Mashonaland, and ruthlessly crushing resistance by the Ndebele and Shona.

61 *Below right*: In the later nineteenth-century Scramble for Africa, Britain sometimes had to take its conquests on the terms on which they came, not necessarily with the willing compliance that it wanted.

62 *Above left*: Anxieties over the security of the bolt on the back door into British India: it irked Whitehall that Afghanistan seemed always to be rumbling, and always had to be watched.

63 *Above right:* They are there because they are there: the East Lancashire Regiment defending British commerce abroad from Gibraltar in the 1890s.

64 In matters of imperial trade and security she helped to hold the waters: the battleship HMS *Camperdown* of the Mediterranean fleet in Malta dockyard, 1897.

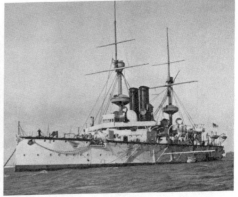

65 *Above left:* Officers of the household troops of the Nizam of Hyderabad awaiting the British twenty-gun salute, which was their ceremonial due as trusted 'natural leaders' of traditional India.

66 *Above right:* A bargaining chip up the sleeve of the British consul-general in Shanghai: HMS *Centurion*, Royal Navy flagship on the China Station at the end of the nineteenth century.

67 Punjab regiment's sharpshooters of the 1890s, suffering from British adoration: Punjabi society was acclaimed by the Raj for its perceived martial qualities and favoured for its loyalty. Whatever stabbing was being done by crack Muslim Pathan and Sikh infantry, it would not be of British backs.

68 An Indian-Anglo fop asserts his masculinity: a twelve-year-old Indian prince bags yet another Bengal tiger, protected against the climate and wildlife by fine British textiles, including flannel and corduroy.

69 *Below left*: Making India his own warrior country: the robust, muscular and gorgeously clothed English commandant of the 18th Bengal Lancers.

70 *Below right*: One thoroughbred meeting another: an Asian elephant obligingly accepts sugar cane from the prince of Wales on his later nineteenth-century tour of Ceylon, relieved that it has escaped being added to his collection of sporting trophies.

71 Thanks to British investors, merchants, entrepreneurs and technologically minded contractors, by the end of the nineteenth century the Indian elephant had the enviable travel option of some 25,000 miles of railway track at its disposal.

72 *Below left*: For the Englishman prepared to travel far afield and willing to rough it, there were few rewards greater than a tiger rug for the drawing room.

73 *Below right*: Local colonist and labour agent for the British army in the South African War 1899–1902 holds one of the keys to imperial victory – African camp and transport labour, however young. In its war against the Boer Republics, British forces used roughly 100,000 black volunteers and conscripts for labouring duties.

74 Earning his keep and keeping the flag: Cecil Rhodes (front, centre) displays his knack for choosing financial associates whose business ethics and moustaches were always above reproach.

75 *Below left*: Helping to make Antarctica British: Scott of the Antarctic. Initially offering little other than crisp snow, penguins and frostbite, Antarctica's frozen wastes suddenly provided a new imperial dividend after the outbreak of the First World War. This was whale oil, a valuable source of glycerine for use in explosives.

76 *Below right*: Sir Herbert Baker, the grandiose architect and master of Edwardian conceit. With Sir Edward Lutyens he designed imperial New Delhi in the earlier twentieth century. His worldwide buildings continue to outlive the British dominion that they once serenaded.

77 Cecil Rhodes at the site of his eventual grave in 1902, the Matopos in Zimbabwe. Always fond of rocks, preferably those bearing diamonds and gold, Rhodes (fourth from left) provides a practical demonstration of his famous commitment to 'well-treated and justly-governed black labour from Cape Town to Zambesi'.

78 *Below left*: In 1914 Viscount Buxton, governor-general of the Union of South Africa, prepares to read the Riot Act to its more unruly Afrikaner republicans, yet again disrespectful of the imperial connection.

79 *Below right*: The impetuous Dr Leander Starr Jameson, who led a mounted expedition to try to topple the republican government of the Transvaal in 1896. The Jameson Raid conspiracy was a tactical fiasco, handing the invaders not power but humiliation.

80 Robert Baden-Powell, founder of the Boy Scouts and advocate of world peace around the campfires of the British Empire: the hardy old scout ponders the wisdom of a 1920s trip to the bush by horseless carriage.

81 *Below left:* At times, implanting the cult of games went beyond the mere rituals of cricket. Free of the burdens of club membership, young Africans try out the public-school ideology of competitive athleticism at Fort Jameson, Northern Rhodesia, early in the twentieth century.

82 *Below right:* An unlikely version of the games ethic as the ideological glue of empire: sprinting Africans in Northern Rhodesia.

a dreamy despotism as the self-appointed guardians of an unspoiled, traditional Asian life, and as bloodthirsty enemies of piracy, viewed as prey to be eliminated without mercy. These parts eventually fell under a London 'protection'.

The impulse behind direct British intervention in the Malayan peninsula was somewhat less buccaneering. By the 1870s, officials and merchants in their commercial settlements of Penang, Malacca and elsewhere were increasingly jumpy over frontier unrest and other turmoil caused by hard-fought Malay succession disputes and intense trade wars involving Chinese bands. Another anxiety was the possibility of some foreign power exploiting turbulence in the Malayan kingdoms to nose its way into a vital sea-route stretch of British influence.

A restoration of peace and order to stave off any slippage of the British position became an issue of ever-increasing urgency, and in 1873 the Colonial Office sounded out the appointment of resident British officers in the Malay states to rein in what had come to be viewed as a set of irresponsible local princes. This move turned into treaty-based political domination over a large area, as a series of Anglo-Malay agreements through the 1870s and 1880s sanctioned the installation of British residents.

These had the usual peculiar attributes of colonial treaties of this period. In principle, Britain confirmed the autonomy of the Malay kingdoms and the sovereign rights of their rulers, while binding sultans to following the advice of British officers in all affairs except custom and religion. Sultans extracted some advantage from this accommodation, as the British looked after their pockets and helped to conserve their petty powers over those beneath them. Maximum advantage, of course, accrued to the British as the real arena of power was filled by incoming residents and their administrative establishments. That colonial administration became more regular and centrally co-ordinated with the incorporation of the main peninsula territories in a Federated Malay States in 1896, with a capital of Kuala Lumpur into which was deposited a bossy resident-general and staff.

Among the Malays, tenderly inscribed in British policy as 'princes of the soil', there were sultans and others who dug in their heels periodically, insisting on acting on their rights and sovereignty in contrary ways. But with a steady and uniform Federated Malay States government in place, there were few worries for British industrial and financial interests which romped into agricultural and mining sectors.

Initially, Chinese capitalists and immigrant labour were influential in crop production and tin mining. Alongside them, British planters soon found what best suited the Malayan climate and soil. Estate production of coffee and sugar was supplanted by rubber enterprise at the end of the nineteenth century, with energetic exploitation of incoming Indian Tamil labour and very rapid plantation growth. Rubber estates and tin mining companies soon became as redolent of British Malaya as did the sugar plantations of British Jamaica.

Also associated with Malaya was an abiding British attitude towards its older ways of life. Cloyingly condescending and tinged with myth, this portrayal cast Malays as harmless and lazy, useful for minor chores and light administration. At their pastoral best in green village fields, the modern and frenetic ways of colonial capitalism were not for them. The Victorian civilising mission was not improvement but conservation, with the consequence that the Federated States took shape around a government controlled by British officials and a thriving export economy angled completely towards the dividend requirements of European and Chinese business enterprise.

Dividends were certainly especially attractive in what had become 'British India'. A grand part of the formal empire, its identity was neither that of the empire of influence, like Argentina, nor that of settlement, like Australia, nor that of authority, like Malaya, nor that of crown dependency, like Gibraltar. In the early decades of the nineteenth century, India became an increasingly vital market for Britain's staple export, cotton textiles, and for the absorption of its iron and steel goods, including machinery. Around 60 per cent of its imports were British at the beginning of the 1800s, producing a healthy surplus that Britain used to make up its deficit on trade with North America, as well as continental Europe. Behind this lay the helpful workings of British policy in the first quarter of the century, which suppressed the local textile industry to free Lancashire mills from competition.

Nor was this all. Through its large export surpluses with the Far East, British Indian interests were able to control trade relations with other economies in the area. It ought not to be forgotten – but often is – that much of what was exported regionally was opium, a narcotic that was still flooding the Chinese market in the 1870s. Almost from the outset, its regular production for raising revenue was nurtured as a dynamic state monopoly. For the idealists of Britain's *laissez-faire* world capitalism, it made India a part of the empire in which to be embarrassed or merely to be silent.

Its handsome trade surpluses were then drawn off to sustain British prosperity through an intriguingly artificial political arrangement, which made it look as if it was a liberal London that was keeping India on its feet. Its levying of municipal-sounding Home Charges or payments by India for the privilege of being administered by the British helped in creating an Indian trading deficit with Britain. This dependent relationship was underpinned further by bloated interest payments on Indian public debt to gentlemanly City investment houses. Not for nothing was this country the jewel or the great honeypot of the nineteenth-century empire. Britain was putting in a lot, but nothing compared to what it was getting out.

On top of its vital importance to British business, India's further advantage to the empire was its army, roughly one-third of it British. By the early years of the twentieth century, its fighting strength had stretched to over 160,000 troops. Representing roughly half of Britain's global military strength in peacetime, the Indian army was considerably more than just a garrison for the defence of India. For a state that did not have conscription at its disposal, it was an essential asset for the usual business of colonial warfare, conquest and pacification. On top of its enormous establishment, the Indian army had the further attraction of being cheap. Imperial arrangements were best when they were cut-price and easy on the pockets of British taxpayers. A policy principle tied the government of India to using its own tax revenue to pay for the peacetime army on its soil, and to funding the costs of Indian Army troops serving overseas. On this economical basis, the Indian army was employed repeatedly towards the end of the century to hold down British positions along a great crescent of eastern colonial interests, from far eastern Asia to eastern Africa. In the midst of incessant disquiet over the burdens imposed upon Britain by the expense of defending its colonies, India's almost unlimited military resources made it a most cheering exception.

The need for Britain to retain its absolute political control of India was virtually unquestioned and it was prepared to go far in backing that paramountcy, devoting a large part of its foreign policy, army and naval capacity to maintaining a secure grip there. It is true that for much of the nineteenth century Britain had little need to worry over a serious threat to any of its imperial possessions from rival powers. The United States of America was throwing its shadow over Canada, but would hardly be going on to sink its teeth into a stable territory able to stand on its feet. Canadians, in any event, were not that one big thing, the jewel in the crown. Its glitter looked to be endangered more seriously by covetous glances from Russia.

From the 1820s, Russian expansion into Central Asia and the Caucasus began to look ominous for British India. If Russia extended its Central Asian control and pulled in Afghanistan, Persia and vulnerable Ottoman imperial territory, it would be lapping up against Indian frontiers. Should menacing Russian influence then seep into the country to inflame the political situation, British supremacy might well be split open. To stave off this threat, Britain concentrated on laying down a strong and protective frontier in north-west India, and on strengthening its spine of influence in Afghanistan, the Middle East, and on the Persian Gulf. India would then be chained in.

Trying to link all the loops proved to be a testing business, involving the use of raiding by expeditionary armed forces across Indian frontiers to try to establish client, pro-British government in adjacent territory. More than once during the century there were disastrous incursions into Afghanistan, in which dashing regiments of Lancers were expected to help in persuading its rulers to admit British agents and to follow their enlightened guidance. In the 1830s and 1840s, and again in the 1870s, British bullying landed them in the soup. It took a major campaign in 1879 to beat off Afghan opposition and to turn its regime in a more favourable direction for the security needs of British India.

After the last irascible Afghan rebel had been cut down or hanged by an occupying imperial army, their state effectively became a British protectorate, with control of its foreign affairs passing under British paws. But Afghanistan remained stubbornly insecure, its ceaseless ferment a continuing trial for the neighbouring viceroyalty of India. Never a strong plug for the gap into India, that insecurity nestled at the centre of what later became known as the imperialist 'Great Game' of Anglo-Russian intrigue and influence in Asia.

Britain's position within India itself was severely jolted by the great rebellion of 1857, often still described as the Indian Mutiny. This started out as a mutiny of restive Indian cavalry at Meerut over the violation of sacred religious custom. These troops struck out in solidarity with East India Company *sepoy*s who had been demeaned publicly and imprisoned for refusing to handle a new cartridge issue, which was rumoured to have been greased with a compound of pork and beef fat. High-handed arrogance had long been a marked feature of British conduct, and this shameless enforcement succeeded in aggrieving both Muslim and Hindu.

A uniformed service mutiny rapidly flared out into a civil rebellion which spread across a large and heavily populated part of northern India, bringing British authority crashing down. It proved to be contagious. Nearly all classes of the Indian population joined in, from rulers who had been slighted by the company and had lost their standing under British rule, to peasants wincing under relentless British demands for tax revenue and ruined by their brusque dispossession of defaulters. Although causes and motives were almost equally varied or mixed, what seems generally to have brought people out in the hope of expelling the British were widespread fear of their spreading authority and an incandescent hatred of their administration for its costly meddling in the workings of the economy and society of rural India.

Although for a short time Britain completely lost control of a large chunk of Indian territory, it responded with ferocity to regain its authority, and the Raj prevailed. Accompanied by much calculated slaughter on both sides, the human cost of the rebellion was horrific. British civilians, including women and children, were murdered, as were British officers of *sepoy* regiments. Army mutineers, rebels and those deemed to have been conspiring with them were put to death out of hand, either shot, hanged, burned alive or blown to pieces from cannon muzzles.

Marked by extreme racial demonising and hatred, and much baying for blood and vengeance, the rebellion left a sour legacy, stretching an already wide gulf between colonial rulers and subjects. Its orgy of excessive violence more or less snuffed out any flickering liberal optimism that under British dominion India would get the better of its maladies and advance towards the ideal of a civilised freedom. The authoritarian residency was there to stay, and its workaday Indian service would have to redouble efforts at the orderly progress of taxation, law, railways and education.

After the pivotal rebellion, the running of India was no longer entrusted to the company and its collection of subordinate Indian collaborators. Instead, in 1858 government was placed directly under the crown and parliament. As the paramount power over about 600 princely states, some, like Hyderabad, the size of England itself, imperial rule was indirect, filtered through rulers whose operations were watched by a British resident. To him fell the handling of their local defence and external relations, with much depending on his vigilance. Primary British India, regions such as Bengal and the Punjab, was governed directly by a professional civil service, led by a trained elite of Englishmen, addicted to bridge parties and regency villas in the Himalayan foothills, and mostly treading a fine line between punishing the servants and cultivating the necessary convenience of Indian goodwill.

Even here, actual imperial rule was no more than skin deep. At its height near the turn of the century, the European

Indian civil service elite consisted of some 1,300 officers amidst a population of about 250 million. Preserving some measure of themselves as an arbitrator or a mediator, placed above the lines of battle between village moneylenders and peasant debtors, dispersed ICS officers needed a ring of willing clients to enable them to perform their functions. Influence rested on consenting alliances with princes, large landlords and commercial leaders, and on a layer of Western-educated Indian clerks and interpreters who made up the crucial clerical base of British administration. Tied securely to the Raj, these groups looked after British requirements in provincial and village society, scooping up revenue, gathering intelligence on those opposed to the peace, and peopling newly expanding professional and commercial sectors.

In general, crown rule and its elaborate Indian imperial establishment came to rest on a somewhat tangled mixture of impulses. On one hand, seeing itself as the lordly successor of the old Mughal emperors and their tributaries, the British colonial regime came to project an ostentatiously traditional image of authority, its invented public rituals and bejewelled ceremonials reflecting a belief that it was Oriental grandeur which would most beguile the minds of aristocratic and other dutiful Indians. Over-zealous missionaries and other crusading Christians were reined in by a Raj which was solicitous of the customary authority of Hindu and Islamic faith orders, and which largely left Indians to their own cultural, religious and social practices.

On the other hand, while the reforming British had little interest in Anglicising and evangelising India, their security, economic and other interests demanded that they take a modernising leap forward at other levels. Railways, roads, telegraphic and postal services, sanitation, irrigation and associated public works exemplified the Victorians' notion of improvement for those Tennysonian lesser breeds without the law. As to that law, British justice brought not only new and onerous legal complexities to issues of land tenure, land rights and labour contract, which tripped up mostly the rural poor. The rules of the game for an elevated British justice also meant the introduction of a new equality before the law. Maintaining its wider credibility required that at times the courts had to find against the great. Privileged Brahmins and other noblemen could now be imprisoned or even hanged.

For the British state and its empire, Ireland was not quite India but it shared the nuisance of its landlord and tenant enmities and a tendency to lapse into anti-British unrest. The formal nineteenth-century Union of the Kingdoms of Great Britain and Ireland was annexation with a parliamentary gloss, as the Irish situation remained colonial. If anything, its imperial burden was heavier than that of more distant formal colonies which had political control over their own tax and excise systems, did not have to share in keeping imperial services going, and were not being bled to help the National Debt. By the later decades of this period, the Irish tax contribution to the funding of army and naval forces, and other imperial establishment expenses, was seriously overstretched. At the same time, unlike India, British investment interests in Ireland remained slight, with income from railways, banking and insurance fields augmented by a modest flow of rental income from landed estates, which had in the past been an attraction to more bloated English and Scottish settlers.

In other respects, too, the British colonial horizon did not find Ireland especially profitable or congenial. Troublesome internal control required a substantial paramilitary police presence and the permanent quartering of an even larger Irish troop garrison which, in the concluding decades of the century, was larger than that of any other British colonial command with the exception of India. Its occupying soldiers were overwhelmingly English and Scottish, trusted not to be riddled with Fenianism, nor to be unduly tender towards the civil liberties of those residing in their many garrisoned towns.

If anything, the price of Ireland was a kind of crown colony khaki. Apprehension over Napoleonic French designs had hurried on incorporation of the western island, and its close proximity to the British mainland ensured that it continued to be viewed as strategically important, a Gibraltar of the Irish Sea, if not quite as vital to London's maritime security. Notions of resettling it properly with venturesome English and sturdy Scottish immigrants came to nothing, despite the heavy and continuous outflow of the Irish population during the nineteenth century. Such British settlers as there were tended to congregate in skilled urban employment around Dublin and Belfast.

Education in English became the vehicle with which to pursue an Anglicising cultural imperialism, its post-1830s National Education System fanning on English for rude Celtic barbarians at roughly the time that Matthew Arnold was praising the qualities of Celtic literature and language to the insular philistines of his own country. But the implanting of English was more to promote efficiency in government and in communication than a policy to turn subordinate Irish into adoptive Britons. The racial attitudes of British imperial administrators, politicians, generals and others to the manner born continued to lump the Irish with the barbarous hordes from Asia and Africa. In the 1890s, the Conservative Prime Minister, Lord Salisbury, and the Fabian Socialists, Sydney and Beatrice Webb, were not at all unusual in sharing the view that in their evolutionary imperfections, the incapable Irish resembled the 'Hottentots' of South Africa.

Naturally, while Irish separatists and nationalists railed against an oppressive tie to English imperial civilisation, for Protestant loyalists an attachment to empire through the Union made them full metropolitan citizens, rather than colonial dependents. Empire was opportunity. In fact, during the nineteenth century more educated and skilled Irish Protestants, as well as some Catholics, were able to insert themselves into colonial service, doing duty in the ICS or staffing medical services and expanding public sector provision in places like Canada and Australia. And for the sons of the Protestant Irish gentry, as with their educated Scottish peers, there were commissions in the Indian army and in other colonial garrisons. Arguably, it was the lure of armed service which did most to create a breed of bloody-minded Irishness in defence of British interests overseas, a pugnacity which became prominent in several later Victorian wars of empire. At the same time, whether Catholic, Protestant or just dewy over Home Rule, for celebrated warrior Britons like the spartan Horatio Herbert Kitchener, an Irish birth or connection had little to recommend it.

To ordinary nineteenth-century natives of Ireland, what had considerably more to recommend it was emigration to colonies of expanding white settlement. Shipped off with the aid of state transportation subsidies and the promise of colonial land grants, hundreds of thousands of Irish emigrants became a significant part of the colonist population of countries like Canada and Australia by the end of the century. Of course, government-aided emigration to Australia was not entirely without some compulsion in earlier decades. For a colony short on slaves, the availability of incoming convict labour for domestic and agricultural work was a considerable solace to settlers fretting over shortages of cheap labour.

Irish movement to settler colonies was, to be sure, but one contribution to the continuing development of these colonial Britannias. When skinned down to its essentials, rural Canada had a secure political and cultural orientation towards Britain and seemingly illimitable space, but lacked India's hundreds of millions of empire subjects. At this level, the fact that British North America held the largest proportion of the overseas white-settler population by the early decades of the twentieth century is not as noteworthy as it may at first appear. In size, what this represented was no more than the population of Greater London. More striking, perhaps, was an influx of white women and children, the result of special female emigration schemes to alter the coarse masculine character of an emigrant society originally tied largely to the fur trade. Fostered by the classic Victorian spirit of reform and crusading improvement, colonial reformers envisaged that the depositing of tender European wives would raise the moral health and stabilise the loose lives of pelt traders and loggers living in squalid tents, at times with Prairie 'squaws' as rather too intimate personal company.

Turning territories of settlement like Canada into more wholesome repositories of family virtues would strengthen the social fabric and institutions of British Canadians. At the same time, the lot of indigenous inhabitants merely grew more dismal, with disease, alcohol and declining buffalo herds helping to reduce their proportion of the population from some 20 per cent in the early 1800s to at most 1 per cent on the eve of the First World War. As immigrant pressure for cheap land and entitlement to resources mounted, colonial authorities turned to the creation of confined reserves as a way of settling Indian populations down to learn orderly ways and the value of a medicine chest. All other land was conveniently alienated as open 'waste' and was thus available for purchase.

Becoming a self-governing federation in 1867, Canada was a classic example of the portly nature of a British imperial identity in the nineteenth century, of the constitutional capaciousness with which it could acquiesce in an increasing level of political independence for loyal white British subjects. Equally, while English-speaking Canada may have been appreciated as a more responsible North America, it was hardly one of the empire's best commercial customers. Although Britain provided almost 90 per cent of all its investment capital by the 1900s, besides the pull of railways and canals Canada did not exactly throb with markets or raw materials. Once of some strategic naval importance, its timber trade ran at half-mast after the early 1800s, and newer developments thereafter were on a small scale. Mining growth was mostly feeble, and even the brief mania of the Yukon gold rush failed to translate into spectacular British expansion. Unlike South Africa, with its coming mining market of shares called '*Kaffirs*' on the London Stock Exchange, Canadian mineral speculation would not be setting the tone of its ceaselessly bullish or bearish rhythms.

A greater hunger of imperial opportunity lay in the more western stretches of the Pacific region. Awakened in the previous century by the amphibious persuasions of Captain James Cook, British interest in the islands and the Australian mainland assumed mercantile fortunes to be made, settlements to be planted and possibly pagan souls to be saved. In the early years of the nineteenth century, free immigrant colonists from New South Wales made increasingly regular crossings to the territories of New Zealand, which represented a favourable landing for more extended Pacific voyaging and for trade with the Maoris, exchanging both goods and knowledge on the basis of mostly peaceful contact and co-existence. A minority, no more than a few hundred, of traders, whalers and mission-aries made their way in a Maori environment, not only tolerated but valued for their tools, commercial practices and acumen which the robust Maori assimilated for their own independent ends.

Relations became more strained once British visitors and residents turned into major immigration. As interest in New Zealand increased among groups and companies fishing for dependable colonial settlements as the answer to unemployment and social disorder at home, early waves of white township settlement upset a delicate balance of trade and contact. Dubious land purchases by private agents and increasing British interference in the local affairs of the Maori led to flaring disorder and increasingly violent disputes, prompting intervention by London in 1840. New Zealand was annexed to impose order and the sovereign authority of imperial civilisation.

Officially regulated white settlement was authorised in a governing exercise which included the signing of the 1840 Treaty of Waitangi with local chiefs who imagined that its guarantees of Maori rights included the reserving of their prerogative to rule themselves under chiefly authority. The British assumption was somewhat different, namely, that as the sovereign controlling power in New Zealand they were entitled to govern all its inhabitants, Maoris as well as Irish Catholics, Scots Presbyterians or English Freemasons. Faced with a small but tenacious and sturdy Maori society which resisted its loss of land and political autonomy, the new British order failed to capture sufficient consent or compliance and had to be imposed by force.

Adept at taking on campaigning imperial forces, warriors gave a formidable account of themselves in a string of Maori Wars from the 1840s to the 1870s, before crumpling under the weight of massively superior British numbers. Defeat, demoralisation and a consequent loss of political cohesion reduced their independent power, easing British alienation of millions of acres of Maori land. A constant flow of new emigrants also reduced their standing to a minority of a very much larger settler population by the 1880s. Perceptions of the plight or cause of the Maori among New Zealand British missionaries and humanitarians were mixed, but what mattered was that their defeat and dispossession made the territory an attractively tame country for prospective settlers. In advertising campaigns to attract emigrants to a fresh and distant colony, benign portraits depicted the Maori as trusty labour, a keen market and a warm tribal presence which gave lyric expression to the hardy exhilaration of outdoor life in New Zealand. Perhaps colonial New Zealand was on the way to becoming part-Maori some time before it realised that it was.

By the 1850s its commercial agriculture was shaping up around wool as a valuable export staple, but the introduction of refrigerated shipping by the 1880s and 1890s stimulated a very rapid development of meat processing and dairy farming, producing bulging volumes of lamb, butter and cheese at costs that were a fraction of those of domestic British producers. With meat and dairy produce as the mainstay of its export economy, New Zealand became a classic complementary imperial economy, virtually a rainy extension of the farmlands and market towns of Lincolnshire or Wiltshire. For all its establishment of responsible government in 1856 and experience of measured political devolution, British investment capital and food markets bound New Zealand ever more firmly to the financial power of London and to a dutiful younger cousinhood with Britain.

At the same time, and more broadly, colonial ascendancy and imperial power in the Pacific found a firm berth in Australia, as it turned gradually from the criminal damnation of Botany Bay to a vast land of opportunity where emigrant settlers could make good. Australia was another exceptionally long haul out from Britain. But it had the store of the Pacific Ocean, convict labour, an abundance of land over which to clamber, and a thin crust of vulnerable Aboriginal inhabitants which could be torn off and discarded as they became outnumbered by a new and expanding colonial society of British migrants. Land was exploited particularly for massive sheep-runs, and from the 1830s wool became the leading and most enduring Australian export commodity throughout this period. As British agricultural capital began to roll in, other major farming products developed, most notably cattle, wheat and sugar. Refrigerated cargo transport turned frozen lamb and beef into large-volume exports to the global market, which meant almost exclusively Britain. Branching out from continental Australia into the Pacific island trade, trawling speculators created a hungry scavenging engine, scooping up shell, marine animals, sandalwood and other goods for the China trade.

But Australian economic growth was to be based on more than being a distant sheep station of industrial Britain. Minerals like gold, coal, copper, lead, silver and zinc added significantly to export earnings and to the capacity for fiscal independence, which was one of the key pegs of the imperial system. Profitable export production linked the new Australian economy to the international trading system, providing the earnings that could be used to fund essential infrastructure – the development of railways, roads, urban services and so on. Obviously, Britain was the crucial cog for this wheel to turn, both as a consumer market and as a money market. It accounted for at least half of Australian trade, and the City's weighty stake in capital investment reflected the settlement's dependence on London financial markets.

By the beginning of the twentieth century, a newly federal white Australia had not only gained responsible government and a distinct degree of constitutional liberty. It had also begun to fashion a manly colonial identity as a country in which even more effete British stock could be regenerated by a fortifying life in the sun and which could breed sturdy Anglo-Australian boys of a kind who had been challenging English cricket teams since the 1870s. Yet there was still a constraining reality which Australia shared with other settler colonies. Its heavy London borrowings on the Square Mile to finance government, railways, urban infrastructure and all manner of other planks of national development conveyed the essence of ambiguity. Increasing political autonomy was accompanied by deepening dependence on the immense financial power of British imperialism.

By the later nineteenth century, London was the unrivalled financial hub of the world, as British investments overseas, dwarfing those in the domestic economy, rose from £200 million to £4,000 million between 1815 and 1914. A mere 5 per cent of this was going to Europe by 1914. All main currencies were pinned to the international gold standard which, in effect, meant that most of the world's trade was being underwritten by the Bank of England. London was also the capital of the world's greatest empire, with administrative power dispersed unevenly across a nexus of Whitehall departments and agencies. Some, like the India Office and Colonial Office, were exclusive paper havens of empire. Others, like the War Office, were mostly doing steely duties which involved holding it all together.

While that empire had emerged as the loose creation of different interests, including those of merchants, industrialists, explorers, missionaries, emigration societies and the ardour of penal transportation, it was coming to rest on a distinctive sense of British phlegm and its commanding notion of effortless superiority. In many parts of the formal empire, the sword could be sheathed and the howitzer rolled away except for drill, ceremonial parade, salutes and other ornamented show. The patrician bearing and studied expression of a Lord Lytton in India and a Lord Charles Somerset in South Africa proclaimed Anglo-Saxon authority over lesser peoples and ingrained expectations of deference and compliance, even if the peoples encountered were rarely supine in their response.

Within British national culture, public-school ideals of upright character formation were educating a governing and administrative class for which the colonies were becoming the natural finishing schools. With this tissue of guardianship went a thick stock of rituals and practices designed to exhibit British authority: the pledging of allegiance to the crown by traditional chiefs in parts of Africa; kneeling to receive the Most Exalted Order of the Star of India in recognition of some Arthurian service as the rescuer or warden of a heathen domain; the theatrical wig and powder of English law courts in colonial Natal; and the occasional larger and highly ornate paternalist ceremonials, like the 1877 Imperial Assemblage in Delhi to commemorate the proclamation of Queen Victoria as empress of India. For British officials and loyal Indian princes, the Raj and its accompanying sham chivalry looked to be turning Cawnpore into Camelot.

Yet, beneath the glitter and the conspicuous display of great power status lay an old island, certainly expertly schooled in the currents of world trade but also unusually dependent on it for its markets, its raw materials and its investment income. Sooner or later, its early industrial pre-eminence would come under challenge from emerging global competition. Here, ironically, the power of Britain's industrialisation and its free-trade empire gnawed away at its own foundations. For those forces helped to fuel a great world capitalist boom in the 1850s and 1860s, in which the absorption of British capital, equipment, technology and know-how enabled several other advancing states to industrialise comparatively speedily.

Germany's and the United States's industrialisation could not but pose an increasing threat to a Britannic world power. London, to be sure, always had its naval strength to punch open a passage for British goods into obdurate markets, like that of China, and to carry the sea lanes. But it could not compel newer industrial countries to fall in behind the maintenance of free trade. To protect themselves from competition, these powers opted for protectionism, while denouncing free-trade imperialism as a scheming policy to extend British industrial advantage.

From the 1870s and 1880s, as Britain's productive position began to appear more and more precarious, domestic concern and debate grew increasingly acute over how to shore it up. For tariff reformers, the dominant ideology of free trade was now incurring increasingly hard costs as British industrial strength became undercut by American and German manufactures. If its world gains were to be secured, a change in policy had become indispensable, just as the scaly protectionism of the old colonial system had once been jettisoned for the benefits of free-trade imperialism. This squabble over free trade and tariff reform went round and round into the early years of the twentieth century.

For the campaigning reformers of 'new imperialism', dealing with a changing balance of world power required that Britain organise its overseas possessions more efficiently and that it renovate its industry through the protectionism of colonial preference. Binding its empire into an enormous commercial union, free trade could rule internally while duties would block goods from outside. British captains of industry and traders wanted a completely open door to all colonies, not least to those self-governing settler territories which were now seeing fit to nurture and protect their own fledgling industries for modern development. A more formal imperial ring would also ensure the efficient fencing in of vital supplies of food and raw materials for the home population and their staple industries.

In the late 1800s, coming enthusiasts of protectionism like Joseph Chamberlain and James Froude argued that just as general national prosperity resided in the benefits of a trading empire, so another great merit of colonialism lay in what it could do for employment and for the perceived deterioration of British racial stock. An older nineteenth-century refrain was being turned into something more shrill by intensifying middle-class alarm about the degenerative impact of urban and industrial poverty and the growth of more militant working-class consciousness. For the moral well-being of able-bodied but vulnerable British workers, useful colonies could not but be the answer. As assured markets, they would prop up industrial employment at home. No less commendably, they could funnel out poverty, as distressed Britons who found work and income in a Queensland or a South Island or an Ontario would become valued consumers of British goods.

Moreover, protectionist sentiment was not entirely commercial in motivation. More systemically developed settler colonies would also help to arrest a waning Anglo-Saxon racial energy, rejuvenating a virility which was deteriorating in the cramped and overcrowded slums of Victorian cities. Once, too much city life had eroded the vigour of the Romans, leaving them too enfeebled to do anything about the demise of their empire. It was up to the British of the 1890s to make sure that they did not go the same way of decadence and decline.

Overseas, Britons could populate healthy offshoots of an older and healthier England, and be better able to preserve its sterling heritage because they were free of the virus of urban squalor and decay that was now creeping through the nation's veins. In this and in other views, tariff reformers called on earlier notions of transforming the empire into a fully sustainable Anglo-Saxon world empire. An expansionist British Christendom offered the opportunity to create this truly integrated organism. This prospect sought to take account of past decades of spluttering anti-colonial opinion, domestic criticism that colonies were becoming more of a burden than an asset. Sometimes cited as a cause of international friction and rivalry, regularly decried as a drain on Britain's tax revenue, in Disraeli's memorable judgement they had once even been dubbed a millstone around its neck. Equally, no government ever considered parting with any British colony.

To settle such murmurings over colonial policy, tariff reform imperialism would do the trick. Colonies that were merely administered as crown dependencies and safeguarded by force and diplomacy from London undoubtedly came at some financial cost. Yet properly settled colonies of loyal white subjects could be moored alongside Britain to add directly to its national strength. For reformers like Chamberlain, foreign competition could be walled out by an Anglo-Saxon world empire in which predominant British capital, institutions and culture need have no fear of rivalry or dilution. Ideally, an imperial federation of this kind might even come to fulfil roseate visions of the balance and unity of Britain itself. Where this would not be possible, as in India, the ideology of the white man's burden provided for the moral exertion of maintaining an authoritarian and paternalistic administration. Less civilised peoples would be brought on through trusteeship of their affairs, and the beneficial hand of indirect rule through indigenous leaders under colonial supervision. But this was not where protectionists were trying to force the pace of empire development.

That said, it proved impossibly hard going for a radical programme which included the notion of an umbrella Imperial Parliament with direct representation by the settler Dominions. Their governments had little inclination to take a step back for the sake of a more rigid and protectionist imperial unity. Their sprouting manufacturing capitalists were suspicious of a free-trade cordon for the evident benefit of British industrialists. Their farmers were committed free traders for their global export crops. And their populations were naturally keen on cheap goods, not caring much whether those imports were British or American. The election of an emphatically free-trade Liberal government in 1906 which remained in power until after the outbreak of war in 1914 further settled the issue. British policy retained its dogged commitment to free trade and a Chamberlain-inspired thirst for empire as a protectionist trading enclave dried up in the earlier decades of the twentieth century, no more than a historical curiosity of anxious and pleading manufacturers.

There was, in all of this, a critical dilemma of balance for the imperial British state. Its long expansion had created both a formal empire of colonies and an informal empire of spheres of influence, satellite economies like that of Argentina. Notwithstanding being saddled with defence obligations and other fiscal responsibilities far beyond Europe, the British derived varying levels of economic benefit from the exploitation of their trading colonies. By the end of the nineteenth century more and more of their food and industrial raw materials was coming from imperial sources, including almost half of all wheat imports. The proportion of British exports headed for colonial settlements or captive markets in Latin America was also rising.

At the same time, as foreign industrial competition became increasingly acute after the 1870s, the problem for British manufacturing was that of being continuously challenged and surpassed on some fronts. Yet while the industrial capitalists and businessmen around Joe Chamberlain and his tariff reform were trying to set the pace, the real running was being made elsewhere. British industrial power may have been slipping but there was even greater benefit to be gained through the controlling pulse of finance and commerce. Capital built up through earlier centuries of maritime plunder provided the reserves for a major intensification of overseas investment. With the international monetary system oiled by sterling and the international trade system braced by the power-ful shipping, insurance and banking services of London, Britain's financial supremacy over the developing world was perhaps more assured than ever. Between the 1870s and the outbreak of the First World War, the distinctively outward nature of British finance capitalism flourished on an unprecedented level, with around 40 per cent of investment abroad going to the empire. For British rentiers looking to bring home the bacon, a steady annual invest-ment income of about £200 million provided a fairly satisfying sizzle.

The success of heavy imperial investment, especially in fostering the quick development of settlement colonies, such as Australia, also helped to bring an ideological self-image of the British imperial tradition into full flower. As the most enlightened country, the world role which it was discharging was that of opening up commercial opportu-nities and thereafter maintaining the conditions for a free flow of capital, goods, people and knowledge in the world economy. A necessity for keeping up this free-trading ideal was continuing British predominance.

By the turn of the century, one supporting necessity was a *Pax Britannica* ideology. This was a military doctrine or strategic principle that the sea routes had to be kept open by British guardianship and that no rival power should be permitted to become so predominant and controlling in Europe in case it turned into a secure land base from which pressure could be directed at Britain's established domination of crucial ports and coastal territories. Previously, Britain had fought France to prevent it from rising to a position of unchecked European supremacy and endangering its world empire and island security. In the early twentieth century it would be taking on and defeating Germany in another inevitable imperial war between two nations set on colonies and naval power.

The other necessity for ensuring British predominance, viewed as unfortunate by some liberal 'anti-imperialists' to whom it appeared as if Britain was not playing fair, was the continued possession of a formal empire. To its advocates, not only was this entirely fair. It was a selfless British duty, as the purpose of previous vast territorial annexations had been to sustain an open world trade system. Indeed, for an early twentieth-century British seapower strategist like Halford Mackinder, even a democracy was under a compulsion to annex an empire if it meant ensuring its capacity to maintain universal conditions of liberal trade. There could, therefore, be no question of shrinking from any further expansion of formal empire should there be need and opportunity.

As we have already seen, by late in the nineteenth century the British had extended their colonial authority in south-east Asia across the Malay peninsula and had squeezed down on Burma. The quest for vital raw materials of larger range and greater quantity than ever before turned commodities like the rubber and tin of Malaya into major international British assets. Occupation had also rolled up Egypt and the Sudan. But the greatest expansion of the empire in the vintage era of High Imperialism or New Imperialism after the 1870s was in the scrambling partition of Africa, through which Britain gained vast new territorial possessions in East, West and Central Africa, and extended its grip upon Southern Africa. By the early 1900s, Britain had taken a massive jump out of its African coastal lethargy and had secured the lion's share of the gains of European conquest through the last quarter of the nineteenth century.

The main factors which influenced such massive and rapid British acquisition of formal colonies are complex and mixed. One view is strategic. As other creeping powers like France and Germany began to sniff at African territory, Britain was impelled to uphold its prestige by pegging down its claims upon areas in which its traders, explorers and other agents had been quietly active for years. Thus, French movement from Senegal towards the upper Niger at the end of the 1870s had to be stalled, in this case by the old chartered company system of unleashing the Royal Niger Company to occupy and administer British claims on the Niger. Awakened by the colonial initiatives of its European rivals, Britain was obliged to fall in step and demonstrate its political supremacy by annexing great zones of tropical jungle, arid bush and even disheartingly unproductive desert.

Another interpretation puts weight on the particular role of economic interests in British calculations of Africa's value for its world position. For years, trading interests had had at least half an eye open to the advantages of opening up Africa to British capitalism, to clear away barriers to the proper advance of commerce. Only through the extension of direct colonial control could such an ambition be realised, as it would provide for the necessary reform of conquered African societies. Once obstructive traditional rulers had been removed or had had their power tamed, colonial government administration would be free to procure local labour for public projects like telegraph communications, railways and roads, to impose its own taxation system, and to enforce peaceful, garrisoned conditions in which transactions with peasant producers could lead to a more stable and flourishing African commerce.

To this could be added other financial irons. Colonial development in railways, roads, dams, urban infrastructure and other facilities provided a new field for African capital investment, whether as government loans for something like the Suez Canal or as private capital investment in emerging mining economies to the south. Furthermore, in circumstances of mounting capitalist competition and growing international rivalries and tensions, there was a pressing need to secure tropical raw material supplies, markets and investment fields, such as the Niger palm oil trade, ivory and wild rubber. Such interests were expected to be more secure under reliable colonial control than if left in independent African societies which were merely under a canopy of fluttery imperial influence. It is equally clear that the economic case for the formal extension of colonial rule in some regions was not exactly overwhelming, and that despite persistence the environment for profit, revenue and trade remained uncongenial. Africa's population was small, markets for manufactured goods were scrawny, and tropical African colonial trade remained a small proportion of overall imperial commerce throughout this period. But, for a trading Britain, a flight into massive new African dependencies still made prospective sense for control over resources and for the buttoning up of vital economic and strategic assets such as Egypt.

As the basis for a commitment to colonial intervention, this was probably nowhere more evident than in Southern Africa, where the discovery of immensely rich mining deposits turned the region into the greatest prize for British capitalism in Africa. The discovery of diamonds in Kimberley in the 1860s stirred sharp interest in industrial investment, in white immigration, and in the growth of commercial agriculture to feed new urban demand. Britain cooked up protectionist land claims to assert protectorates over African territories like British Bechuanaland which just happened to spread over diamond fields, and the kingdom of Basutoland which was placed under the Cape Colony to keep it out of the hands of the Boer republicans of the independent Orange Free State.

Through its Cape stronghold, Britain then urged on the creation of an amalgamated settler South Africa with a unified economy to ease in investment and aid the construction of an efficient regional system to sort out ticklish problems of African labour supply and labour control. The continuing independence of the surviving strong African kingdoms of Southern Africa, like the Zulu state, was bottling up wanted labour and also creating local tensions. In the closing decades of the nineteenth century, British imperial policy focused on the redcoat subjugation of resisting African chiefdoms.

Slipping naturally into old conquest habits, this time
London provoked a war with the Zulu. Although its troops
were mauled at Isandhlwana at the end of the 1880s, Britain
was determined to squash Zulu obduracy. With resistance
finally broken, King Cetshwayo was exiled and Zululand
was dismembered into over a dozen pieces. A little further
along the way, the British army was unleashed again to
dispose of the recalcitrant Pedi. By the 1880s, British arms
had seen to it that overall white supremacy in the region
was now unassailable, although the imperial assertion of
British paramountcy over South Africa continued to be
a contentious issue for republican anti-imperialist Boers.
But they were a relatively small fly in the ointment. Britain
might have had to mark time in its thrust towards uniting
South Africa, but time was what it had for finally coaxing
its white settlers into a responsible Dominion statehood,
making it a New Zealand with diamonds or a Canada
with the Zulu.

But time suddenly ran out with the discovery of massive gold fields in the independent Boer territory of the
South African Republic or Transvaal in 1886. By the end
of the 1890s the Witwatersrand gold fields became the
largest single site of gold production in the world, dramatically ratcheting up the importance of South Africa to
Britain as its vast mineral deposits were siphoned out to
sustain the value of sterling and the basis of all international trade under the Gold Standard. Under the impetus
of its mineral revolution South Africa began to industrialise rapidly. Its spectacularly wealthy Rand gold fields
turned Johannesburg into an urban honeypot for British
immigrants and a glittering nugget for City high finance,

with its massive exports of speculative investment capital and febrile, slightly seedy or unrespectable South African mining market, its shares known coarsely as the '*Kaffir Circus*' after the mass of cheap African migrant labour fed into deep underground mine work.

For the Boer republicans, this great capitalist enterprise presented a chance to use gushing mining revenue to strengthen their independence and loosen the strangling grip of British regional domination. This represented a challenge that British imperialism had to face down. South African ore reserves were an increasingly crucial commodity for the protection of Britain's commercial and financial advantages in the international trading system. Gold was a vital interest, and any toleration of a defiance of British paramountcy was considered strategically disastrous, for if absolute power dribbled away in South Africa, imperial authority and prestige might be at stake elsewhere. What the Transvaal provided was a turn-of-the-century peephole into some imagined post-imperial abyss.

Resolved upon the need to smash the threat of Boer republicanism, imperial strategy of confrontation with the South African Republic was flagged on by the ruthless and intensely self-seeking Cecil John Rhodes, that leaping local agent of crown acquisition in the 1890s whose chartered British South Africa Company had bludgeoned and bamboozled its way through southern and central African lands to establish what would become Southern and Northern Rhodesia. This made him the only British capitalist in the 'Scramble for Africa' to have his name added to a colonial possession. It made Vancouver look a positive picture of modesty. In 1895, with the winking connivance of Britain's Colonial Secretary, Rhodes tried to topple the South African Republic regime to bag the Transvaal and its gold in the failed armed expedition fiasco of the Jameson Raid. This finished the piratical Rhodes politically.

It also brought on war with the South African Republic and its Orange Free State republican ally in 1899 in which the resources of the British Empire were mobilised to crush independent white-settler republicanism. The Anglo-Boer War or South African War of 1899–1902 was the largest and most testing imperial war fought by the British on African soil, a costly, ferocious and bitter campaign to reach a peace in which Britain could rest assured of its position and reconstruct a unified South Africa which would be safely tied to its purse-strings. British military difficulties in subduing a small number of Boer adversaries provided further fuel for prevailing unease within political and military elites over a physical deterioration in once-famous British racial vigour, and for anxieties about declining efficiency and its implications for imperial security. At the same time, the use by British forces of scorched earth and concentration camp measures against white Protestant opponents aroused a moral din from Quakers and other anti-war pressure groups over government claims to an uplifting empire of liberal ethics and Christian idealism. In the end, what it came down to was the Boers experiencing the price of Britain's African partition, the heavy hand of conquest and annexation.

Whether headlong, as in Southern Africa, or as more tramping gains in other parts of the continent, Britain's interventionist spurt into Africa was accompanied and facilitated by a range of newer industrial, technological, scientific and other developments. Advances in steam shipping, railways, telegraphic communication, prophylactic medicine and sanitary health, cartography and surveying, both eased white penetration into areas like West Africa and East Africa, and cheapened its costs. Lives were no longer typically at risk from malarial mosquitoes, tsetse fly and other inhospitable inhabitants of the African environment. Khaki also ensured that while Britons could not avoid sticking out, it need not always be like a sore thumb.

Superior armaments, the greater killing capacity of disciplined and concentrated firepower, and a calculated and heavy reliance on African mercenaries content to fight for a wage and a share of plunder gave colonial forces a decisive advantage over numerically superior African armies, inflicting great slaughter and destruction while economising on British lives. In one such (oft-repeated) instance in the Sudan in the late 1890s, over 11,000 peasants were mowed down by a British-Egyptian force which only sustained around 600 casualties. Demonstrably superior military and technical capability helped to endorse an increasingly aggressive imperial ideology in the late Victorian and early Edwardian era, with an intensely racist and militaristic popular culture celebrating conquest and subjugation. The annexation of African colonies was ultimately for the benefit of Africans themselves, whose political crises and inability to reform made them unfit to be left to their own devices. Britain's triumph in its wars of colonial conquest had come about because its flag signified superlative martial prowess, as well as an outstanding national sense of moral responsibility. Defiant societies like the independent Boers who would not play fair with the British had only themselves to blame for its grim consequences. War was indeed a terrible business, Lord Salisbury, the Prime Minister, mused in 1901, and those republicans should have thought of its horrific significance before threatening the queen's dominion in South Africa. Also playing its part was the growth of the pseudo-scientific racism of Social Darwinism, a crude application of Charles Darwin's theory of the survival of the fittest species to the idea of a pecking order of fixed racial categories. Black Africans were on the bottom rung, destined to be ruled by an imperial civilising mission because power and cultural superiority resided in the British race.

Racial ideas of national superiority, an indulgent culture of glorification in wars of conquest and the relatively cheap costs of British expansion also lifted the ambitions of a ragbag of frontier British officers, commercial officials, agents and settlers in areas like Central Africa who sometimes tugged imperial rule to far boundaries of their own making. Christian mission societies were no less caught up in the expansionist fever of this period, standing on feet strengthened by public subscription and private patronage, and bathed in the favourable publicity generated by saintly missionary figures, such as David Livingstone, the Victorian light of Africa. To them fell the more divine portion of the imperial mission, converting Africans from barbarism and savagery into worthy Christian communities. Yet zeal was not entirely without some ambivalence. Like those West African British merchants who disapproved of colonial wars because they were killing off Gold Coast and Nigerian customers, not all missionaries found the destructive warfare of colonial expansion to be righteous.

In trying to resist the extinction of their independence, those African states which turned to the final, mostly barren, diplomatic strategy of garnering support for their cause in London found it in hives of missionary and humanitarian influence. The nature of the Scramble for Africa was another factor which helped to ensure that early twentieth-century imperialism was not without its accompanying controversies, not least that of why morality seemed stuck as a poor relation.

5

Lingering Sunset
*c.*1914–2000

By the opening years of the twentieth century, the safety of empire had come to loom large in British national obsessions. Within ruling circles, worries about national defence and security were fanned by scaremongering over the possibility of a surprise invasion of the British Isles by a continental rival, and by the strategic implications of the great expansion of empire through the last decades of the nineteenth century. Of particular concern was the issue of how a small imperial homeland with a small professional army of no more than 200,000 regular troops could be expected to defend not only Sussex and Kent against possible invasion, but an empire made vulnerable by its size. Given its recent growth and consolidation into an expanse of more than 12 million square miles holding one-third of the world's population, how was it to be defended against the nightmare of insurrection or the threat of intervention from imperial rivals? On the eve of the First World War, most colonies were lightly administered and few had effective permanent defence administrations. There were limits to what could be damped down by swapping stretched resources around crackling frontiers.

What alarmed pessimists was the intensification of Anglo-German antagonisms after the 1870s. Britain's welcoming of the emergence of the German Empire in 1871 as a strategic counter to French pretensions in continental Europe soon cooled when the implications of German expansion became clear. Here was a strong European nation with a booming industrial economy, a formidably efficient army, and a gathering resolve to construct a strong navy and acquire colonies for its own place in the sun. Anxiety about Britain's competitive capabilities gradually turned into an antagonistic conviction that Berlin's goal was growth at London's expense. Absolute clarity seemed to be provided by the German move in the 1890s to develop a high-seas battlefleet, making it an oceanic power capable of mounting a direct challenge to British naval supremacy. German ambitions for dominance over France and parity with Britain were steps towards the creation of its own immediate land empire, a renewed expansion of its African colonial empire and the establishment of a world power which was seen as a direct threat to the British role as the leading imperial power in the world economy. Sooner or later, an Anglo-German imperialist conflict was inevitable.

By the time that great war came, the British Empire had expanded to its largest extent. While more bemused contemporary observers continued to wonder quite what it was for, it bounded a great range of differing and unevenly developed territories which were obviously significant for the British economy, providing raw materials and food, investment opportunities, markets, and destinations for migrants. More recent colonial annexations had swollen those destinations to include East and Central Africa, where the commercial reach of small numbers of early twentieth-century white settlers in places like Northern Rhodesia and Kenya was tending to exceed their grasp. Land grants spooned out vast tracts of good arable and pastoral land for noisy and demanding settlers, most of them British, but the competitive enterprise of African peasant farmers and their retention of desperately needed cheap labour did little for the deserving cause of highland white farmers in Kenya, that quintessential white man's colony.

In a number of other early colonial possessions like rural Uganda or the Gold Coast, the touch of a few officers, missionaries and immigrant Indian traders was so light that inhabitants went on with their lives as if for all practical purposes the British were not even there. British officials ventured gingerly into often hostile outlying areas, but the pith helmet was more noises off than occupying the centre of the scene. Their commercial objective of gradually transforming entire regions into cash economies by obliging Africans to pay taxes in cash rather than in livestock, produce or other goods ran into some tiresome times. In parts of East Africa, for example, Africans' fuddy-duddy desire for sticking to commercial barter in livestock and grain meant that it was cattle rather than the shilling which continued to be capital. For colonial administration and its desire for the adoption of civilising progress there was considerable frustration.

When this was added to other rumbling issues like various colonial budget deficits, taxing expenditures on defence responsibility, and the leeching of colonial treasury funds by squirming settlers needing agricultural subsidies and other revenue supports to remain healthy, for more sceptical Liberals and other critics it seemed that the British were somehow still resolved on empire first and deciding on the dilemmas of its development afterwards. In newly acquired dependencies, beyond a greed for cocoa and minor speculation in Nigerian tin deposits and Gold Coast gold fields to stimulate exploitation of the tropics, and confirmation of southern and eastern Africa as kith-and-kin empire, not much was being done for renewal and integration through more effective administration and stepping up the treadmill of long-term development. All the while, though, the flow of investment income from formal (and other) British assets overseas ensured that for the wealthy of Edwardian society there was no question that the empire of capital export had its use.

That use was demonstrated in other ways in 1914–18 when Britain took on Germany to destroy its world power ambitions and to preserve its own supremacy. Through a remarkable effort of worldwide social and political mobili-sation, and economic exploitation of imperial resources, Britain not only avoided the unmitigated disaster of a military defeat, but also continued to hold on tightly to its empire and to come through the Great War with gains, as well as losses, for its position of global power. Imperial territories furnished vital raw materials for the British war effort and crucial supplies of foodstuffs, with the settler Dominions functioning as massive stockpiles or granaries to keep the British fed while the German food chain ultimately crumbled. They also provided great numbers of colonial troops and labouring servicemen: 1.3 million soldiers from the Dominions; around 1 million from India; 70,000 from West Africa and East Africa; and close to 10,000 from the West Indies.

Reared on a kinship of the imagination with the Mother Country, many combatants from Australia, New Zealand, Canada and South Africa were loyalist volunteers, some travelling to Britain at their own expense to enlist in the home army. Female nurses and Red Cross volunteers further widened those bonds of imperial kinship and moral obligation by coming in from overseas to do duty at the bedside of mutilated men. But joining Britain to adopt its wartime cause was not an option for all its imperial subjects. Black African and Jamaican doctors who had been educated and trained in British hospitals had no luck in turning up for commissions in the Royal Army Medical corps, as officers were defined as having to be of 'pure' European descent.

A large proportion of West African and East African troops and labouring auxiliaries were coerced into the ranks, often as levies supplied by local chiefs to meet Britain's appetite for recruits for its African theatre of war. This was a wartime benefit of colonial policies of Indirect Rule through tribal authorities. Another of those benefits to expeditionary campaigning was that enlisted men came cheaply. West African Hausa privates were paid 3d per day, went barefoot and had to provide their own rations. It goes virtually without saying that the vast majority of black and Asian imperial troops were illiterate rural non-Christians with little if any inkling of why they were engaged in a British imperial war.

But educated middle-class social and political elites, recently emerging nationalists and urban trade union leaders, Indian princes, Nigerian emirs and other pragmatic traditional aristocracies through whom Britain ruled were for king and empire. Most suspended grumbling or agitation against discrimination and other hardships of the colonial order on the grounds that this was no time for disloyal slacking by subjects of an empire fighting for a civilisation of democratic liberty. Some hoped that patriotic service might bring a victory dividend from a Whitehall that would begin to take its pledge of an empire of universal rights and freedoms more seriously. Those wincing under levels of racial discrimination and oppression in white settlement colonies or in a Dominion like the new Union of South Africa, which put the average British district officer or merchant to shame, were ever hopeful of direct custodial intervention by parliament in London to check the legislative excesses under the responsible rule of white colonists. Others rallied to the cause of war because of a sense of aspirational connection to the power and influence of a crown imperial Britain. That vision was of the imperial state as a mythical monarchy in which the decency of an Edwardian bigwig paramount chief ultimately stood for the welfare and protection of all subjects, without distinction of colour.

British wartime propaganda was certainly careful in its brushing over of that distinction. It was not enough to extol the fighting valour of the empire's white Gurkhas, a breed of colonial supermen made up of hot-blooded ANZACS, brawny Canadian lumberjacks and Springboks bronzed by the veld. They were joined by unflinching Indian *sepoys*, brave native police from Central and Southern Africa, blood-curdling Muslim warriors from Northern Nigeria and the dogged British *Askaris* of East Africa. No longer the enemy of past colonial wars, they had become part of the rhetorical appeal and power of the imperial family, loyally united in the great British cause.

That cause prevailed in the sense of total victory over Germany in 1918 rather than any earlier negotiated peace. A major political consequence was a repartition of the colonial world, and the toppling of the position in Africa which Germany had acquired in the Scramble. German South-West Africa passed to the sub-imperial administration of South Africa, Kamerun and Togo were carved up between Britain and France, and the British acquired German East Africa, renaming it Tanganyika. In principle, former German colonial territories were under a trusteeship mandate of the League of Nations. But their official proclamation as a sacred trust of civilisation, to be looked after by their occupying power only until they could stand on their own feet, was of little practical consequence to the running of these assets in an essentially British imperial interest.

Losses to Britain were not only those of the Germans. For the Turks, a fighting alliance with Berlin was the kiss of death. In the Middle East, the fraying Ottoman Empire, which rested on an area of British strategic interest as it straddled the channels to India, had continued to arouse contempt among upright Liberal imperialists. In 1914, Lloyd George, the politician who had romanticised South

Africa's Boer republicans as champions of the cause of the small man against the conspiratorial greed of the City and its monopoly financiers, denounced the Ottomans as an irredeemably rotten and cancerous growth that would have to be removed in order to save the health of their oppressed subjects.

Now the British had a wonderful chance to assert their prerogatives, war having raised an itch for another round of territorial acquisition. To hasten the break-up of Turkish power, Britain encouraged Arab peoples to rise against Turkish rule, implying and sometimes even promising that emancipation from the Ottomans would lead to independence and the creation of future free Arab states on the basis of self-determination. Such prodding was aided by extensive military intelligence activity from 1916, in which the flamboyant figure of T.E. Lawrence, 'Lawrence of Arabia', played an influential and effective game.

An irregular warrior and prominent British Arabist, Lawrence was not one for dressing for dinner in the wilderness of the Arabian deserts. For him it was industrial Britain that had grown vain and incontinent, whereas the *Bedu* tribesmen of Arabia were an almost utopian alternative kingdom, governed not by money and machines but by the qualities Englishmen had lost – simplicity, toughness and the life-enhancing lessons of hardship. Back in post-war Britain Lawrence would go on to become deeply disillusioned and distressed by what he saw as the cynical betrayal of Arab aspirations. Surely their war had not been fought to change Turkish masters for British or French replacements, but to win the right to have what he was fond of calling a show of their own, in a confederation of friendly states.

Wartime imperial expediency also led Britain to promise the creation of a Jewish homeland in Palestine through the Balfour Declaration of 1917, an inducement to rally Russian Jews in that climactic year in the hope that despite the revolution they would work to keep Moscow in the war against Germany. Britain also dealt adroitly with other allied claimants to Ottoman possessions, agreeing to divide Arab territories in the Near East into fixed London and Paris spheres of influence.

All the while, by 1918 Britain had other leaping ambitions of its own in this region, what with Jerusalem having fallen at the end of 1917 and Baghdad a few months later to its mainly Indian armies. Fleshing out its regional position in Palestine and Mesopotamia, Transjordan became another British Mandate, as did Iraq. The British secured a shaky Iraq by helping up their client Arab monarch, King Faisal, and by the use of the RAF to cow rural insurgency with terror from the air, a new strategic option cheaper than having to commit a large army.

In Persia, although the Bolsheviks repudiated a 1907 Anglo-Russian agreement which divided it into formal spheres of influence, and despite the rise to power of a pro-Russian Shah in the early 1920s, Britain retained an underlying grip on its essential economic and strategic interests. As the Royal Navy had dumped coal for oil shortly before the outbreak of the Great War, by no means the least of these were the booming operations of the Anglo-Persian Oil Company in which the British government had lost little time in acquiring a controlling share. Ground of a similar kind was also held quietly elsewhere in the Middle East, the most valuable of which were Gulf sheikhdoms with appealing oil prospects like Bahrain and Kuwait. There, the British alone could benefit from any oozing holes through their exclusive hold on company concessionary rights.

What this all added up to for the post-war world of the 1920s and 1930s was Britain's consolidation of a position over rivals as overwhelmingly the dominant foreign power in the Near and Middle East, ending any further worries about the passage to India. Fenced to the north by the garrison of an occupied Palestine, Suez was now watertight. Despite nationalist rumblings over the infidel British and some other tactical problems, what the experience seemed to demonstrate was the viability of a renewed phase of British informal imperialism, through the embracing of cliques of upper- and middle-class clients and the furnishing of wise British supervision to their cabinets in making their self-governing countries ever more responsible.

Looking at what had apparently been achieved with a stable Iraq, given the cheap outlay on informal empire there still seemed plenty of room for a future of commanding influence. Egypt was just another state which illustrated this. The outbreak of war had nudged London into declaring Egypt a British protectorate and turning its Victorian strategic occupation rights in Cyprus into formal annexation. For a fuming Egyptian nationalism, however, the swing of a protectorate pendulum was against all the rules by the time war ended. As continuing British occupation was intolerable, it was made unsustainable by large-scale popular discontent. In 1922 the protectorate was abandoned and declared by a conciliatory Britain to have become what it termed a sovereign independent country.

It was, though, sovereignty of a somewhat emasculated variety. Under new treaty terms Britain reserved control over foreign policy, the position of the Sudan, imperial communications and defence. With assured easy access to the Egyptian cotton that was so vital to its textile industry and complete freedom of movement for Tommy Atkins to tramp about the country, London could shrug off any serious worries about the daunting social and economic difficulties of Egyptian development.

Equally, on other fronts there was little in post-war instability to indicate that the British were facing the incipient stirrings of decolonisation, even if their power was shaken. Certainly, war-related food shortages, the disruption of shipping, biting inflation, the arbitrary requisitioning of property, and the imposition of more oppressive labour regimentation fuelled grievances across imperial economies, bringing out discontented south-east Asian peasants and rice mill workers, South Asian artisans and West African transport workers in various kinds of agitation.

As the upsurge stimulated the growth of trade union movements in places like India and the West Indies, disturbed colonial authorities cranked up the scale of intelligence operations and cashed the authoritarian cheques of special censorship decrees and anti-sedition legislation. But nationalist anti-colonial challenges after 1918, whether in East Africa, Trinidad or the New Hebrides, were mostly swatted aside by police forces. Those revolts which were less half-baked were dealt with ruthlessly, suppressed with considerable violence by military forces. In British Somaliland, the cutting down of rebels by the RAF gave early notice of what could be done on shoestring airpower.

At Amritsar in 1919, the massacre of an unarmed Indian crowd by British troops broke street opposition, even if it came at a discrediting moral and political price for the imperial order.

At the same time, there were prudent political concessions and compromises to rebuild a peaceable contract between prickly colonial politics and imperial policy. In India, the 1917 Montagu Declaration had already committed Britain to the development of a fabric of self-government to lead to the flowering of a responsibly ruled India as an integral part of the empire. Legislation in 1919 transferred agricultural, education and other government responsibilities to new administrations under Indian ministers responsible to elected local assemblies. And by the 1930s the costs of the war to India, billions of rupees in artificial new debt, were being relieved by massively increased tariff rates at the expense of Britain's own cotton export industry.

The crisis in Ireland seemed also, in its way, to be the making of a second innings. Following failed Liberal attempts to grant the usual imperial device of Home Rule or autonomy in domestic affairs, and the failed nationalist Easter Rising of 1916, rebelling Irish nationalists declared an independent republic at the end of the war. The British government would not countenance this, declaring that a free Ireland or even one with Dominion status would be likely to welsh on its share of the costs of the war and might well also levy harmful tariffs on British goods. In the eyes of Lloyd George it would make war and a full reconquest of Ireland unavoidable, as if he were a Welsh Cromwell.

While it did not go all that way, during 1920 and 1921 martial law and a policy of counter-insurgency was imposed by British troops, backed by the Royal Irish Constabulary with a trailing division of ruffianly auxiliaries and a mainstream force known as the Black and Tans, recruited from non-Irish ex-servicemen. Largely left to run their own show of colonial pacification, they quickly became notorious for their iconic brutality and harsh repression of the civilian population, treated almost indiscriminately as murderous Fenians. With the tide running towards an implacable and permanent parting, Britain lurched into a vicious and bitter guerrilla struggle with nationalists whose Irish Republican Army or IRA well deserved its own rough diamond reputation.

Then in 1921 the British government changed step and opted to parley with its nationalist enemy. An Anglo-Irish Treaty produced an Irish settlement based on partition, conceding Dominion status to most of the country, while several mostly Protestant counties in Ulster were granted a Unionist Home Rule within the United Kingdom. Several factors played their part in this outcome, none of which had anything to do with a sudden burst of imperial enlightenment on the issue of national self-determination. Repressive handling of the Irish troubles had sparked off American protest, raised the political temperature of the Dominions' Irish flock and aroused some domestic revulsion at colonial methods of pacification usually reserved for native people at the further ends of the earth. Brute force on naked display so close to home suggested that the moral language of a liberal imperialism was losing something of its veracity. The not inconsiderable cost of a large army presence also took its toll. On Ireland, the political corrosion of war-weariness led to a fundamental loss of will in British ruling circles.

While the Irish Free State remained within the empire only under constraint, other white self-governing states continued their measured tread on the path of a safe imperial centrifugalism. The 1931 Statute of Westminster provided paper confirmation of what had already become general practice, namely that the London Parliament had no rights to legislate for the Dominions, although the British monarch would naturally remain as head of state. However, crown ties remained strong among Australians, New Zealanders, English Canadians and English–Afrikaner loyalists, as well as numerous black South Africans. Theirs was still unequivocally an imperial citizenship, in which they defined themselves as British subjects. Before the Second World War the only Dominion to define its own citizenship was, unsurprisingly, the Irish Free State in an impertinent 1930s Nationality and Citizenship Act, which defined the British as aliens along with all other non-Irish subjects.

British political accommodation of increased Dominion autonomy by the 1930s was just that and no more. High levels of dependence upon, and indebtedness to, the capital markets of the City ensured that Britain maintained its underlying economic influence right through the terrible crisis of the inter-war Great Depression. The creation after 1931 of the sterling area which tied in most of the recog- nised empire, as well as states dependent on British markets such as Argentina, Iraq and Egypt, was an effective calcula- tion on the ledgers of gentlemanly investment financiers, as it helped to sustain London's leading position as an international currency market.

Colonial reliance on the pound sterling as the medium of exchange and dependence on the sanctity of London vaults for the deposit of reserves kept the imperial currency system purring. The value of the empire for British overseas investment also rose in the inter-war era because of the particular advantage of stability and security that it provided. Even during the worst turbulence of the Depression, big investors in the stock of colonial or Dominion governments were not making much of a gamble. Whereas any number of sickly foreign borrowers routinely defaulted on payment of interest, returns on imperial lending through government issues could be counted on with certainty during the 1930s.

A resort to greater trade regulation through the establishment of preferential tariffs was also advantageous to British interests. Protective British trade duties introduced in the early 1930s provided exemption to their colonies and Dominions for agricultural, industrial and other goods. In return, Britain squeezed hard, negotiating terms which lowered the export cost of its goods on Dominion markets and compelling its colonial dependencies to grant preference to empire imports over any foreign goods. There were other cushioning layers, too. Those classic invisible earnings generated by sectors like shipping and insurance gave little serious sign of drying up. Nor did the empire market for British-manufactured goods. This held up well in otherwise dire conditions for the export economy of the 1930s, aided by the natural political inclination of virtually every colonial government to procure British products, by education and advertising in regions like Asia and Africa in the superior quality of such names as Raleigh, Humber and Enfield, and by the consumer preferences of South Coast expatriates. By the middle of the 1930s, while the overall level of British exports had slumped by almost 30 per cent, the drop in empire exports was only half of that loss. As a result, although Britain had accumulated a modest general foreign trade deficit of just under £2 million towards the end of the Depression decade, its takings in the markets of the imperial economy had landed it a favourable balance of trade with the empire of well over £150 million. There was a further benefit to add to those which more than restored any shine lost through the capital costs to the British treasury of a large commitment to imperial defence and associated colonial administration. One outcome of the growth and increasing sophistication of colonial bureaucracies in these later pre-Second World War years was the creation of Marketing Boards to control the development of cash-crop production by African peasant agriculturalists, setting prices as a declared means of holding up the income of peasants suffering in the Depression.

Exploiting its ability to pull the purse-strings, Britain used the boards in arranging direct bulk purchases by the London government of particular export crops. In colonial dependencies which had no negotiating hand, prices were kept artificially flat, fixed at well below world market prices. This was the basis on which the British state undertook to purchase the entire cocoa crop of British West Africa at the end of the 1930s, an agreement which was extended to virtually all major tropical raw material and food imports, including strategic minerals, early in the Second World War.

British government bulk-buying schemes saw to commodities like cotton and sisal from East Africa, tea and rubber from Ceylon, bananas and limes from the West Indies, and citrus from Palestine. Empire products could be presented as being good for the morale and nutritional health of citizens of the Mother Country, but the decisive benefit lay elsewhere. The convenient profit generated by bulk buying was pulled in by Whitehall ministries or by the various Marketing Boards themselves. These large sums were then deposited in Britain as a useful balance to back sterling. It has to be said that demand for imported commodities and a system of big government purchases, which ran into the 1950s, did something to shield many rural producers from an economic abyss, and even to create pockets of prosperity for small minorities of better-off peasant growers in African, as well as Asian, territories. And Colonial Office rhetoric made much of the great value of these trade strategies for development and welfare, through improving the productivity and organisational efficiency of rural economies, protecting and helping to raise the earnings of impoverished mass populations, and stabilising restless social conditions. Yet for the most part, they represented a transfer of income from colonial growers to the reserves of the British state.

In addition to the bulk purchase of many colonial exports, there was another advantageous trade strategy for the British. This was the imperious imposition of quotas on their colonial markets. Bruised by a decline in its textile and other exports to the colonies in the 1920s, and menaced by rising competition from foreign manufactures in the 1930s, Britain slapped on quotas to control the share of imports from trading states outside the sterling area. With proportions of dollar-based purchases by colonies effectively curbed through to the 1950s, there was much cursing of the British government. The discontent came not only from the colonies but also from British merchant traders, put out by the laying of tripwires on the high road of liberal free trade. Those who were not put out by imperial quotas were their natural exporting beneficiaries, such as the textile and clothing interests of Lancashire and Northamptonshire, and those of the pale plutocrats of dark British chocolate, Cadburys at Bournville and the Rowntree Cocoa Works in York. Their Quaker owners knew well the advantage of good works, even in trade.

None of this is to suggest that the Great War was not a very serious blow to Britain's Empire and international position in the post-1918 world. The British were obliged to relinquish their position as the world's leading creditor nation largely because to muster the resources required to fight Germany they liquidated a massive portion of their investments in the United States of America. Britain's heavy indebtedness to the Yankee merchant bankers of an eastern seaboard it had once possessed ensured that in turn the USA ended the war as the greatest international creditor state. In order to preserve their imperial power at the expense of Germany, the British had serviced the rise to world power of the United States.

No longer able to export virtually endless supplies of capital, London now had to take account of New York as a major new force in international finance after 1918. It had also to ally itself with a country with some irritating domestic characteristics and an international line that would have stung any old European imperialist nation. American politicians ignored local susceptibilities on Irish freedom at great peril to their electoral organs, and had constituencies which were readily responsive to all manner of populist anti-British sentiment. In the early 1920s, a Congressional Representative for Montana, a State known more for its bears than its Latin Primers, championed a Bill to replace English with what it defined as 'The American Language' as the official language of the United States. Declaring that immortality would follow if Americans would only begin to write authentic American, Representative Washington Jay McCormick called upon Bostonians and the other white Brahmins of New England to kick away their top-coats and walking canes and to embrace the rough and honest diction bred by a brawny frontier heritage of the moccasin, the buckskin and the tomahawk. Congressman McCormick's desire has probably come to be more than adequately fulfilled today, if not in ways which James Fenimore Cooper, Walt Whitman or Dashiel Hammett might have envisaged.

Internationally, a new American world power had virtually no stake in the maintenance of a system of colonial rule, liked to strike isolationist anti-imperialist and anti-colonial poses, and did not always muffle its hostility towards the direct rule component of British imperialism. An early manifestation of this could be seen in how maritime power relations were restored at the end of the war. One important British war aim had been to preserve their seapower superiority over that of Germany and by default over all other states. But at the post-war Washington Disarmament Conference, sulky but debt-ridden British delegates were served notice by an American Secretary of State that maintaining such absolute naval superiority would no longer be tolerated. London meekly consented to a limiting of the power of the British Admiralty.

Reputedly coached by Senator Charles Borah from Idaho, a former hick Shakespearean actor, Secretary Charles Hughes even rattled off the names of almost two dozen Royal Navy warships that would have to be decommissioned to bring down the size and capacity of the British fleet to reach an acceptable balance between the USA, Britain and Japan. In the 1920s, suspicious of the Anglo-Japanese naval treaty, the US Navy Department pushed for the construction of a navy equal to that of Britain and Japan combined, and made no secret of its contingent readiness for a possible maritime confrontation with the British. What this represented ultimately was something less dramatic, the gradual building-up of American supremacy at sea.

After 1918, second-to-none Whitehall imperialists like Arthur Balfour and Winston Churchill were appalled by the possibility of being put in a position of having to swallow orders from the US about the conduct of imperial policy in, perhaps, Egypt and Canada. Churchill also in this period saw that beneath the humbug of American anti-colonialism lay an expansionist ideology of its own, electrified by a business order with a rising desire to establish power and influence in the trade networks and raw material resources of colonies dominated by Britain and France. An unflinching defender of the existing imperial system and its preference, and of the prestige of the Gold Standard, defunct in wartime but restored fully in 1925, Churchill feared that the USA had undermining designs upon the British Empire.

There were other Great War knocks to British standing. A resurrection of the fabled Gold Standard, designed for a British lead in major international currency exchange, ended with it having to be run down again in 1931. America cut into British markets in Latin America, although in Argentina and in Brazil they managed to see off challenges from the USA, as well as from Germany in the inter-war decades. In India and East Asia, the increasing uncompetitiveness of British exports widened doors for Japan to squeeze in. While Britain maintained its place as the dominant foreign investor in China through the 1920s and for most of the 1930s, its share of the Chinese import market almost halved, while Japan greatly enlarged its portion.

The necessity for wide wartime mobilisation and conversion to the mass production demands of total war after 1915 promoted marked industrialisation in Dominions like Australia and in prize colonial South Asia. In India, to take a random example, Indian mill magnates were well served by the inevitable boom in the price of vital jute manufactures, such as canvas and sandbags, and large catches from a sudden sea of speculation in jute, as well as in other lucrative commodities, brought in capital which in the post-war period was used to found the first jute mills owned by Indian capitalists. In cities like Bombay, Indian industrialists and speculators were also beneficiaries of unsettled wartime conditions for British home business, as their cotton textile industry experienced a phase of substantial growth at the expense of the mills of north-west England.

Up to a point, the weakening of Britain's position in some of its imperial assets, its loss of reserves and the increased force of international rivalry can all be viewed as signs of some diminishing of British imperial power in these earlier twentieth-century decades. But that need not lead one to exaggerate its very relative scale. Nor, necessarily, to conclude, as some histories have done, that the outcome of the 1914–18 conflict for the British was that of winning the war yet losing the peace, as their power began to drift and they surrendered their leading world role to the boardroom of J.P. Morgan and the bridges of the Sixth Fleet. At the very least, the imperial mission could still blaze an explicitly colonial path, free of having to do the fagging for an Anglo-American world dominion which those men of destiny, the sherry-sipping Woodrow Wilson and the megalomaniac Rhodes, were both prone to dream about from differing angles.

Lord Curzon, a viceroy of India whose tenure bridged the transition from a Victorian to an Edwardian Empire and who had an endless capacity for dazzle, had once remarked of that imperial mission that there had never been anything as great in the entire history of the world as the British Empire, the finest known instrument for the good of humanity. For all that this rang hollow to the ears of many of its more outlying subjects, including some of those across the Irish Sea, Britain's later mandarins continued to have little difficulty in justifying the basis for its imperial possessions.

Throughout the 1920s and 1930s they simply ran true to type, in a way reasonably shrugging off the anti-imperialism of encroaching American imperialism as disingenuous. By the time of the Second World War, this attitude had become particularly constipated and dismissive of what was seen as wilfully ignorant criticism from Washington's Middle Eastern diplomats that lumped British imperialism together with those of Germany and Italy. In one classically grumpy riposte in 1943, Churchill was more than unapologetic. Declaring that some of Washington's notions of the British Empire were enough to 'make me rub my eyes', the Prime Minister was scornful of charges that Britain was failing to face up to an irrepressible world conflict between imperialism and democracy. They had failed to grasp the British genius in conjoining the two, Churchill asserted. In his view, the political point about the British Empire was that it had spread and was spreading democracy more widely than any other system of government since the very beginning of time. Coming from a high politician who earlier in the 1930s had publicly expressed scepticism about the virtue of rule by universal suffrage in Britain itself, he may have been hypocritical but not completely fraudulent.

The handing down of peaceful order and good governance from a plate on high was what provided a balance to more immediate and more worldly imperial matters, like the measure of profit rather than power. In these years, that included wartime Anglo-American squabbling over economic privileges, as American oil companies and other businesses which were wheedling for concessions from the government of Iran were trying to do in the trade monopoly of the United Kingdom Commercial Corporation.

On this front, there was the memorable reassurance of President Franklin Roosevelt's promise to Churchill in 1944 that America was not making what he called sheep's eyes at Britain's oil fields in Iran and Iraq. Whether this made it all fine by Downing Street is not clear. Yet, by then, there was certainly no shortage of other local problems for Churchill to ponder, such as the threat to orderly rule in Arab affairs from troublesome nationalists, especially those whom he denigrated with characteristic crudity as Egyptian *wogs*.

In immediately preceding decades, numerous British politicians and colonial authorities had also made repeated announcements of their staunch ruling commitment to generate revenue and maintain order for the economic and social development of their possessions, and to lead their inhabitants towards a vague or opaque future stage of 'political maturity', which would be appropriate for the ultimate granting of self-government to indigenous peoples. Political thinking about this was still not very systematic by the Second World War. Still, the consensual growth of self-governing white Dominions, the begrudging promise in 1917 that 'self-government' would be countenanced in India, the constitutional establishment of Legislative Councils in Nigeria and the Gold Coast and the granting to Jamaica of fully elected internal self-government in 1944 suggested some directions.

These paths were tolerable even if they included having to gulp down the prospect of conceding Dominion status to India by the early 1940s. What mattered was the essential provision of guidance to ensure that what the wartime Secretary of State for the Colonies, Oliver Stanley, called 'colonial' people remained on the straight and narrow. That was the road to self-government with the British Empire as an undercarriage. Cooperative and fraternal Anglo-Dominion relations would survive moves by Canadian or Australian governments to sup with Washington, however short the spoon. In 1930s India, significant political reforms could be implemented in response to pressure from the Indian National Congress, Indianisation of its civil service and army could advance, and elected Indian politicians could be entrusted with any number of palatable governing portfolios, from welfare responsibilities like health and education, to the custodianship of agriculture and transport. By the end of that decade, India could even reach fiscal autonomy.

What such financial health emphasised was the great credit of the Raj, and its capacity to guarantee the cycle of interest payment from Britain's investments back to the cream of its society in its City clubs, Mayfair mansions and Brighton and Hove seafronts, rather than any taciturn resignation to soon sell off the jewel of imperial assets. On the eve of a war that would end with imperial power backed onto the ropes, the British continued to assume an interest in India, which would preserve their role as natural guides and guardians, with their professional personnel at the elbow of India's civil service and massive armed forces, and with those harder governing portfolios which mattered more, like defence, justice and finance, still reserved to them. Indeed, even at the end of that war, Britain's khaki strategists assumed that in the event of full Indian independence, any such transition would be conditional on a favourable defence treaty with a new Delhi government, having identified the maintaining of RAF bases in north-west India as being crucially important for a retaliatory strike capability on Soviet Russian cities.

Despite all its increasing untidiness for the British, India seemed to be one good illustration of the vision of colonial nationhood that Oliver Stanley had articulated in 1943. It was certainly less authoritarian on the great issues than Britain's man in Egypt in the 1890s, Sir Evelyn Baring, later Lord Cromer. Like his Indian contemporary, Lord Curzon, who found it unimaginable that there could ever be Indian political participation in the shaping of British India, for Cromer the rock of empire was the virtue of guardianship by an altruistic autocracy.

Policies of colonial development would have to ensure that it stood fixed for generations, even countless centuries. After all, leading imperialists like Curzon and Cromer had felt it in their garters. Modern representative self-government was unsuitable for those crown subjects who were not white men, those stuck with the infant capacities of the minds of South Asian 'Orientals' or African 'Aboriginals'. Racial and cultural differences confirmed not just the inadvisability but the danger of something warned against by Cromer, that of ever succumbing to the fancy of transporting institutions 'whose natural habitat is Westminster' to the unforthcoming soil of a Calcutta or a Cairo. This was proconsular vindication of the British doctrine of indirect rule through chiefs, sultans and princes at its clearest, and without tricks. On the other hand, a more liberal notion of India becoming a free nation state within some continuing British imperial clasp was not liberal enough for Mahatma Gandhi and the other all-or-nothing men of the Indian National Congress. What they had in mind was the attainment of full national freedom, on the basis of their legitimate rights and political maturity, to control state power in order to construct a new national India.

The empire had, of course, made that an especially challenging and often fraught political business, and not only for India. In its best image, through a nurturing British Empire colonial subjects would eventually assemble into budding nation states, based almost always on the individual colonies created by British expansion. Needless to say, few plural colonial populations could be said to have naturally constituted nations in the sense of having had a deep unified past or of sharing a common language and culture. In that perspective, one could say that the peoples of the colonial dependencies of a British India, a British Malaya, a British Gold Coast or a British Nyasaland were no more pure a nationhood than, say, a nineteenth-century European Belgium or Italy, or, for that matter, even a much earlier Britain.

India was a South Asian subcontinent with a jostle of varying Hindu, Muslim and other religions, different languages and customs, and discrete ethnic identities and cultures, with modern boundaries defined by the limitations of British imperial conquest. Malaya was a conglomeration of tight communal identities, Malay, Chinese and Indian. African colonial territories had been brought into being through the calculations of European partition and the convenience of varied treaty settlements. The colonial borders they fixed were largely random or arbitrary. Thus, populations within new colonial dependencies were not brought together through the adhesive of language affiliation or shared ethnic identity, as with Britain's Yoruba and Islamic Hausa subjects of Nigeria.

The displacing impact of nineteenth-century conquest had also done much to foster migration and intermingling among Africans, further complicating tribal identities and making tribal affiliation variable. At times, ordinary African people themselves made the most of a fluid environment, passing themselves off as something or other to British employers or officials through necessity, convenience or choice. In the case of the Union of South Africa, some imaginative, wily individuals played the colonial game all too well. During the First World War, a line of men who turned up to enlist in response to a recruiting campaign for a South African Native Labour Contingent to serve on the Western Front declared themselves to be either Zulu or Basuto. When this was queried by an old white police hand, who instinctively recognised their names as being of Xhosa origin, volunteers were said to have responded that they knew that what the king wanted for the defence of the empire were the toughest tribes available. To them went the greatest prestige and the better perks.

Whether on the basis of uninformed perception or as deliberate political manipulation, those who administered colonies, either directly as officials or indirectly through the overseeing of indigenous authorities, had developed a complicated range of racial stereotypes of 'native' peoples, colonial cultural vocabularies and social recognition by the twentieth century. The Zulu were just one admired 'martial' race. To the east of Afghanistan, the fearsome Pathans were not far behind on the scale of warrior admiration.

Where, as in West Africa, political officers needed traditional chiefs to exercise authority, they had to choose with whom to make the most fruitful alliance, or even to raise new chiefs themselves who would do their bidding. New anthropological knowledge, in the form of any amount of hocus-pocus about traditional African identities and customs, played its part. Christian missionaries played another, as their creation of standardised vernacular languages in written and printed form was seen as being useful in helping to sort out definite tribal identities. Obtaining a firm grip upon the identity of crown subjects was also a distinctive concern in Central and East African colonies, where there was a need to ensure that the boundaries of white men's country did not become too porous. In Northern Rhodesia, Nyasaland and Kenya in the 1920s and 1930s, one issue for attorney-generals and their courts was the status of so-called 'mixed race' or 'half-caste' inhabitants. Those judged to be living in the 'manner' or after the 'fashion' of African communities did not tax the administrative mind. Those who were educated, had aspirations and contested being treated as 'natives' did pose problems when they objected legally to being taxed as Africans and to being denied land tenure rights in areas set aside for occupation by 'civilised' residents. They were an annoying flaw in the creation of neat compartments in colonial societies.

Other annoyances were the black and brown clerks, journalists, lawyers and other white-collar or professional classes produced under British rule. By and large, the British preferred the chiefs, princes, sultans and *emirs* at the top of their colonial societies, and the stalwart peasants and hardy warriors towards the bottom. Particular disdain and even animus came to be reserved for those Western-educated men, African mission 'sixpences' and Indian *babus*, corrupted by European influences into trying to get themselves above their station. Yet colonial government could not do without its ranks of literate Christian clerks in Nigeria or Western-educated Bengali officials in South Asia. Nor could it avoid stepping up investment in education to keep them coming. Justice, planning, census and all manner of other routine colonial activity needed locals with the training and skills to maintain the discipline of bureaucracy, taking minutes, keeping records and drawing up paper estimates. Naturally, the British did not see themselves as shaping modern, educated elites who would be making increasingly assertive political claims upon rights and liberties. But the increasing proficiency with which disgruntled modern elites were mobilising colonial nationalist discontent by the 1930s was being kindled by the very forces that the British had brought to their Asian and African colonies, from education and the press to the growth of railway, road and postal systems. These fostered the spread of broad-based coalitions animated by mounting opposition to the injustices and burdens of colonial rule. For a few wealthy individuals, even a British education was not calming – Jawaharlal Nehru was at Harrow and Cambridge.

Reports by some military strategists in the later 1930s that the empire would be in trouble if it were to be attacked by more than one large power were not calming either, and with good reason. By 1942, the British Empire appeared to be tottering on the edge of an unimaginably steep precipice. If not entirely as imperialist in range as the Great War, the Second World War was still being waged by Britain as much to preserve its imperial position as to defend the shires from the booted menace of a Nazi German totalitarianism. Even the least of any of those guilty men of 1930s appeasement, whether it was Prime Minister Stanley Baldwin or Prime Minister Neville Chamberlain, were in no mind to see the empire liquidated as a consequence of keeping peace with Adolf Hitler.

With war instead of an Anglo-German understanding, the gravest threat to the British imperial position nevertheless did not come from the European axis powers. In North Africa, British forces combined with imperial contingents including Indian, Sudanese, Cypriot, East African, West African, South African and Southern Rhodesian troops to rout Mussolini's Roman legions. Although stronger German pressure made the strategic picture stickier in the Middle East, it was not yielded to the empire's enemies. Despite everything thrown at it, Malta stayed in their way and helped to prop up British power and communications in the Mediterranean as, in their way, did the holding of Suez and the desert oil fields.

In the early stages of the conflict, Iran, Iraq and Syria were all overrun by British and Allied troops, while by 1942 Churchill's General Staff had their feet up in Cairo. There, Britain exercised its vigilant control over Egypt's defence affairs to deal with the installation of an anti-British government in a manner that would have impressed any of Palmerston's gunboat captains. Calling up an armed convoy, Whitehall's ambassador to Cairo, Sir Miles Lampson, thundered up to the royal palace, barged into the king's chambers and ordered him to sack the Prime Minister and oversee the formation of a new government that would be friendly to British interests. One of those enraged by such humiliating servility was an infantry lieutenant, Gamal Abdel Nasser.

It was Tokyo rather than Berlin that had the empire staring down the barrel of a gun in the early 1940s. In the light of the bungled Malayan campaign, which cost the Japanese fewer than 10,000 troops and the British close to 140,000, most of whom had been forced to surrender with the fall of Singapore, few British interests in Asia were left looking secure, starting with rubber trees and tin mines. This included seapower, its weakness exposed by the airpower of those whom Churchill, true to form as ever, had called the *wops* of the Pacific. And it also included the old allure of British imperial prestige and invincibility, the assuring motor of morale by which politicians and officials had set so much store for so long.

Australia was in a state of panic over where the Japanese invasions were going next. General Indian support for the British war effort was not merely lukewarm. Popular desire and striving for independence was leading many inhabitants to support the enemy's enemy, falling in behind the Asian liberty propaganda of either the pro-Japanese Indian National Army or the pro-German India Legion. The exiled nationalist radical, Subhas Chandra Bose, found a bed with the Japanese and in a radio address from Germany crowed over the toppling of Singapore as a sign of the collapse of a foul British imperialism.

As if this were not enough, internally the Raj was soon also up against the Quit India movement, a mass body of civil disobedience breathed into life by Gandhi and other leading Congress Party figures. By the end of 1942, this campaign had become the gravest threat to the Raj since the rebellion of 1857. Clement Attlee, the Labour leader, pleaded with Churchill to take a statesmanlike step, as to continue dithering would be to lose India completely to a hostile coalition, behind signs saying 'Boycott British Goods' in at least five languages. Constitutional initiatives for a form of Dominion status for India were one response to the alarming scale of its political challenge to the British in the 1940s. Another from authority in New Delhi was its ferocious crushing of the Quit India campaign, and its abridging of the liberties of Indian subjects, to continue screwing down on resistance.

With India on the brink, and Australia seemingly on the ropes, Hong Kong and Burma with its vital oil and supplies-bearing Road had also to be added to the loss of Singapore and Malaya. Had war with the Japanese continued much beyond the cessation of hostilities in Europe, the security crisis of empire might well have turned into catastrophe, for Britain lacked the wherewithal, as well as probable public backing, for an arduous campaign of continuing attrition in Asia and the East.

In this context, the American atomic bombs on Japanese cities were champagne corks to British imperial recovery. Sudden surrender by Tokyo brought relief to lengthy, exhausting and bloody campaigning by British, Indian, African and Chinese soldiers to drive Japan out of London's interests. In the Far East or south-east Asia, small and highly mobile British forces retook their colonial territories fairly rapidly, with the urge and the guile to stay a jump ahead of US forces. Their accompanying assistance in recapturing them would probably have obliged London to accept a disagreeable arrangement of international trusteeships imposed by American will, rather than the reassurance of seeing familiar colonial government back in harness. By the end of the war, what the imperial balance sheet reflected was the fact that not a single British colony had been lost permanently to direct enemy conquest and occupation.

Meanwhile, the war effort had also renewed the imperial system on other fronts, some of them routine. As the British mobilised the campaigning resources of their empire to unprecedented levels, inevitably there was a general increase in authoritarian control from the centre. With overseas finance once again an Achilles heel in world war, there was much tighter regimentation of the sterling area to ensure that colonies and Dominions pooled and conserved all foreign exchange earnings in London. Dependent economies were regulated extensively by official controls over their output, prices and marketing arrangements, and in the case of some colonies there was a widespread resort to labour conscription, in some instances under extreme duress.

Thus, in Northern Nigeria, some 100,000 peasants were forcibly conscripted for the mining industry after 1941, to boost open-cast production of vital tin supplies following the loss of Malayan metal to Japanese invasion at the end of 1941. Similarly, in Tanganyika, around 85,000 inhabitants were rounded up and set to work producing urgently needed agricultural commodities, including sisal and rubber, on estates and commercial farms. In many other colonial parts, low-key democratic forms which had been spreading through the 1930s, like trade union rights, civil rights, habeas corpus and a free press, were either curtailed or mostly squashed. Sir Miles Lampson was but one among many in observing that as Britain was fighting a war to the death in order to preserve an empire, it could hardly be expected to tolerate having its colonial subjects still marching around with banners in their hands. Or, even worse, sticks. National survival depended on exploitation of the power and resources of the empire. That required the firmest possible colonial control which, in turn, had to be backed by credible force, as numbers of striking African industrial workers on the Northern Rhodesian Copperbelt and activists of Ceylon's Marxist Sama Samajist Party found to their cost between 1939 and 1945.

Even so, alongside authoritarianism and force the British did not altogether abandon old colonial plans when caught up in a new crisis. In fact, the war crisis seemed only to breathe new life into their imperial system. True, loose and inevitably woolly propaganda from London's Ministry of Information on the issue of the great British and Allied fight for the cause of democracy and freedom failed to raise much more than a shrug or a smirk from many Indian and African colonial nationalists. While declaring themselves to be in dread of Fascism, they were possibly even more weary of the endless hypocrisies and racial discrimination of the empire. Yet, effective worldwide co-ordination of a fighting imperial war effort in a battle of what was beamed as the British Commonwealth family or partnership paid off, even handsomely.

Countless material and symbolic moments illustrated this, a phase in which many frozen differences that beset colonial ties to Britain seemed suddenly to thaw. To the relief of its treasury, the Dominions took up the financial burden of maintaining their very large forces. South Africa was taken to war by its Jan Smuts' coalition despite not having a popular mandate from a white electorate divided between English and Anglo-Afrikaner loyalists and a sizeable rump of disaffected anti-war or pro-German Afrikaner nationalists and republicans. Even Ireland patted the imperial connection with the enlistment of over 40,000 of its citizen volunteers in British forces.

In West Africa, authorities in the Nigerian city of Kano had little difficulty in raising more than £10,000 from public subscription for the cost of a Spitfire fighter aircraft. Meanwhile, in Accra, capital of the Gold Coast, prosperous Muslim cola-nut traders made spontaneous financial donations to the war effort, while their sons tramped off to confront the Italians in Abyssinia and the Japanese in Burma. There, they served out the war as a black Tommy Atkins on Rudyard Kipling's 'Road where the White Men tread', if not almost on to the 'Dawn of the White Men's Day'. Of course, racial segregation and discrimination was a routine experience for the empire's hundreds of thousands of non-European servicemen in Africa, the Middle East and the Far East. For educated West African clerks, when a posting to duty in the Empire Overseas turned out to be a 'white man's country' like Kenya, Nairobi's own settler apartheid was a particular affront to dignity. Off-duty West Africa regiment NCOs who regarded themselves as a good cut above those they considered to be local 'houseboys', 'primitive tribesmen' or 'raw *askaris*', were dismayed to find themselves barred from clubs, canteens and hospitals open to white troops.

On the other hand, 'home' service for British-based empire volunteers may well have been the token saviour of 1940s Churchillian rhetoric about the supple yet steely bonds that united those from all parts of His Majesty's Dominions in a struggle for the cause of democracy in which all would either go down together or prevail together. Although there were incidents in 1939 of middle-class West Indian and African volunteers being turned away from the Tank Corps and the RAF, a reform-minded Colonial Office found racial discrimination in the armed services discomfiting and politically untenable. Increasingly concerned with the broader question of accommodating the aspirations of an educated African elite, it pressed hard for the repeal of discriminatory Army and Air Force Acts.

A month into the war, all colonial subjects, irrespective of race, were rendered eligible for home voluntary enlistment and for commissions. By 1940, a home regiment had its first black officer. Understandably, as the most modern of Britain's services, the RAF had the largest crop of commissions. They included two Battle of Britain pilots, Flight Sergeant James Hyde from Trinidad and Indian Flight Sergeant Mahinder Singh Pujji. Although not familiar with Northern Nigeria or with its famous exponent of Indirect Rule, Hyde had a pet mascot called Lugard. His compatriot, who flew while wearing his turban, did not have a charm named after a governor-general, but perhaps piloting a Hurricane titled Amritsar over the Weald of Kent was sufficient as a way of making do.

For its part, the Colonial Office had for some time prior to the war been preoccupied with weightier matters than mobility in the Mother Country for black and brown armed service patriots. This involved increased planning for the needs of colonial economic development and community improvement that were being hampered by deplorable rural and urban social conditions – poor housing, sanitation, nutrition and inadequate basic schooling. Picking up pace in the 1940s, colonial personnel worked hard at expanding peasant cash-crop production for the market, at promoting social reform and at ameliorating acute poverty. Tens of millions of pounds were earmarked under measures like the 1945 Colonial Development and Welfare Act for initiatives aimed at stabilising conditions, including mass rural medical campaigns and the provision of higher-level education. It did something to repair the image of what Lloyd George in the 1930s had decried as a slummy empire. But it would take something other than a passion for development and welfare to slow down what was about to become a fairly hasty colonial retreat.

It is commonplace to point out that the British Empire emerged from the end of the Second World War with its essential territorial integrity intact, and with a sense on the part of its masters of the prospects of its renewal through an honourable colonial policy of 'constructive' development and inter-racial 'partnership'. Fairly immediate self-government was on the cards for India and had a future spot in the deck for the rest of the colonial empire. This rested on the belief that it could all be planned and controlled. It is equally commonplace to point to the illusory quality of that historical moment. For the fate of Britannia's Empire after 1945 turned out to be that of rapid and complete disintegration within a remarkably short space of time. In little more than twenty-five years, a stream of colonial territories became constitutionally sovereign independent states, and an entire world system of British formal rule and informal power shrivelled up. No longer able to hold it all together with its military and economic power, Britain plumped for imperial retreat.

The old jewel in the crown of Empire had, for instance, become a mess in which the British had lost control of the pace of events as they confronted the massive presence of the Indian people. Their wartime incarceration of Hindu Congress leaders and alienation of their nationalist following had led to a deepening of old divisions between Hindu and Muslim as the Raj turned to tactical collaboration with a rising and increasingly important Muslim League. Old colonial governing habits of favouring alliances with some groups and keeping a lid on others had had a particularly long run in India. Once, control by the Raj could be helped by regular audits to ensure that so-called martial races like the Punjabis were enjoying a favoured position in the ranks. Now, control through manipulative division acquired explosive potential.

Prospects of an orderly transfer of constitutional power to a friendly government had been sunk by irreconcilable Congress demands for a united India and League insistence on the creation of a separate Pakistan. Already tenuous for some time, and now impossibly fragile, British capacity to maintain order over a rising tide of communal violence drained away. By 1946, Lord Wavell, the Viceroy, was already planning what he drily termed Operation

Madhouse, a complete British evacuation with women and children first. The shambles of a partitioned independence under Nehru and Muhammad Ali Jinnah did not fit well with Colonial Office vision or with the residual defence strategy of the Committee for Imperial Defence. But it lay immediately ahead of the last Ferret armoured car.

Palestine was another mess which boiled over through the inherent contradictions of British imperial policy. Cultivation of Zionist sentiment by the need of Great War diplomacy was cut back to meet the requirements of Second World War diplomacy in 1939 to cultivate Arab goodwill by restricting the rate of Jewish immigration and making it subject to majority consent. Britain's intention for its Palestinian mandate was an independent Arab-Jewish state with a permanent Arab majority, in which its chiefs of staff would be able to secure the strategic air bases which they insisted were essential for a credible post-war defence posture in the Middle East. As civil war intensified between Palestinian Arabs and Zionists determined on making the whole of Palestine a state of their own, the embattled British were unable to maintain order or to hammer out an agreed transfer of its mandated power. For the Labour Prime Minister, Clement Attlee, who saw the 1946–47 analogy, Palestine and India were all of one or one of the other.

But Palestine was also an international issue in the shadow of the Holocaust, not a British colonial dependency. Watching a declining British power exhaust its revenues and its credit in a territory that was overwhelming it, President Harry S. Truman courted the American

Jewish vote by demanding the resumption of continued immigration and the creation of an independent Israeli state, while refusing to assume any international responsibilities for peacekeeping in the mandate.

Attacks on British personnel and installations by Zionist terrorist groups forced the authorities into protected security zones, which armed anti-British gangs derisively titled 'Bevingrads', after the Labour Foreign Secretary, Ernest Bevin. This was despite the deployment of around 100,000 men at an annual cost of some £40 million. Naturally, a few histrionic press commentators were all for hanging on, even if it meant one soldier for every eighteen inhabitants in a territory not much more than the size of Wales. In that view, the British were not well fitted by their imperial history to be the kind of nation which would just lie down and give up the ghost. But even Churchill, so fallible on Gandhi and India, could see no point in flailing about in Palestine. As leader of the opposition, he called for the return of conscripts to more useful service at home, helping to regenerate failing industries. In 1948 Britain shed its mandate, leaving it to turmoil, Arab-Israeli war and the displacement or exile of much of the Palestinian Arab population.

The ghost twitched in several other hot spots, as British forces were drawn into a succession of other little wars in possessions like Malaya, Cyprus, Kenya and Aden. But, at best, these could only delay decolonisation in the belief that there could still be a controlled devolution of power. Through reasonable concessions to middle-class Asian and African nationalist elites, and through what the Colonial Office termed gradual, orderly and tranquil evolution towards democratic forms of government, circumstances would be ripened for the withdrawal of formal British rule at the right time – the time when British investment in the economic and strategic stability of independent dependencies could be judged to be assured.

Clearly, where ultimate responsibility still mattered, as in a valuable dependency such as Malaya, Britain remained up to a fight. Malaya was a most profitable part of the sterling area, whose dollar earnings from mass rubber and tin supplies to the USA were handily on call as low interest loans to London. Threatened by a Communist Chinese insurrection, the British imposed an emergency from 1948 and spent five years breaking radical guerrilla opposition. Here, there was no question of hurried withdrawal. Much the same applied to East Africa. There, the Mau Mau revolution of the 1950s produced another rolling emergency contest, which the British were determined not to lose in fear of its consequences for a transfer of power to moderate nationalist politics and the preservation of vital British Indian Ocean regional interests after independence.

For all this, for most of the dozens of colonies that had attained free sovereignty by the 1970s, the formal independence granted by Britain led on to a far more complete political separation from its influence than had been foreseen, as countries bolstered their sense of independence and freedom. By and large, official British involvement in their post-colonial states continued to diminish, even those in which they maintained Cold War defence, intelligence and surveillance establishments into the 1970s, over which they were careful not to splash the red paint.

After 1945, the old imperial policy idea of federations, long favoured as a governing framework for large and complicated areas, also tried some translation into power. In south-east Asia, one pet objective was an amalgamation or union of Singapore and the Malayan states. After stamping down Mau Mau rebels in Kenya, Britain attempted to weld together an East African Federation through closer 'Union' in which African elites in Uganda and Tanganyika would be hitched to a multiracial Kenya in which immigrant whites would have decisive government power. Further south, a Central African Federation, formed in the early 1950s from Southern and Northern Rhodesia and Nyasaland, was floated to check any potential South African expansion northwards. Its Nationalist Afrikanerdom was viewed as a threat to the settled 'British way' of the Rhodesias, and its apartheid influence as a threat to Britain's more enlightened and well-intentioned race relations. As Gordon Walker, the Labour Secretary of State for Commonwealth Relations, put it darkly in 1950, Britain had no meaningful power to control its white emigrant communities in Africa, and to avoid the advancement of Africans, disgruntled East African and Central African whites might well end up repudiating their British loyalty and hitching up to the Union. If left to the pull of South Africa, a risk was the nightmare of seeing Kenya and the Rhodesias turning into 'American colonies', resolved to have their head. The Central African Federation spluttered on for a decade until 1963. Then, it foundered on the rock of implacable opposition from its African majority to an artificial ploy in which federal power-sharing or 'partnership' to blunt white minority rule was also being used to head off black majority rule. The other experiments came to nothing, too, abandoned as lost causes. After all, they were no good if they could not iron out the constitutional wrinkles at the end of the imperial era.

The only legacy of the white-dominated federation was the intransigent problem of Southern Rhodesia, whose vociferous settler minority were itching for immediate independence on the basis of white rule. When Britain refused to consent to this, they *did* turn into rebellious American colonists, and declared a unilateral and illegal independence in 1965. Pulling a tired British tail at the end of the imperial era, white Rhodesia managed to get away with it for a decade and a half, surviving watery sanctions until a bitter guerrilla war with destructive regional dimensions brought on a negotiated transition to African independence in 1980.

By now thoroughly used to a post-war role, even if it was not one to be cherished, the British returned to haul down the flag. For a time, Rhodesia had been a last redoubt for a shrunken tribe of reactionary old imperialists, men of the Mother Country for whom the disaster of decolonisation was the loss to black and brown people of the educational discipline and standards of white British rule. There were no deep traps after this to seriously complicate the cutting of losses which had to be cut quickly. Retreating informal empire in China culminated in observing island leasehold terms and packing up when it was time to go. Having only had Hong Kong on lease from China until the 1990s, Britain bowed to the Chinese assumption of sovereignty over its former crown colony in 1997.

Beyond Palestine, few crises of the end of empire became watersheds of truly major international significance. An exception was that famous moment of truth in 1956. Set on nationalising the Suez Canal to assert Arab rights of control, Egyptian President Gamal Abdel Nasser provoked an incensed reaction from the British government, whose overheated Prime Minister, Sir Anthony Eden, likened him to Hitler and declared that not intervening to halt the move on Suez was the equivalent of a Munich appeasement. In secret and unsavoury collusion with France and Israel, Britain embarked on a foolhardy Suez expedition to invade Egypt in order to reassert British domination of its eastern Mediterranean interests and restore national self-confidence at a time of declining prestige. What ensued was chaos rather than triumph, and the humiliation of being forced into a humbling ceasefire just hours after botched Suez invasion landings.

Britain's Suez fiasco appeared to turn out far worse than anything anyone could conceivably have predicted, including its motorists who suddenly faced petrol rationing for the first time since the war. Far from securing American indulgence in its late-colonial enterprise, the Eden administration found itself up against more than the usual irritation of sly Washington neutrality over imperial matters. At the United Nations and elsewhere, the US vigorously opposed Britain's connivance with France and Israel in the invasion and was openly critical of its Suez policy. It also put a financial squeeze on London. America had, of course, already decided that the British hour in the Middle East was well and truly over, something already being felt earlier in 1956 by General John Glubb as he was sacked as commander of the Jordanian armed forces by King Hussein. At the end of the squalid Suez War, the US Under Secretary of State, Herbert Hoover Jr, suggested a formal approach to the British government with the observation that as Britain appeared to be 'through' in the Middle East, Whitehall might be asked if it wanted America to 'pick up' its commitments in the region. Even President Dwight D. Eisenhower found this a little too blunt to be conveyed to Harold Macmillan, standing in for a post-Suez Eden, who had limped off to Jamaica in the hope of resting and recovering his nerve.

The last militant episode of an old imperial past came almost three decades later, off Argentina. By then, Britain's weakening post-war economy had long ceased being able to satisfy Argentinian import needs, which had moved on a long way from Barbour coats and Highland whisky. In fact, its share of Latin American trade had slumped to less than 2 per cent in the 1980s, which meant that the United Kingdom was exporting more to Norway than to South America. Despite a peaceful record of calm withdrawal from the assets of an enormous regional informal empire, Britain went to war in the Falklands in 1982 to drive out Argentinian invaders and recover a barren maritime flake of its formal empire. If it was nothing other than a bizarre imperial episode, unlike Suez, military victory this time seemed to do something to atone for a catalogue of decline and failure at home. And the lesson of conquest in the South Atlantic was beamed out to remind other foreign peoples that whatever the appearances, Britain was still a world nation to be feared. Yet, despite the undoubted magnitude of the Falklands War accomplishment, it was no way forward. Aside from its domestic political advantage for Britain's governing party, it was the sudden and unexpected last action from a veteran rearguard.

Well before this, of course, the end of empire had come and gone, both speedily and unexpectedly. Why the end of the Second World War brought dissolution rather than continuing colonial development remains a general question that continues to lead to a general kind of answer, although historians of varied stripe continue to debate the relative weight to give to the range of factors chosen as explanation. One of these is that as Britain shook itself off from the Second World War, its overseas investment finance settled down into new grooves which no longer needed the coating of empire. Fields in China were lost to Communism in the late 1940s, and large British interests in Latin America were muscled aside and all but vaporised by an American economic offensive through the 1940s. Prime Canadian and Australian investment positions were also lost to American capital.

Another lost position was India. The war had gobbled up so much extra British expenditure on the defence of Indian interests that by its end a £1.3 billion bill had turned the British into debtors. With India one of its creditors, there seemed to be little need to keep up the mounting costs of the Raj. Interest, dividends and profit from most peasant-dominated economies of tropical Africa had never been all that elephantine in value, and there seemed no reason to doubt the willingness of the nationalist leadership of independent states to keep up conditions for the protection and furthering of financial and commercial interests. The terms of Kenyan independence in 1963 enshrined private property, and its coffee production would continue to grow, if no longer exclusively as a profitable settler monopoly then also as African capitalist enterprise in the former white highlands. As to white-settler economic regimes, the country which mattered most, South Africa, continued as a comforting customer. Whatever the anti-British bile of its Afrikaner white supremacist rulers after 1948, the Union retained its dependence on British finance, in particular through its tie to the sterling area up to the early 1960s, and its commitment to the protection of Anglo-South African trade.

More broadly, when post-war Britain was able to resume major volumes of overseas investment, its City institutions concentrated on the rewards and risks of the booming capitalist economies of the USA and Western Europe. Attracting any number of foreign banks to set up in London, the heart of the British financial system directed its arteries even more into serving as a global financial centre. Empire no longer provided a focus for the economic endeavour of bankers and brokers.

To economic change and the behaviour of British investment can be added several other considerations in explaining the dismantling of empire. After 1945, seapower, industrial power and financial power had passed quite decisively and irrevocably to the USA. Britain's Second World War victory was only nominal, for thereafter it had neither the strength nor the capacity to match American power and resources as a dominant global force. As its military and industrial power ebbed, the continuing (and now rising) costs of imperial administration and defence became an untenable burden for a declining industrial state. Inevitably, the survival of empire could not but come to rest on American consent or sufferance. Several years before the Suez crisis, Washington's move on the new Pakistan, stocking its armoury and advising its British-trained Punjabi warrior elite, was already providing evidence of what the USA had in mind for a British imperial future.

Pressures produced by the increasing force of international opinion critical of imperialism and its colonial systems also took their toll of morale and will within imperial ruling circles. Whatever was done to paint a positive image of empire as a rising Commonwealth of loyal and equal subjects under the crown or as a constructive partnership of multiracial development, it could not disguise what delaying decolonisation in Kenya or resisting a radical nationalist insurgency in Aden looked like to critical world opinion. It looked like nothing so much as a peeling imperial citadel, prolonging an overdue demolition through its temporising struggles to defend each separate rampart.

In this, the American public outlook was distinctly cool towards any preservation of colonial empire, gingered up by a foreign policy which supported self-rule around the globe, by talk of the right of oppressed peoples to exercise their democratic rights and to be free of foreign oppression, and by visits from anti-colonial nationalists in the 1950s, who told their audiences that life under the tyrannical British was no better than life in Soviet Russia.

Whatever the special relationship of war alliance, economic bonds and kinship, American sniping at their colonialism was painful and wearing for the British. It was especially so for their older and more experienced desk mandarins on such spots as Middle Eastern Affairs at the

Foreign Office or the Africa Department of the Colonial Office. What they disliked was what the USA had on offer as an alternative. An imperialism of intruding commerce and strategic anti-Communism, so reliant upon sheer cash and brash undertakings, cut against what they thought of as the ultimate underlying spirit of a Britannic Empire. It could never be a civilising mission. But there could be no holding out against the next hour which had come.

Lastly, at least some importance might be given to the growth of politically nervous opinion within Britain itself by the end of the 1950s that the use of imperial force to maintain colonial positions and hold the line against decolonisation was becoming a discredited cause, and endangering traditional views of the British as a reputable colonial power of liberal moderation. It became increasingly less comfortable to suppress self-determination at any cost, particularly when the force of nationalism seemed to have become so unstoppable. In its way, shame over the violence of Britain's wars of decolonisation in places like Malaya, Kenya and Cyprus among Labour, trade union and other sections of British society also eroded public confidence in any idea of continuing imperial mission.

To leave until last the influence and power of colonial nationalist movements in bringing on the end of the empire is not to suggest that the growing local nationalisms of its subjects were the least significant factor in pushing the British back. But it is to suggest that any explanation which sees the ending of colonial rule as the inevitable triumph of nationalism over imperialism is probably too simple, however much those political leaders who followed in British footsteps celebrated independence as the fruit of united anti-colonial struggle and nation-building. Of course, mass opposition against British colonial rule and the gathering force of nationalists' demands shook London's power in some cases, sapped control in others, and were influential in forcing through independence arrangements at stages which did not suit the British time-table for a planned decolonisation and transfer of power.

But anti-British nationalisms themselves were not the product of single visions. India was but one leading and early example. In Cyprus, a Greek Cypriot campaign in the 1950s for independence as union with Greece was hardly an inspiration to those Cypriots who happened to be Turkish. The prominent pan-Africanist, Kwame Nkrumah, kept up unity appearances in the Gold Coast up to independence in 1957, even as his Convention Peoples' Party was quarrelling with the Ashanti-based National Liberation Movement and other regional interests over who should be recognised as top dog for the collar of independence.

In other words, if the nerves of colonial rulers were getting frayed as their hold on internal security swayed between treating nationalists as diabolical ogres and having to strike political bargains with them once they became dignified men in good suits, nationalist movements them-selves were not necessarily entirely cohesive or possessed of an agreed vision of what an independent future might mean. Ultimately, the local colonial pressure which they stirred up against British administration was but one pull among others tugging imperial policy towards transfers of power. After all, those under trusteeship in the High Commission Territories of Bechuanaland, Basutoland and

Swaziland were hardly learning Tswana, Lesotho and Swazi nationhood at their mother's knee. When it came to the theatricals of their formal independence in the 1960s, the vast majority of men and women were probably remaining stolidly at home. Perhaps, in the words of T.E. Lawrence, they had always known that it was their country, their way and that the time of their imperial rulers was short.

6

Pondering Pomp and Circumstance

This book opened with the observation that Britain lost its last, retired empress early in the twenty-first century. Japan, on the other hand, retains a glossy living Emperor. Yet as his subjects happen all to be Japanese, when he dies he is unlikely to follow the legendary example of King George V and ask after the empire on his deathbed. China is no longer an empire, unless perhaps you are an aggrieved Tibetan monk. Nonetheless, not all that long ago, on the eve of the First World War, these states were among the dozen or so which ruled most of the world beyond the Americas.

From then on the others, all European, mostly faced nothing but trouble. Germany, Russia, Austria-Hungary and Turkey nailed their own coffins by warring against other empires and doing badly. Those who prevailed picked up the pieces, and put on a display of overseas vigour and determination in the inter-war years. But the undermining consequences and severe costs of another great war did for them, too, and those empires were duly washed away in the post-1945 decades. They were joined by the more lame-duck modern empires of the lesser European powers of Belgium, Holland, Portugal and Spain.

By the 1960s and 1970s, empire was over, or certainly finished in any meaningful formal sense. What was left of it was the Soviet Union and its rusting claim to anti-imperialism. But it, too, would shortly find its own ramshackle empire, inherited from Tsarist times, striking back and shrivelling up. Today, empires defined by political boundaries or by highlighted spots on a map no longer exist, to say nothing of having become almost universally unfashionable.

The march of contemporary history suggests that the time is long gone when, driven by one or other imperial mission, any upstart nation or people can see themselves as gifted or destined to govern the world as the lords of humankind. In this, as in anything in history, it may of course be too soon to tell, but it is difficult to imagine the world ever being formally recolonised. One of Georges Clemenceau's more memorable and acute observations was that war was too serious a business to be left to soldiers. Today, the global order is too big and messy a business to be left to a Colonial Service and its District Officers, and even less to any Uncle Sam equivalent on one or other khaki-clad Operation to Restore Hope or Rebuild Freedom.

To be sure, there is still the unrivalled power of the United States of America, ever inclined to behave as the police cruiser of humankind or, more accurately, of its coveted oil and other strategic resources. But that country's ominous combination of hubris and self-deception saddles it with great power expectations which are probably far too extravagant and unrealistic for its own good. It is one thing to have spread railways, tea, the Christian Gospel, the English Dictionary and the notion of the rule of law around much of the globe. It is quite another to try to direct the world through repeated shows of massive military force, the installation of airbases in client states, and the provision of air-conditioned lavatories and *Time* magazine.

In other respects, inevitably, the modern traces of a vanished global greatness are mostly faint or present only in patches. German remains quite widespread in the Balkans. Francophone language and culture pulses across its former colonial empire in West Africa and North Africa, and the heavy tread of formal French imperialism has bequeathed a fairly intrusive post-imperial influence in former colonies. This can include the Parisian armed services and intelligence operations staging a sideshow every so often, through the dashing habit of despatching paras as latter-day gunboats to secure French interests whenever one of their former colonies catches alight.

For the rest, Spanish, Dutch, Italian, Portuguese and Belgian imperialism have left comparatively little behind. Contemporary Latin American republics originating in the first Spanish empire have their versions of Spanish, but barely any real kinship with European Spain. For South African Afrikaners, the Netherlands ceased to be 'home, sweet home' countless years ago. What remains today of Italy's sacred mission of civilisation in Africa is espresso in the odd pavement cafe in Addis Ababa or an antiquated Turin steam locomotive in Mogadishu.

Angola still has its urban Lusophone tint and several American oil companies where once there used to be *prazos*, the feudal estates of Portuguese-speaking potentates. It was Albert Camus who once mused that everything faded except memory. One can only wonder how much of it there still is of that Portuguese African pretension, and its rose-coloured map, which so ambitiously united Angola and Mozambique. The present-day Democratic Republic of the Congo has virtually no trace of Brussels at all, save for an urban husk of French and a whiff of Chanel from its fleshy elite. While the buried deposit of these empires may continue to shape indigenous peoples' lives and identities in intricate ways, it seems mostly to be somewhere in their bones.

It may not simply be the arrogance of the English-speaking to suggest that aside from the *imperium* of the Romans, it is surely the British Empire that is most widely remembered today. That would no doubt have satisfied Rudyard Kipling, who viewed all history as a succession of empires, with the British Empire as the culmination of a seamless world history, starting with the Romans. Certainly, at its Victorian zenith, in the old-school-tie and play-the-game era, the British *were* identifying themselves as the modern Romans. Seemingly salted by the mystical power of English soil, their appetite for colonies, commerce and migration was second to none, as were their daydreams of reposing in the Punjab, Plumtree and Penang.

Just as the Roman Empire had incorporated a tangle of cultures, religions and races, so the British Empire had bound together heterogeneous peoples and ways of life. The famous cry of the succumbing Norman soldier, 'England hath taken me!', in Kipling's *Puck of Pook's Hill* (1906) was being echoed, if at a greater distance, by a mind-boggling array of people, from the Maori to the Malays. The Roman past was also in the mind of the novelist Henry James, for whom London was as ancient Rome, 'the city to which the world paid tribute'. Both the Romans and the British had 'the same vast and multifarious needs, gratified on the same huge scale – in the one case by conquest, in the other by industry; the same immense development of practical and material resources'. With the fall of Rome came the snuffing out of a sacred flame of empire and a relapse into barbarism, until the coming of a British thin red line restored the civilising influences of law, justice and mercy. And as in the Roman tradition, these always had to be imposed in the face of overwhelming odds.

The extent to which the ruling British wanted their empire to be like that of the Romans, and whether their imperialism can ever be imaginatively remembered in those terms, may be one positive way of accounting for its wider impact. It is, needless to say, but one among others, not all of them sanguine. From this ample viewpoint, it was the later empire which most realised its real Roman potential. What mattered was not the long, underlying momentum of worldwide extraction, trade and exploitation. Nor was an empire of migration and settlement of serious account, such as the so-called First British Empire in North America. After all, its consequences were rather mixed. On top of having to get over the grumpy business of white settlers snatching their freedom, there was the nerve of Thomas Jefferson, a turncoat English gentleman, taking over the myth of Rome for America, this time as the unruly model of republican virtue.

In the Roman vision it was the creation of a second British Empire, notched up across Asia and Africa, and then held in benign custody, which really counted. Empire-building there was not rooted solely in the grubby economics of frenzied colonial conquest, as in the earlier Caribbean frenzy. Neither was it a business of heavy overseas settlement, or certainly not until later in the nineteenth century, and then mostly in lands viewed as empty, like English Canada. Instead, what emerged was an empire lifted a fair rung above narrow self-interest by a flourishing and creative industrial power in the service of essentially well-disposed intentions. This was the epic empire of Roman significance, one of custodianship and civilisation built upon an elevated devotion to duty and decency.

Of course, the power of custody brought great advantages to Britain, of an economic and strategic kind. Thus, Malaya had rubber, Northern Rhodesia had copper, Jamaica had sugar, Ceylon had tea, South Africa had gold, and Aden was an important gatepost to vital oil resources and a bastion on the vital waterway to India. But it was always more than this, for the imperial ethos derived in some part from ideal notions of human progress. Through enlightened conversion, legal, cultural and political life could be gradually moulded by a paternalist and public-spirited hand for the improvement of varied masses of people.

Nor was this the only sensibility which showed the British at their Roman best. The British Empire was also, like the Roman, committed to the construction of great public works, a virtuoso parade of durable railways, bridges, harbours, canals, roads, dams and decent postal, telegraph and telephone services, all of which would provide a permanent infrastructure for the modern economic development of many African and Asian continental economies. These were nothing if not monuments to usefulness and logical purpose, whether it was opening up a country for trade and investment, making it easier to find a stranded missionary, or increasing the speed with which a beleaguered post could be relieved.

More than just putting the best face on empire, this was the mission to which the British supposedly gave of their best, with their proud and idealistic Victorian empire-builders bent on leaving the world a better place. In sensibility, it was the empire of thought and dedicated work, assiduous investigation and calm enquiry, of positive trust and interaction between colonial subjects and their administrators, and of incremental progress and improvement towards the right habits of self-reliance.

Then there was the long and passionate commitment to the market liberalism of free trade. This distinguished the British as the most enlightened imperial nation in the world economy as they were willing to shoulder the responsibility for maintaining the conditions for a free circulation of capital, goods and labour in the international system. Their period of *Pax Britannica* was essentially a national undertaking to uphold the orderly, civilised conditions required for reliable trading, which was improving the wealth and sustaining the development of all the societies participating in the global economy.

As if this were not enough, the lure of empire also gave able members of British society, by no means least those with a public-school pedigree, something new and necessary to do, such as serving as Traffic Manager for the Federated Malay States Railway in Kuala Lumpur or riding about

Burma as an Assistant Sub-Deputy Opium Agent, Second Grade. And anyone for whom the midday sun proved all too much could also count on thoughtful care. Colonial officials who succumbed to mental illness in India and Africa were secreted away in special asylums for Europeans. It would have been unthinkable to have colonial subjects gawping at clinically demented Britons, their disturbed minds and feeble bodies in breach of governing status and standards. In the raw hinterlands of empire, it was the mullahs who were meant to be mad.

For a classic cast of the barracks, the court, the club and the orderly administrative office, this cosy empire hummed along to the robust tunefulness of Kipling's 'The Roman Centurion's Song'. In that work, an ageing soldier begs the imperial legate not to recall him to Rome. His simple remaining duty, he pleads, is 'staying on' to do good deeds for a cause:

> Let me work here for Britain's sake – at any task you will –
> A marsh to drain, a road to make or native troops to drill.
> Some western camp (I know the Pict) or granite Border keep.
> Mid seas of heather derelict, where old messmates sleep.

That cause held out the prospect of worthwhile service for those bread-and-butter men and women prepared to take on messy, humdrum jobs for no more than a reasonable living in the sun. Bravely squeamish, they knew how to endure the miseries of long separation from home and loved ones, and to cope with reading *The Times* six months after publication. Devoted to duty and work, they craved little more by way of recreation or entertainment than a scratchy gramophone record, a pensive pipe, a stock of

Bombay Sapphire Gin and getting spruced up for a regular visit from a neighbouring assistant district officer or chief district forester, who were usually hundreds of miles away.

The key to it all lay in the distinctive meanings and mythologies of British – or, more exactly – 'English' character and its level-headed adaptability to a colonial way of life. Its core image was far from the empire of the mystical and muddled General Gordon, the vain and boastful General Wolfe, or the borderline Victorian insanity of Stanley and Florence Baker, whose search for the source of the White Nile muddled on despite debilitating bouts of malaria, near-fatal sunstroke, and being tossed by an enraged bull hippopotamus.

Rather than the archetypal dramas of heroic endeavour and privation in a foreign wilderness which so galvanised the Victorian imagination, or the usual repertoire of faked heroics, or other theatrical postures to uphold the white man's dignity, what most defined the imperial temperament was a stereotypical British quality, described most aptly as being down to earth. In its determination always to stick closely to the facts, it represented a dispassionate kind of inverse Romanticism, built on plain-headed simplicity. 'Grit' and 'mettle' captured the solidity and dependability of the ideal laconic type who sailed out from Liverpool for West Africa, individuals like Alec Cook, father of the acclaimed comedian, Peter Cook, who slept all the more soundly in the knowledge that Nigeria was administered 'not by Huns but by Britons'.

Fiercely proud of what he saw as the incorruptibility of his fellow district officers in Nigeria in the 1930s and 1940s, Cook at the same time had a nice streak of irony and self-parody about what was required to cut it among the Ibo as a representative of British civilisation. As he once hinted, behind the white uniform with its uncomfortably tight collar, the ceremonial sword, and the shiny black boots always worn on occasions when he had to deliver an uplifting speech on the duties and privileges of the British order, there lay a hazardous quagmire. The edge of that quicksand was the slipperiness of the iron steps he would have to descend gingerly on public occasions. While invariably emerging from it all well-composed, for Cook there was a constant, nagging fear that one day it could end up with him falling on his face. In the end, moral authority rested on physical agility.

Alec Cook also possessed a modest, self-deprecatory sense of exactly what constituted his portion of the white man's burden. It was not any of the risks to health or life, as he considered 'the average bout of malaria' to be 'no worse than a bad cold or a slight touch of 'flu in England'. The determining test was mental, as 'it is the mind and not the body that is most severely tried here'. Cook recounted how the effects of his youthful inexperience, his ignorance of any of the Nigerian languages and his clinging reliance on a trusted local interpreter combined to produce 'tremendously alarming circumstances to live in', especially when having 'to reach moral or judicial decisions over a society about which, at least when you arrived, you knew absolutely nothing'.

In this setting, Cook was seldom ever fully in control of his circumstances. He was always having to tread a fine line in transactions with traditional village authorities, wandering from one canny local chief to another to get to the bottom of witchcraft or 'trickery and juju', and unable to reach any shared understanding with Africans of many of the fundamental religious, customary and cultural codes of their everyday life and being. In a myopic predicament, to stay afloat 'the trick of it' was to bet on having found the right African agent, 'to hope that you'd chosen an honest interpreter, because otherwise, it was just all nonsense'.

Towards the end of his service, one of Cook's tasks was to assist in the setting up of councils, authorities and law courts to prepare West African citizenry for life in an independent, post-colonial state. This was not an unwelcome prospect for one who believed the legacy of British colonial policy to be sound. His only personal misgiving was that independence might arrive before enough had been done to inculcate 'moral integrity' in Nigerian society, to insulate its officials and traditional rulers against the present and future corrosion of the 'graft and corruption indigenous to West Africa', so long a cause of 'great mental distress'. There was no backing away from that nagging question: had the firmness of British colonialism sufficiently stiffened a morally flabby Nigerian world?

Equally, however unsure of the answer, Alec Cook knew that there could be no political successor except the people of Nigeria themselves. His duty, as he saw it, was to show the right way forward, not to forever be that way. With a slight hint of halo hovering over him, he would have achieved much of his purpose once he had got back from Calabar to his green lawn in Eastbourne. The tone of the wider story represented here is worth recalling again, however often it may have been touched on in histories before, as it addresses what undoubtedly remains an influential British perception of the imperial past. For the handling of decline and the retreat from empire continues to be seen frequently as a remarkable achievement, or certainly as something which showed classic British good sense. As befitted a country of easy-going compromise, the lightness of its custodial and civilising touch overseas had produced a liberal empire, an unusually subtle weave of formal and informal control, influence and power, meshing together modernity and tradition in an orderly way. Viewed like this, it was the fine balance of a lax yet well-run empire of the middle ground that had enabled the British to maintain the innumerable cushy benefits of global power, while ducking its most crushing burdens. Skilled in the arts of adaptation, adjustment and compromise, it was also no great surprise, then, that the British were able to relinquish their empire relatively calmly when the pressures for decolonisation eventually became too strong to withstand. Even in dissolution, what was lost in power was gained in prestige.

Unlike, say, France over Algeria in the 1950s and 1960s, or Portugal over Mozambique and Angola in the 1970s, Britain was not convulsed by profound national crises over decolonisation. Granted, there was the perennial problem for London of Ireland. But that aside, within domestic politics there were no intractable and powerful interests prepared to go to the wire to resist lowering the flag for colonial independence. This meant that even if late-colonial crises were unavoidable, such as the chaos accompanying disengagement from Cyprus, compared with French decolonisation their metropolitan impact was much less extreme and bitterly divisive. For all that figures such as Churchill and George VI were so fed up over Indian independence that they never quite managed to get over sulking about national loss, their long-winded remorse did not matter much. Amid the drama of imperial retrocession, this also meant that withdrawal was less protracted and disruptive for most British colonial subjects than in other cases of European decolonisation.

This all ensured a swift and graceful British retreat from empire, even if extrication from India and Palestine in the late 1940s subjected the unfortunate inhabitants of those countries to horrendous suffering. When set against the bloody catastrophes of the sluggish French withdrawal from Indochina, or the Dutch from the East Indies, or the Belgians from the Congo, Britain played a remarkably poised and peaceful final hand. If it was a considerable accomplishment, it was equally no more than to be expected of a country with the uncommonly practical, level-headed and sturdy virtues of the Scout-master.

Seen like this, there could be no greater final underlining of the contrast between the mature management of British imperial affairs and the heavier controlling hand, over-dramatised power and doctrinaire ideologies of more prima donna continental European empires. Crucially, it ensured the difference between dignity and trauma in becoming reconciled to the decline of national power. Put another way, even if glum Conservatives did what they could to put up a rearguard resistance to the post-war dissolution of empire, the more astute among them were already wondering whether it was really worth the candle. And, after Suez, they settled down to relinquishing their dominion over palm and pine. No French politician of the mid-1950s, least of all Socialists and Communists, could contemplate any sort of French withdrawal from Algeria, a territory still indissolubly part of the national identity of France.

The point of so sunny a sketch is not to mock complacent memories of the winding-down of empire. There is, arguably, something to be said for its embossed mandarins, from Louis Mountbatten in India to Christopher Soames in Southern Rhodesia, cloaking their ruthlessness and resentments to pull down the flag, and hand over power to local nationalists with dignity and decorum. There may, also, be something to be said for the illusory theatre of benign decolonisation, a beguiling sense of metropolitan self-assurance that independence was what had always been prepared for, and that peacefully relinquishing power to the right people was exactly what the situation required, as various independence leaders puckered up to turn their colonies into loyal states of a multicultural British Commonwealth.

After all, with so experienced an eye turned to the main chance, it seemed that Britain was not only able to avoid being hurried into a handover of rule, it could even be ahead of the game. Tunku Abdul Rahman, who became the first chief minister of a self-governing Malaya in 1955, reminded us of this in a radio interview years later. He was asked why he had refused to stiffen a rather mellow independence speech in order to address radical nationalist concerns, and by doing so had he not risked giving the impression that the people of Malaya had not sacrificed and fought fiercely for independence? Abdul Rahman's retort was, 'but we didn't'.

Lastly, there may also be something to be said for the view that at the end of empire, British hands ended up less bloodied than those of more bungling rivals like the French or the Belgians. After all had it not long been thus? One has only to take the notoriety of Belgium. King Leopold's empire had eaten the Congo in the later nineteenth and early twentieth centuries, subjecting inhabitants to a genocidal forced labour system notorious for its routine practices of rape, torture and murder. Perhaps as many as 10 million Congolese died as a consequence of the organised violence and culture of sadism brought to Central Africa by the good works of the Belgian monarch's International Association for Philanthropy in the Congo. Not for nothing did Cecil Rhodes, no great milksop himself, describe Leopold II as Satan.

Back in Edwardian Britain, it was Joseph Conrad's *Heart of Darkness* that had helped to carry the anti-slavery outrage of British humanitarianism up the Congo River. Of course, and perhaps all too predictably, those fired by indignation over the degradation of shoestring Belgian imperialism were seemingly oblivious to the conduct of Lever Brothers, also deeply implicated in Congolese forced labour through its Belgian palm-oil subsidiary. Although not another Leopold, William Lever was no soft soap, but then empire moralism invariably involved staring the other way.

Decades later, there was the grim cost of the French refusal to read the writing on the wall after 1945. De Gaulle's stubborn insistence on forcibly rehabilitating the glory of France's *mission civilisatrice* in Indochina ended in bloody disaster. In a futile nine-year struggle to keep Vietnam French, at least half a million and possibly as many as 1 million civilians perished, while the 300,000 Viet Minh combatants who were killed took almost 100,000 French colonial troops with them. The doomed 1954–62 colonial war to keep Algeria as French as the Languedoc was no better. It is true that French forces got off fairly lightly, with a casualty rate which for most of the war was actually lower than that claimed by road accidents in France. But the experience of Algerian Muslims was a war death total of perhaps 1 million, and the uprooting and expulsion of 1.8 million from their homes during the conflict.

In contrast, from the nineteenth century, liberal free-market capitalism, a flourishing parliamentary tradition of critical scrutiny of behaviour overseas by the Mother Country, and a rich Christian mission legacy of ethical purpose and respectability preserved Britain's subjects from forced labour and its atrocious heart of darkness. Fittingly, at the end, rather than spatter blood and trigger chaos and destruction, shortly after the end of the Second World War Britain began to let slip those colonial territories that had simply grown too independent to be held. Unlike the panicking French columns in Indochina in 1950, marching down a *Route Coloniale* to the worst overseas defeat in French history since Wolfe overcame Montcalm in 1759, the British thrashed about far less ruinously in their death throes of empire.

Such recitals of the imperial past are still fairly commonplace and can often tend to fuel a sense of emotional nostalgia or complacency about archetypal British moderation, and the praiseworthy intentions reflected in the rhetoric of an uplifting colonial mission, an endeavour to leave behind territory in an improved condition. It may just present a history easier to write about than ever to have lived through. For, by and large, it remains true that it has been far less common to acknowledge the more seamy aspects of British imperialism, not least in that famously orderly transition to independence. Then, the vain Mountbatten was fond of portraying Indian independence as a magnificent triumph of statesmanlike panache, leaving India the bounty of parliamentary democracy, the Great East Indian Railway, the thriving commercial and industrial infrastructure of Bombay, the cricketing ethic of fair play, a proper appreciation of regimental colours, and a shrewd commercial understanding of the value of First Day Covers from the post office. All the same, this has also to be set against the scrambled partition of the Indian sub-continent, and the consuming panic and unrestrained violence that it unleashed, resulting in roughly 1 million deaths.

Africa had the woeful Central African Federation, judged a police state by one of its very own government commissions, in which dozens of African protesters in Nyasaland were gunned down in the early 1960s. Earlier, to its north, with the camp incarceration in Kenya of some 80,000 Kikuyu peasants in the Mau Mau rebellion, and the notorious beating to death of some detainees, the British response to anti-colonial insurrection was not exactly that of killing with kindness. In Asia, the cut-throat latitude provided by emergency proclamations was also worked to the full. This saw the collective killings of Communist opponents and troublemakers in Malaya by British infantry, the implacable hunting down and summary despatching in Perak of rebels demonised as bandits or gangsters, and the carpet bombing of Malayan villages and defoliation of large strips of the countryside.

Efforts to subdue opposition in Aden in the late 1940s led to the levelling of villages by intensive bombing, and a resort to torture and widespread killings under the tactfully named Operation Nutcracker in the 1960s. In tough times, it is important also to be reminded of the eagerness with which Churchill in the 1940s had nodded at a crushing French reoccupation of Indochina, fearing that any slackening of colonial control there would prove contaminating, eroding Britain's hold over India and the rest of its Asian Empire.

With its own fair measure of brutality and bloodshed, the final era of the empire was not, then, altogether an edifying sight. Granted, in some wars of decolonisation in territories like Kenya and Cyprus, more liberal or left-wing sections of the British press attacked the manner of counter-insurgency operations against what they accepted as legitimate nationalist struggles for independence. There was also condemnation of instances of administrative ineptitude leading to civilian suffering and of prominent incidents of military atrocity. By and large, however, the press parroted the official Whitehall line, which painted a demonology of shadowy subversives, criminalising anti-colonial insurgents as gangsters, bandits, or terrorists who were plunging stable and well-regulated places into bestial chaos. Those who had lost their heads politically, of necessity, had to have them bitten off – embittered and hateful opponents of colonial rule could not expect to be treated with kid gloves.

This picture is well recognised by some historians, as are various other, and earlier, examples of imperial atrocity, not least the extensive use in the 1920s of phosphorus and shrapnel bombs to cow troublesome Afghan and Iraqi villagers, viewed as otherwise ungovernable. As the RAF headquarters for India stressed in a 1922 report on its efficiency in dealing with the country's Northwest Province, it was loss of life that had the greatest impact on the morale of recalcitrant Afghans.

Such gruesome episodes have to be part of the main story if memory of the British imperial record is not to be wilfully selective. Equally, the point of taking due

account of the inter-war bombing of Iraqi villages or, for
that matter, the earlier sufferings of slavery, the cruelties
of forced labour, the harsh deceptions of indenture or the
virtual decimation of various indigenous peoples is not to
imply that Britannia's Empire should now be viewed more
as the creation of Lucifer than as the work of a St Francis
of Assisi. Nor, for that matter, is it to drum up an imperial
parade of ancestral atrocities and crimes, for which one
or other member of the House of Windsor or the British
Cabinet should at last apologise symbolically, virtually a
ritual requirement in twenty-first-century politics, with
any middle-class therapeutic credibility.

Moral penance for the Irish potato famine, the concentration camp deaths of the South African War or the
Amritsar massacre may be all well and good as palliative
national compensation. Yet, other than providing a fleeting
sentimental spectacle based upon a busy politician or a
lounging royal reaching for the nearest cliché, it is hard to
know what meaningful effect an apology for history has
on the lives of ordinary Irish assembly workers, Kenyan
peasants, Afrikaner bank tellers, Punjabi street hawkers, or
Jamaican cane cutters today.

Finally, and perhaps least of all, the purpose of taking
proper account of the authoritarianism and brutal extrem-
ities of the imperial experience is not to grind historical
axes. This can take the form of condemning the impact
and influence of the British Empire or posing the counter-
factual question of a modern world which would have
been better off without that interventionist colonial era.

As to the first stance, the job of history is surely to avoid
comforting simplification. That means being wary of dewy,

coffee-table myths of the Raj of peace and progress or of the trimmed lawns, bouncy Labradors and tractable retainers of Malayan plantation life. It is also to be equally wary of blanket judgements, whether of unequivocal denunciation or of golden achievement. The latter can sometimes seem all the more golden for having been followed, as in so much of independent Africa, by decades of political ferment, violent dictatorship, chronic economic crisis, raging corruption, plunder of public revenue and tottering state administration.

Equally to address the second, speculative issue – any backwards prediction of how the world might have turned out without British intrusion cannot be anything but hazy. It is, in any event, something to imagine rather than ever to know. And, given the immense diversity of conditions across the colonised world, reaching definitive judgements about questions of impact and consequences is not easy. All the same, this is not to say that one cannot make some reasonable suppositions when weighing up the effects of imperial rule and influence.

One basic factor is that British imperialism skewed or distorted the history of many countries, removing the autonomous capacity of pre-colonial societies to dictate their shape and to mould their own patterns of growth or development. Inevitably, external domination, with its extinguishing of sovereignty and its denigration of indigenous people and cultures as primitive or inferior, involved humiliating subjugation and the erosion of human dignity. How much greater an indignity could any society endure than to be lorded over by some overbearing and racist alien power?

While it is important not to overlook the ways in which those under British rule were able to exploit the vulnerabilities of their superiors and to negotiate the terms of their domination, everyday racist currents of a black hole of Calcutta and a darkest Africa created a legacy of backwater inferiority among colonised groups of Asians and Africans. In time, a national sense of pride, worth and independence would be retrieved in many ways, including imaginatively. In 2004 Nelson Mandela, the first post-apartheid President of South Africa, became an ancient recommended nominee for the even more ancient honorary title of Lord Warden of the Cinque Ports, giving him ceremonial responsibility for ensuring that South Coast naval ports supply ships to the crown and keep the Channel clear of enemy vessels. Even as no more than a delicious slice of post-imperial British baroque, this act decrees that the birthright to be a protector of the realm may now extend to the right kind of chiefly Xhosa. Sir Harry Smith could never have foreseen this performance.

For some, however, the past burden of an enforced colonial servility can continue to smart today, like an inherited toothache. Or it can serve as a politically usable past for bankrupt nationalists, in which virtually all the current ills of a post-colonial state can be attributed opportunistically to the past misdeeds of a wicked Britain.

Generally more serious in impact was the nature and direction of capitalist economic development under later colonial rule. Central to Victorian Britain's imperial exertions was the sustaining of its international trade and financial interests through manipulative policies, which were destructive of numerous captive economies by pinning them to lower-grade, single-commodity export production and looming parasitically over their markets. Whether as the broader exploitation of colonial empire as the source of cheap raw materials and cheap labour or as the specific blocking of a natural drift to industrialisation in a country like India, the lopsided or sub-standard growth imposed by British power sowed the seed of the floundering underdevelopment experienced by many impoverished ex-colonial countries today. At the same time, we should certainly not *assume* that there was no grinding poverty and economic calamity in the pre-colonial past, whatever the romantic visions of those inclined to imagine it as a flowing Eden of sweetness and egalitarian plenty, until it all crumbled under the hammer blows of British occupation and money-making.

What can probably also be said with a fair degree of historical certainty is that had it not been Britain's empire, it would almost certainly have been that of another European state. By the sixteenth and seventeenth centuries, the likelihood of a continuing epoch of independent development for regions like Asia and Africa was in any event slight. The British were not the only Europeans too restless to make do with a more modest northern place in the world, and with an edge in seaborne capability, weaponry, technology and the economic incentive to do something about it. If not Britain, then before the end of the nineteenth century some other dominant colonial system, or combination of systems, starting with France, would probably have been drawn out to impose its dominant power beyond Europe.

What remains is the importance of explanation or of getting the British imperial past in fair perspective. The easiest thing to say is that at the height of its power, the empire was undoubtedly the greatest moment in the history of the British people. But there is clearly more to recognise than this. As already suggested, one green view is that however unevenly it started, empire surely ended well. Looking beyond that transition, British rule or domination becomes a catalogue of facilitating improvements left behind at the setting of the sun. From these, one might list the raising of literacy and the creation of a major world language, with over 800 million people having English as a first or second language, and its influential integrating role in administrative, commercial, cultural, intellectual and sporting life. Even more than this, interaction with English-language use has enriched a variety of other native languages and cultures, with Hindi, Arabic and other language speakers switching to expressive English idiom or vocabulary to ginger up their daily speech.

Then, it would not be difficult to pinpoint institutions, such as advanced medicine and public health, formal education, the press, parliament and a civil service. To this could be added modern aspirations towards representative liberal democracy; universal values of law and constitutional legality; literature and the arts; the irreligious enrichment of football, cricket and rugby; and the spiritual infusions of Christian religious values and morality. Indeed, vigorous Christian rites and rituals permeate Africa while in Britain itself they are falling increasingly into disuse. When it comes to active Anglican adherence, West Africa easily dwarfs Britain.

Numerous modern former colonies live in one way or another by the secular institutions, tax and treasury administration, and practices and habits passed down by British rule, even where its duration was short-lived. Furthermore, there are multi-ethnic and multilingual states that live well enough on the basis of a tolerable compromise between local notions of rights and law, and those implanted by Britain. Some of these, quite apart from being difficult to dismantle, show little sign of having outgrown their usefulness in serving a range of contemporary human needs. Indeed, even where derivative British models of governing authority and judicial administration have become a deep dilemma or a source of turmoil, as in partially Islamic states like Nigeria or Sudan, it remains moot whether a quandary over national cohesion and identity can simply be resolved by expunging the influence of a protectorate past. If anything, where a modern judicial system left by colonial rule may bring the predatory customary authority of traditional chiefs and other hungry patriarchal rulers within inhibiting constitutional controls, so active an inheritance is not something to be belittled, least of all discarded. In the end, the only protection from arbitrary, unbridled power may be the man or woman with a wig, trained on the *Cambridge Law Journal*. Thus, for the distressed Swazi family of Zena Mahlangu, a teenage school-girl abducted by royal aides in 2002 to become the tenth wife of King Mswati III, the only available medium of self-defence against royal absolutism was a Full Bench of the High Court of Swaziland.

For the most part, ordinary African and Asian men and women whose lives accommodate the Cambridge International Schools Certificate *and* the ritual of *lobola* or bridewealth, or Harvey's Bristol Cream *and* the festival of *Diwali*, are not necessarily locked into some civil war of the mind and heart. Theirs is the construction of an imaginative citizenship, geared to a post-colonial era. Nor are they necessarily as gullible as some of their more pseudo-traditional leaders may suppose them to be. Like the metal workers of Port Elizabeth, South Africa, and the dockers of Port Harcourt, Nigeria, they will not always be swept off their feet by the first portly politician who swops his navy blue blazer for chic ethnic attire.

Similarly, the millions of Indians who swoon over a wicket-taking leg-break from Anil Kumble are unlikely to be hushed because one or other Hindu chauvinist moans that the mass popularity of cricket in the sub-continent shows that infernal English culture continues to dominate the minds of Asians. Understandably enough, those assimilated colonial legacies that resonate with people's concerns and values, be they a claim upon equal civil rights, a tradition of independent trade unionism, expanded civic opportunities for women outside the domestic domain, or the compulsions of cricket, continue to be re-affirmed. There can be little doubt as to their preferred place in the natural conditions of everyday life.

What, then, are we to make of the role of long-term British expansion in the development of the world? Applying the law of averages might well lead one to conclude of its impact that some part of it was positive, some of it negative and the rest of it ambiguous. Perhaps as important though, is the fact that the dead hand of the imperial past seems to have burdened its histories with the constant need to rebalance the scale between what was good and what was bad. Hence, in the eyes of its most dutiful servants and their most charitable historians it was overwhelm-ingly a positive force, standing for a modernising, tranquil and integrated world. While British economic, political and cultural objectives were rigorously pursued, for most undeveloped peoples the colonial experience was one of enlightening, orderly and peaceful progress under author-ity which was starchy, firm and fair rather than capricious and swaggering.

From a more qualified angle, the record can still appear favourable. However authoritarian or paternalis-tic in nature, British imperial power was appreciably less coercive and sordid than its Russian, French, Japanese or Belgian counterparts. In the 1930s, foaming anti-British rebellion and insurrection in the Middle East and in India was met by a pacifying Royal Commission, regulating judicial controls over orders to shoot, and the tempering hand of an effortlessly self-assured John Glubb or Glubb Pasha, a virtuous soldier who saw his mission as weaning desert Arabs off their morbid addiction to violence. What was this viewed next to Italy's wanton use of saturation bombing, gas warfare and rampaging Fascist death squads in Abyssinia?

On the other hand, flat anti-colonial denunciation might see the empire portrayed as one of the nastiest interludes in the long history of a continent like Africa, a despica-bly exploitative enterprise, which brought enslavement, plunder and misery, leaving independent states bounded by borders drawn for colonial convenience, and poorly equipped to remedy the consequences of capitalist greed, and the various failed reform and development experi-ments of colonial rule.

Ultimately, though, it is probably more fruitful to shift perspective from historical justification or historical charges to the record of the modern imperial age as a whole. Viewed in that context, British experience was inextricably part of a specific stage of European historical experience, however much the liberal assumptions of its nineteenth- and twentieth-century empire were clearly very different from those of its more autocratic continental counterparts. In practice, for all their lofty claims or uplifting intentions, modern empires, not merely those of King Leopold a century ago or of Benito Mussolini seventy years ago, or even Charles de Gaulle fifty years ago, produced greater or lesser instances of governing maladministration and callousness, as well as military atrocity and acts of terror.

Today, as the wheel comes full circle, new pretenders to world empire seem also to learn little from the bumbling of those who preceded them. In its way, the handing down of a creed of freedom and democracy branded by Walt Disney and Coca-Cola is a crude echo of the nineteenth-century intentions of Victorian Christendom to rescue benighted parts of the world for the just civilisation of a Gladstone and Disraeli.

Both moralising and ruthless, in its 2003 relieving of Iraq and its mineral resources from the tyranny of a Saddam Hussein dictatorship, the White House seems an uncanny echo of Downing Street in 1956. Then, as now, the declared target was not the Arab people and their interests, but a rogue regime – that of Colonel Gamal Abdul Nasser. In his haste to unseat a defiant Middle Eastern dictatorship, President George Bush Junior turned into a lowbrow version of Anthony Eden, without the Oxford First in Oriental Languages. There is also another – military – irony. In the 1950s, a fading British Empire failed to carry military support from a maladroit America for its disastrous Suez incursion. Today, a diminished Britain could be counted on to send its armed forces into the Middle East once again, subservient in its support of the Anglo-American alliance, come what may.

As unavoidable consequences of imperial expansion, wilful brutality, as well as the unintended outcome of fear and panic among those on the spot, would all have played their part. Yet explanation is probably best sought not in the realm of human mistakes, catastrophic blunders, ruthless levels of greed, or abnormally malevolent racism. It is, perhaps, no more there than it is in defining the essence of empire as the romanticism of doughty pioneers like William Mackinnon in East Africa or the fluttering flags of the Bengal Lancers along the Northwest Frontier. Yes, General Dyer removed a glove too many at Amritsar in 1921; landlessness, mass rural poverty and culpable negligence in India contributed to millions of deaths in nineteenth- and twentieth-century famine; Rhodes took unscrupulous and malign conduct to dizzy levels in Southern Africa in the 1890s; and nineteenth-century Queensland ranchers poisoned maize and drinking wells to exterminate Aboriginals regarded as a sub-human pestilence requiring eradication.

However, the larger question is one of more than callous or twisted human temperament, or of a mismatch between good motives, means and ends, in which it can be said that the British Empire failed to live up properly to its ethical and visionary liberal mould. The answer has to be the arrogant sense of power and superiority associated with imperialism. Inevitably, there would be a lacerating impact, if no more than as 'the consequences of consequences', or 'the fruits of fruits', in the words of the great Russian writer, Boris Pasternak. In this sense, the British may not have been entirely unlike the confident Spanish ahead of them and the French alongside.

Resolute belief in Christianity, capitalism, the Enlightenment, investor opportunity and telegraph cables encouraged the British to see themselves over a long period as a model of Western civilisation for lesser peoples around the globe. That commercial and colonising appetite reached its grandest heights of interference in the affairs of others in the later Victorian age. Then, however disquieting the realities behind the *Pax Britannica* image, however contentious the rising cost of things like imperial defence, it is hardly surprising that people were so mesmerised by the trappings of power at Queen Victoria's Diamond Jubilee in 1897.

National power, and the mix of tangibles and intangibles which formed its central nervous system – military force, prestige, insouciance, credibility, racial arrogance and fear – seemed to have acquired its shape spontaneously, just as the foaming commercial plunder that preceded it had established itself seemingly without any English national strategic plan or deliberate design. Thus, in some depictions of national self-image, what defined the British ruling classes was a rarefied tinge of Protestant self-denial or self-restraint. Maintaining a kind of restrained minimalism, they presided over palm and pine as reluctant imperialists.

Viewed in this light, much of the empire tended to be scooped up as a by-product of the economic and strategic dynamics of Britain's worldwide market expansion. So, rather than owning their empire, the British were its nightwatchman. London was content with patrolling its trade, investment and settlement interests, relying on the comfortable consent of Dominion autonomy, mildly liberal neglect of crown colonies, self-limiting indirect colonial rule, and the bejewelled ceremonials of the Raj. True, garrison force was always there on land, but essentially as a large pet guard dog to protect the calm, befitting the image of a small and independent commercial nation which saw itself as fundamentally peace-loving. The same military doctrine applied to the navy, whose job it was to keep strategically key coasts and ports free of anything foreign that menaced reliable trading exchange.

In this respect, the general notion of Britannia's Empire is turned into a fairly placid show, certainly a far cry from any greedy reflexes or splenetic displays of national power. In style, British imperialism appears as something of an anticlimax, run as a card game. One side held a small but potent body of Colonial Office bureaucrats and speculative City usurers holding a strong suit in Union Pacific or Consol or Tanganyika sisal bonds. The other held their client societies, mostly playing the same card back, as gold, copper and cotton returns, commercial concessions, harbour facilities, good land to absorb emigrants and the like.

Such an angle may have its interest, even though few of those staffing the empire were inclined to see it as incidental, as if it were some chastity belt of Victorian reticence. One could take the writer Joyce Cary, for whom

British expansion was all about striving to remake countries sorely in need of a spring cleaning – inside and out. Just over sixty years ago, Cary produced a treatise on the politics of British colonialism in Africa, *The Case for African Freedom*. 'With all its faults', he concluded brightly in 1941, British 'conquest has brought incomparably more good than harm to Africa.' The good was modern schooling, social services, a modern communications infrastructure, and the humanitarian commitment of educated and incorruptible officials, public order, and the rule of law. On top of this, there was the cultivation of an increasingly universal English language as a boon to newly literate local elites busy in politics, law and administration, and to sociable African entrepreneurs with ambitious trading and commercial aspirations.

It was an imaginative world reflected in Cary's classic novel about colonial Nigeria, *Mister Johnson*, in which the chameleon-like Johnson, a character with rather too much of England in his mind for his own good, sings of the power of the advancing Fada road in levelling the jungle:

> Out of our way, this is the king road.
> Where he flies, the great trees fall
> The sun and moon are walking on our road.

Clearing a more decent way for affairs to be run, Cary's British brought a sheltering emancipation, starting with the delivery of West Africans from the mendacity of Arab slave traders and the malpractice of idolatrous and unscrupulous tribal chiefs, and ending with district health clinics and drainage systems.

George Orwell penned a characteristically astringent foreword to the first edition of Cary's volume, hailing it as an antidote to the muddled anti-colonialism and left-wing sentimentality which imagined that African peoples could be 'set free' by the stroke of some pen, and that 'their troubles will thereupon be ended'. That may still strike a certain contemporary chord, if perhaps not quite in the way envisaged by Orwell. If the mass of African people did not deserve the various troubles brought by the authoritarian British resident, all manner of other dismal troubles have continued long after he had cleared out. For these, Alec Cook and other cadets from the Imperial Service College, Windsor, cannot continue to be held entirely responsible.

Ultimately, it remains well to be cautious about the use of any single, catch-all descriptive phrase to define British imperialism. Put simply, empire was too big, too diverse and too scattered for there to have been a universal experience for the governing and the governed. Equally, this need not mean abandoning all generalities. In the first place, it might not be too much to suggest that the British took the notion of a European world mission to its peak, and did more than any other empire to bring the world together. This went further than international financial flows and trade circuits. Emigration to trans-continental imperial destinations like Australia and New Zealand produced a British diaspora threaded together by family, occupational, sporting, religious, educational and all manner of other links. However great the difference in white Commonwealth culture between an Australian Greater Britain in the 1920s and the nation holding a republic referendum in the 1990s, the identity of a graduated Britishness has played its major part in international integration.

Secondly, for all that their empire became the largest ever, the British still knew one important thing: that they could not dominate or bully the whole world. The quintessential *Pax Britannica* of the nineteenth century was for those pink portions on the map. It was never for lording it over South America. Nor was it ever a claim to supremacy within Europe itself. There, all that Britain required was a share in international exchange and a stable balance of power.

Thirdly, African and Asian societies should not be seen as helpless victims or dupes of imperialist oppression and racism. Inhabitants of colonised countries had the knowledge and capability to influence the shape and terms of British rule in numerous and complex ways, and to tussle endlessly over the limits of their domination. Everywhere, long-term colonial rule was insupportable without the consent and complicity of African and Asian collaborators and their entitlement to a portion of its dividend. At the same time, uncertainty, unease and foreboding was the lot of all who were bound up in responsibility for the civilised order of trade and taxation, the British as much as those they excluded from power or installed into office.

Indeed, formal colonial power was if anything mostly finely balanced, short on resources, unable ever to fully resolve its contradictions and to overcome its acute dilemmas of governance – which Central African chief, and on what hierarchical claim to legitimate authority, was a district commissioner to recognise? If his administrative approval turned out to be unsound, what lay ahead was possibly a devil's country of endless disputes and head-aches. Supreme self-belief in colonial achievement from a retired admiral in Cheltenham in the 1930s was one thing. The frustrations of inter-war veterinary services, battling to overcome resistance from East African pastoralists scep-tical of livestock quarantine measures, was quite another.

A fourth point is, once more, relative. Compared with more languid, oozing empires, the pedestrian centuries of, say, earlier Byzantine or Ottoman rule, what Britain brought were more trained colonial bureaucracies, the radical transformations of industrial capitalism, formidable technological advances in control and destruction, and a large volume of long-distance migration. In that respect, what was noteworthy about this imperialism was not so much its staying power, nor even its extended scale, but the heat of its determination to open up promising territories for exploitation, and to collar those bits of the world that were essential to security and control.

New worlds were moulded as a consequence, a pro-cess which brought both costs and gains. Sometimes, this involved the bloody fragmentation and disintegration of vulnerable societies that had been there previously, as in native North America or Australia. At other times, it was through edgy adaptation to, and dependence upon, the resilient customary powers of indigenous institutions and cultures. The rule of colonial market capitalism had to co-exist with tribal law and traditional practices, which sought to conserve entrenched interests, as in East or West Africa. Tax administration under Indirect Rule was only ever possible through co-operation between colonial officials and traditional authorities. The result for the crown was frequently frustrating and sometimes comic. Equally, many cases of colonial 'civilisation' also unleashed those key historical elements of force and exploitation that constitute the effective building-blocks of virtually all modern nation-building and economic development.

The heart of the matter is that British imperial conduct was always bound to be Janus-headed, reflecting opposite sides of the same coin of the realm. In one guise it could be foul-mouthed, brutal and buccaneering. Alternatively, its appearance could be prim, stuffy and matronly, swinging a manual rather than a cutlass, and scrupulously tending to its duty. In another such picture, it could be a martinet in khaki, bristling for retribution at the slightest sign of colonial insolence. Or, again, the guise could be that of a missionary doctor, shouldering village welfare burdens without much fuss, and carrying the battle of vaccine and linen against what was viewed as stubborn rural ignorance and enslaving superstition. In a way, there can almost be no end to the painting of these miscellaneous imperial creations. A further stroke could produce a ruthless, shamelessly exploitative Caribbean planter whose degenerate lust for wealth and immersion in vice made him a kind of Caligula from Kent. Or the touchstone might be a prim, tireless, copy typist in a railway junction office, with a maternalistic decency towards the servants' children and sufficient Malay or Swahili to cajole 'cook' into baking something special for the ladies' tea.

Naturally, a mythology of a phlegmatic, common-sense empire without *too* much blood was an idea which fitted well the liberal English notion that national success derived from exemplary institutions, ideas and habits, which provided a model for a developing world. Furthermore, especially in its most bloated Victorian version, it was also about having the right temperament to go off and govern colonies through sterling qualities of command, something best possessed by men who had survived cold school showers, had once taken six of the best without flinching, could command respect and exert credible moral authority, knew the value of cultivating native goodwill, and would not mix up longitudes and latitudes.

Alongside that, back in those wet islands, it is commonplace enough to observe that empire had a pervasive impact on metropolitan life, both as conscious propaganda and as a taken-for-granted reality. The Victorians had a queen who was empress of India, sons who served in the army in Egypt or the navy in Singapore, daughters who became colonial wives, teachers and missionary workers, men who bought shares in great imperial companies or invested in land in the colonies, women who wore silks from the East, and industrial workers who cycled on rubber from Malaya, drank tea from India and China, and smoked cigarettes made from Trinidadian or Southern Rhodesian tobacco.

Through far migration, family branches set down roots half a world away, with a London pension supporting someone's living in Tasmania or Ontario. Even standard English novels found an imaginative place for the colonies, usually as a spot to which to consign burnt-out characters or from which to retrieve slightly dubious male figures, whose raffish presence smelled of tropical sexual scandal or speculative land bankruptcy. For twentieth-century Britons of the inter-war years, there was empire as a moving feast of ideology, an earnest world of make-believe peddled through cinema, wireless, exhibitions, dioramas, billboards exhorting British consumers to buy empire goods, commemorative days, popular juvenile fiction, the monarchy and the idolatry of established religion. From Lambeth to Lichfield, from music hall to the Middle Common Room, the empire paraded as symbolic proof of Britain having gained the world through its qualities of courage and ingenuity, aptitudes on which its commercial and moral superiority had come to rest.

For all this, it remains easier to talk of the appeal of a national imperial past, or of selectively mythologised versions of that past, than to know what the empire actually *meant* to a wider British public. Even in its later pre-Second World War era, outside of recorded popular responses to the varied drama, spectacle and excitement of imperialism, understanding of the nerve it touched in everyday sentiment and attitudes remains fairly elusive.

On the face of it, the growth, maintenance and continued toasting of the empire affected all classes and institutions, while anti-imperial sentiment also influenced some. Yet its place within the more humdrum sensibilities of daily routine, whether of the household, the workplace, the pub, or the dole queue, looks still to be open to some debate. Whether it was an industrialist whose grasp on empire was buying cheap and selling hard, or a High Tory grandee for which it was speculation in an overseas mining venture, experience of colonial affairs largely remained that of a distant, cigarette-card aspect of British life. Although a great deal may continue to be made of the power of empire in British consciousness, that need not be a reason to inflate it beyond what it actually was. When it came to knowing something of the colonial world, the average inhabitant of Englefield Green or Sutton Coldfield was no George Orwell.

Life within an ambience of colourful empire marketing board advertisements in the 1920s, royal visits to supplicant tribes out in the colonies in the 1930s and dinner table warnings to British children in the 1950s that Mau Mau would come for them unless they ate all their food should not lead one to assume automatically that the general British public was in any deep sense aware of what the act of empire represented. In that respect, perhaps, the sun has not yet set on H.G. Wells's famously dismissive shrug that nineteen Englishmen out of twenty knew as much about the British Empire as they did about the Italian Renaissance.

There is, then, something to be said for a view that outside of jingoistic bouts of militant imperialism, sensational colonial episodes, or hand-wringing over shameful British conduct overseas, empire was mostly taken for granted or experienced as a sideshow, a far-off reflection of the gains of national power. Generally, people merely went along with it. If anything, the overseas remoteness of empire and ignorance of its real conditions may have been part of its delegated character from the beginning, as the outer plating of a practical and knight-errant civilisation. When the Union Jack needed some hot breath as late as the early 1980s, even the Gurkhas were still on hand for the Falklands expedition.

So long as Britain was all crown sovereignty and derring-do, it could despatch its fleet to virtually any part of its coastal territories to shell troublemakers, loop its armies, traditionally small by continental standards, around the world in various minor conflicts, and mount air raids in the twentieth century to bomb Middle Eastern villagers. The most remarkable aspect of this was not the feat of immense logistical organisation, but the fact that it could be managed without imposing anything like the authoritarian militarism of the European mainland upon society at home.

Accordingly, several grim and brutal colonial wars could be waged at once by what always remained a deeply civil society, held together by a broadly liberal-democratic parliamentary system of free citizens. By the nineteenth century, routine suspensions of Habeas Corpus and absolutist rule by decree were primarily for export, to resolve threats to law and order, and to secure peace in troublesome spots overseas. To another extent, too, formal territorial empire also provided a functional use for antique, outmoded or decaying home institutions, which would otherwise have had their day. The enforced levies and militia lists of later eighteenth-century Britain lived on for further centuries to deliver colonies from crisis. Similarly, old and repressive class legislation such as Masters and Servants statutes, which had become politically indigestible in the Home Counties, could be transferred to the colonial realm for a new lease of twentieth-century life, such as imposing British labour discipline under the East African sun in the inter-war decades.

On the other hand, occasionally the truculent side of the *Pax Britannica* could be felt at home or on the London doorstep. In the 1880s, Charles Warren, a snappish

Metropolitan Police commissioner with a healthy pedigree in cracking Asian and African heads, set about radical London protesters with no particular regard for life and limb. And, less than a century later, renewed IRA troubles from Ireland brought police-military surveillance and a thinning of customary civil liberties. The liberal ethos had always found it hard going in many offshore places, and the experience of bluff colonial men who understood that was invaluable whenever it looked as if British streets could no longer be ruled by restraint. Nevertheless, up to at least the earlier twentieth century, a relaxed metropolitan society remained largely distanced from what the empire at times represented to more restive colonial inhabitants.

There, it was the spiky, illiberal underside to the constitutional magic of Westminster freedom, its hob-nailed boots drumming under the dining-room table. In turn, this suggests a certain irony. When non-European empire for the British was truly *empire*, little knowledge of its human reality came from personal experience, but for scattered or episodic deposits. These might have included the peppery settlement of black colonial subjects in port cities like Bristol, Cardiff and Liverpool, the enrolment of some Asian and African students in boarding schools and universities in the nineteenth and twentieth centuries, the posting of West Indian aircrew to Bomber Command squadrons in the Second World War, and the occasional African nationalist, like Jomo Kenyatta, bedding down amidst British anti-colonial sympathisers in such fashionable fortresses as Hampstead.

It was more when its parades were over, when British power, in a sense, started to *de-imperialise* after the Second

World War, that empire became a more commonplace and lively reality. To be more precise, rather than striking back, the empire sloshed in on a human tide of old ties, active connections, and intermingled assumptions and expectations. The Irish, naturally, were always coming to England and continued to do so, forming by far the largest post-1945 settlement group. What really changed the insular look of metropolitan society was post-war immigration and settlement from the so-called New Commonwealth. Caribbean, Asian and African incomers brought in not merely their industrial labour, commercial acumen and professional skills, but also a rich and sustaining cultural and social drapery of customs, arts, religion, food, music and sports participation.

The growth of 'non-European' British communities also reminds us of yet another of those paradoxes of empire. For centuries, up to the earlier decades of the twentieth century, a steady dribble of Africans, Asians, or Arabs from British areas had generally encountered no statutory obstacles to entering Britain as its colonial subjects. It was the crumbling of the black and brown empire which saw the multiplying of barriers from the 1960s. Today, the only remaining colonial subjects defined as fully British subjects with free rights of entry and settlement are the odd crop of loyalist islanders, notably those of the Falklands or Gibraltar. They also happen to be largely of white British ancestry. Such racial convenience aside, they are in any event unlikely ever to clog up the immigration queues at Heathrow Airport.

Still, despite no shortage from the 1960s onwards of toothy immigration controls, deportation orders, and rigid

Nationality Acts designed to make it exceptionally hard for ex-colonial subjects of the wrong skin colour to settle and to acquire full citizenship, post-imperial Britain has gone on to acquire the grain of a diverse, permanently multiracial, multicultural society. While a soggy climate and general greyness may have altered little over the centuries, the 'other' British have invigorated almost every conceivable sector of life. Whether dispersed and assimilated or concentrated and alienated, ethnic minority immigrant communities have made a 'Mother Country' contribution sufficiently extensive for it to be counted as an integral strand of modern British history.

In short, the histories of a European Britain and once-colonised non-Europeans have become shared, almost interdependent. Just as the Maori Te Atiawa had a piece of their shore rechristened as Wellington in the early nineteenth century, so Londoners in Southall found themselves passing commercial property Hinduised as Dhansay in the later twentieth century. This time, the British are the natives who find themselves accommodating to a habitat which has been translated to reflect another identity.

Naturally, recognition of all this is a far cry from the early 1950s, when around half the native population had never ever seen a black individual, when a West Indian might have had his or her skin touched for 'luck' or 'fortune', and when many black and Asian immigrants faced bilious racist hostility, enduring a repetition of the lot of Irish labourers in the previous century. While contemporary Britain is by no means free of its share of disfiguring racism and xenophobia, levels of popular feeling about 'immigration' and 'aliens' fluctuate according to changing political and economic circumstances. Overall, it is probably reasonable to venture that nationalist intolerance has grown less blatant compared with sentiment of just a few decades ago.

Politically, the molecular growth of a more capacious society has also ended up raising the notion of what has now come to constitute Britishness. For the parochial idea of an ancestral island national community safely massaged by ancient blood ties and some agreeable absorption of white Commonwealth kith and kin has haemorrhaged, obliging an old racist metropolis to confront the changing meaning of nation, and stark relationship to such factors as race, culture and identity. One part of this continuing post-colonial story is the distinct tendency for many black and brown Commonwealth settlers to personify themselves fondly as British, whereas 'home' islanders are perhaps more likely to identify themselves instinctively as English, Welsh, or Scottish.

In a way, the slow assimilation of minorities into a *national* British community has come as a late test of those old, self-serving myths of a liberal nation of basic decency and fair play. For most of their existence, the older landed empires, mostly glued together by dynastic loyalty or religious sentiment, had handled the accommodation of cultural or other minorities with less fuss and somewhat more tolerance. On the other hand, perhaps the self-indulgent Habsburgs might also have had a fiercer and more obsessively tribal mentality had they been infused with the nationhood magnetism of a King Arthur or a Wellington, or the Spanish Armada, to say nothing of Agincourt.

In this light, however much of Britain's future may lie in a growing European integration, its edgy problems with adaptation to the European Union, and its rather tepid showing of a shared European identity, are entirely understandable. It is not simply the difficulty in having had to come to terms with a loss of power, and rather slowly at that – after all, there is nothing unusual about an inflated nation finding decline humiliating and difficult to handle. Nor is it just the continuing reluctance of successive governments, whether Conservative or Labour, to abandon the risible posture of a world power role, when the operation of much British foreign policy has for decades become all but subject to the whims of the White House.

Beyond this, it is hard to miss another store of residual emotional capital. This is the archaic, almost intangible element of the redcoat and red duster. Irredeemably English imperial and imaginative, it is almost a fathomless historical image of itself. At this deeper level, the offshore independence of the British lies also in the weight of their hundreds of years of history which tugged them away from continental Europe, and in the survival of fusty oceanic sensibilities, an orientation towards a maritime global economy and societies which felt the touch of a tiller from Tilbury, Bristol, Portsmouth, or Liverpool. In an old country nourished for so long by the appeal of high water, force four to five winds, sailors and the navy, it is not for nothing that so many public houses are still called the Lord Nelson, the Crown and Anchor, the Mermaid and the Admiral Drake, or that boozy test cricket crowds at The Oval have 'Britannia rules the waves' on their lips. For times of insecurity, the empire always had its khaki and blue serge guardians, those armed banks of regulars, militias, police and expeditionary forces. Yet, its primary defensive screen was always a shrewd and commanding control of the seas. Gibraltar, Malta, the Falklands, the Cook Islands, St Helena, Ascension Island, Bermuda, Singapore and other deep water bases and small islands were the arterial annexations that supplied Britain with its necessary strategic oxygen.

The unity of its blue-water empire rested on highly effective control of the sea lanes and occupation of scattered chunks of shoreline territory to power the Royal Navy, the Royal Marines and oceanic cable terminals. This was a seamless, enduring strategy, which was always more likely to last than any alternative, not that there were many. Perhaps the least promising was a feeble aviation fantasy of the inter-war years, based on the idea of airships ballooning through an empire of the skies, binding together Croydon, Cairo and Cape Town in a kind of helium soufflé. Within this overseas residue lies much that remains hopelessly non-European about the British, inhabitants of a post-imperial country which seems somehow still to live midway between the reality of decline and the perpetual hope of renewal.

Understandably, also quietly buried there are other ingrained and fairly fiery reflexes. Something of their iron-clad ironies could be seen in the 1982 Falklands crisis, what can be termed Britain's last truly authentic independent act of empire. It was, after all, down once again to the paramount role of the Royal Navy. In a symbolically powerful showdown with Argentina, the naval romance of Palmerston and Portsmouth was hauled back into the realm of popular imagination, with a fleet putting to sea to recapture crown soil, blown on into the South Atlantic by a gale of popular jingoism. Had the Royal Navy still been able to pass through apartheid Simon's Town, the illusion of an undisputed reconquest of the waves could have looked all but complete.

In a half-comic but brilliantly euphoric judgement of what the Falklands war had represented, Margaret Thatcher turned back the clock far enough to pass earlier end-of-empire scenes, like Suez. Any impudent foreigners who tried to write off Britain would be doing so at their peril. And as for the dishonourable faint-hearts at home, those:

> who thought we could no longer do the great things we once did, those who believed our decline was irreversible, that we could never again be what we were, that Britain was no longer the nation that had built an empire and ruled a quarter of the world. Well, they were wrong.

Arguably, the Falklands success proved little of the kind, serving only to confirm the primordial survival of an imperial nerve within British society, and popular backing for war against an enemy aggressor. Once the surf had settled after the clamour around a seaborne expedition which bore the classic stamp of gunboats and colonies, it could be seen for what it was. It had been a fleeting, compensating spectacle of the waves being ruled once again, in which people could come out from making the tea to applaud the revival of an audacious Britain that was great. In vintage Palmerstonian maritime style, the unsheathed claws of the British lion had left a brazen foreign despot dripping blood.

Yet with Hong Kong relinquished, the continuing retention of superannuated small islands like the Falklands remains an historical anomaly. In time, it is surely inevitable that they, too, will be cast off. Indeed, in all but name that fate has already befallen some shuttered relics of crown dependency. Since the mid-1960s, Diego Garcia, in the territorial waters of the Chagos Islands or British Indian Ocean Territory, has been on free lease to the United States as a base for its navy and airforce. To meet the standard Pentagon demand for a cleared area, between 1965 and 1973 the Foreign Office obligingly scooped up the permanent native population of Ilois islanders and dumped them on the islands of Mauritius and the Seychelles, although not without some liberal parliamentary and press censure. British crown colony subjects were forcibly exiled so that the State Department could create its Indian Ocean version of Gibraltar. Today, there is still a quixotic island administrator with a fine mandarin hat. But with the Diego Garcia base under the command of some admiral in distant Honolulu, it is no longer the 'Queen's Peace' which is being held.

Early in the twenty-first century, it is easy to see why there remains seemingly little to do but trail behind a tubby America, seconding its most recent punitive invasions of Afghanistan and Iraq in its exorcising 'war on terror' following the attacks in New York and Washington in September 2001. For a Whitehall without an empire, there is more than a touch of irony to this revisiting of the yesterdays of Kabul in the 1870s and 1880s, and Baghdad in 1917. It is no longer the Britain of General Stanley Maude's marching Anglo-Indian Army of the Tigres, even if this may have escaped the notice of most of its tabloid dailies. For this side of the Anglo-American alliance, what seems to be left is responsibility without power. As well as a disregard of the fateful lessons of its own dubious history on bringing freedom and prosperity to Middle Eastern peoples through military invasion and occupation.

There remains the closing question of what we are left with beyond Britannia today, a point on which this book started. It still holds some of its most remote islands, like St Helena and Ascension, rocky leftovers from a time when naval power and humming cable stations held good. Assuredly, there is the Commonwealth and its useful maze of co-operative institutions and developmental organisations, but as just another member country Britain does not exactly enjoy blue-chip status. In international relations the political loyalty of most Commonwealth countries to London is at best lukewarm. Granted, the crown continues to be embedded in the constitutions of most members of the old white Dominions' club. For that matter, too, the queen continues to head the Commonwealth, but she is also the least mystical Great White Mother one is ever likely to be given.

In any event, the anachronistic palace, which resembles nothing so much as an imperial hangover, can have precious little meaning for most Third World societies or, for that matter, republican-minded Australians, South Africans, Canadians and possibly even one or two New Zealanders. The crown's Christmas message to its British subjects and citizens of the Commonwealth may well continue to prick up ears in Wiltshire, Gloucestershire and Sussex, but it cannot be expected to do much to divert Wazirabad, Khartoum and Sydney.

Many inhabitants of the ex-American colonies continue to have a nostalgic liking for all things English, not least the products of its fine-craft manufacturing traditions. Their conservative politicians, too, have a seemingly endemic weakness for the sayings of Winston Churchill. This is a habit which extends even to the current White House occupant, whose usual literary instincts can be presumed to run little further than the Western novels of Louis L'Amour. But America has been too flamboyantly republican for too long, and too concerned with its own great power standing, for its colour-postcard Anglophilia to be of any serious cultural consequence. Those like Cornwallis who bungled that War of Independence and ushered in a premature colonial freedom may have a lot to answer for.

For a sober and meaningful legacy one has to look elsewhere. Understandably, large numbers of ordinary British people today travel, work, study, or play sport in Anglophone countries, free of the old, encumbering baggage of national power and influence. Invariably, they encounter welcoming friendship from citizens of former dependent territories, where there appear to be remarkably few hard feelings aside from ritual spasms of Australian pommie-bashing.

A wider British world, centred upon the former white Dominions, but by no means exclusively confined to them, has comfortably outlived the burden of empire. Its shared, clubby cultures of language, architecture, the arts, sports, the nuts and bolts of industry and the grammar of finance attest to the vibrant legacy of British overseas expansion. Britain itself has always been a patchwork of cultures.

The gastric juice of its imperial experience has made that immeasurably more than Morris dancing, tossing the caber, or spooning mushy peas. Through their mastery of English and an English cultural literacy, Africans and Asians have added double languages and identities.

Still, in thinking about the living influences of Britishness abroad, a long view leaves us with one final thought. Just as high-water nineteenth-century imperialism preserved and fortified a particular kind of aristocratic or governing class, with its traditionalist personality and stuffy manner, so that elite and its ethos became a great export staple. Emigrant gentlemen and ladies, and younger sons and daughters who picked up jobs in colonial administration or other outlying service, went out to *be* the police, the barracks, the firm, the hospital, the school, the bench, the bar, the veterinary station, the Stock Exchange, the Anglican community and the tea planter.

Inevitably, perhaps, the dominant image of the visiting British (or English) which modern empire transmitted to much of its large global 'family' was that of a breezy, conservative, *possessing* community, keenly aware of the duties of its station – military, juridical, monied, philanthropic, religious – and with a mannered confidence, which was high-handed if not always high-minded towards those considered to be racially and culturally inferior. Bonded by authoritative accent and aloofness, it also sustained a high seasoning of 'character' quirks and oddities, exemplified by figures like the unflinchingly philanthropic Eleanor Rathbone. In her mission to protect the purity of Indian women against the corruptions of Indian men, she memorably called upon the assistance of well-heeled female

Britons, as 'the natural custodians' of 'that portion of the Imperial burden'. In the creation of a popular stereotype of the imperial British, it is surely the case that rarely in modern history has so prominent a role been played by so small a number of men and women.

Long after the closing down of their varied stations of authority, and the retreat of those pale proconsuls who used to glide about like princes in their Phantoms, a cast of ramrod soldiers of fortune, explorers, patrician law-bringers, sharp merchants, crusaders for good causes, literary and musical laureates of empire, and colonial eccentrics retain their grip upon popular imagination. Indeed, in some respects it may be easier to debunk the empire as having been a ragbag of disparate territories than to slip the hold of these festooning images. For all that the life of the Bengal Lancer has long been fading, it remains no more than half-forgotten, no more so than nostalgic views that distil the British imperial experience as a chirpy, idiotic heroism, which carried epic expeditions towards brave defeat or brilliant success, or as sentimental paternal trusteeship to develop colonial Africans and train them for a self-governing future.

What is the story of wretched Burmese coolie labour in the steam rice mills of Rangoon against that of a deluded 'Chinese' Gordon – Christian fundamentalist scourge of the heathen, whose fate it was to be martyred by those Islamic Mahdists of the Sudan, the Taliban of their time? What story is there to match that of the will of the vainglorious T.E. Lawrence in changing the course of Arab history? Even stories of planning enthusiasm which ended in hapless defeat, like the Tanganyika Ground-Nut Scheme of the 1940s, can be a cherished historical memory.

Yet the British spirit which went out into a colonial world was not only that of a Bristol Channel *ancien regime* wanting that world at its feet. There was also, almost always, contraband of one kind or another. In the sixteenth and seventeenth centuries, it was the 'White Mughals', wayward Englishmen who, instead of minding the white man's burden, melted into Indian life and immersed themselves in Muslim and Hindu ways, bridging worlds and fostering tolerance. In the later eighteenth century, it was the dissident democratic and republican instincts of British Jacobinism, the radicalism of Britons who came to regard themselves as spiritual Americans. Prominent among them was Thomas Paine, whose influence crossed the Atlantic, and for whom 1776 meant the end of corrupt imperial power and a coming spring of liberty.

In the nineteenth century, it was the emigration of English, Welsh and Scottish coal miners and textile workers to settler societies that implanted a smouldering urban tradition of trade union organisation and industrial action. Elsewhere, it was the fiercely crusading nature of some of the more formidable English Victorian women in Africa, who took up the fight against colonial injustice and imperial exploitation as an impassioned public duty. In the early twentieth century, it was the Marxist tint of campaigning anti-war London dockers, carrying their case against imperialist war and the greed of capitalist arms merchants to far-off industrial cities and ports, such as Johannesburg and Sydney.

Decades later, in the 1960s, it was the radical critics of colonialism who criss-crossed the Commonwealth, advocating its development on egalitarian or even socialist principles into a multiracial body of free equals, freed of any idea that it represented *the* British Commonwealth. For an impassioned writer of that era, such as Colin MacInnes, it was important to ensure that the Commonwealth notion did not become a homely, comforting substitute for bruised imperial feelings. In his weekly *New Statesman* journalism, MacInnes detected what he thought a larger British public wished to be told, that the creation of the Commonwealth was a sly and ingenious fix through which their country could continue to maintain all the great power benefits of imperial influence, without any of its awkward or shameful burdens. This, he snorted, was 'idiotic vanity'. However hard it might be to digest, people would have to learn that Britain had lost its power.

That meant an empire displaced, not rehabilitated into something else. However, trade would continue. Then, by finding a more modest spot in the world as the historical cousin of more populous or much larger countries, such as India and Canada, the British might come to terms more easily with their limitations, and become as realistic about their world role as they are about the capabilities of the English cricket team. After all, the imperialist British of the later nineteenth century had been perfectly aware of the relative limits of their supremacy: strong, but never strong enough to claim the entire world. In the end, they had probably been all the more effective for it.

For MacInnes some four decades or so ago, having straddled the world as a precociously unified European people, it meant the British embracing the inheritance of a wider ethnic diversity, confronting racism and discrimination, and facing up to a future of bumpy relations with the

Third World over the more cruel legacies of colonialism. It also meant the British adjusting to the reality of living as a survivor society, certainly destined to be a life less hard and uncomfortable than that of most of its ex-colonies.

Those home truths probably still hold some water now, as Britain edges ever closer to the continent, while remaining a fairly flat chorus aboard the bandwagon of European unity. If this is carrying the torch of the Labour Prime Minister, Clement Attlee, who in the late 1940s declared Britain's future to lie 'apart from America and beyond an empire', in some respects it remains in danger of falling down on the job.

Anthony Burgess was another celebrated British novelist who had no need to be told such things. He read signs early and well, not least in the defining last volume of his Malayan trilogy, *The Long Day Wanes*, in which Sayed Omar, an arthritic colonial retainer, eventually jettisons the self-deceptions of class and empire to serve a brash new master, the US Information Service. It was a shrewd conversion, which would be adopted by many others. Nothing is immutable, not even in an old country.

This is usually not the kind of image that springs instantly to mind when taking the popular measure of Britannia's Empire. Still, everything that has been said about a pious and florid imperial repertoire is all the reason, and more, for paying due regard to the grubbier elements of over-seas expansion. After all, selective, smothering nostalgia for some flag-waving world of Elizabethan ventures, a buoyant Victorian bulldog-market and the 'King's Peace' over colonies and protectorates which once were 'ours' need not be the price people pay for reminders of the imperial past.

In taking due account of that, it is as well to take account of other worldly circumstances. Many of the national masters and mistresses who have replaced the British can hardly be said to represent a humanitarian post-colonial age of labour emancipation. Trailing their baggage of monied power and influence, in some ways affluent modern Asian and African elites bear more than a passing resemblance to the old tea and rubber estate *sahibs*, with their snobbish clubs and their incessant whining about the idleness and fecklessness of the natives. It is at best debatable whether conditions for tea plantation labourers or mineworkers are very much better these days simply because capitalists and managers happen to have become natives-of-their-parts.

As for the remains of empire, its extinct forts or prisons and disused harbours or sugar mills will continue to be appropriated by the burgeoning heritage industry. Also, of course, long after the final curtain its histories can go on being remade. Much scholarship now underlines the ambiguous impact or contradictory consequences of colonialism in many places, where the unfolding of British influence and practices brought not only burdens and constraints for people, but also new opportunities for advancement and chances to extract resources in the organising of their livelihoods.

Yet, whatever the versions of empire history, it is what goes into putting them together that matters. A cue of one sort might be taken from Churchill, who in 1942 decided that empires of the future were the empires of the mind. Then, again, there is always the more prosaic vision of the impish playwright, Edward Bond. For him, 'the English sent all their bores abroad, and acquired the empire as a punishment'. Today, their financial services and technology companies appear to be sending many of their jobs abroad, acquiring cheaper workers in former parts of the empire like India. There, a sound modern education in English may convince a Surrey bank customer that she is speaking to someone in a call centre in Croydon, when it may actually be in Calcutta. This may be one of the more quizzical legacies which the East India Company has left to the great global divide between North and South.

Whatever else may be said of them, it is unlikely that the likes of Drake and Raleigh or Wolfe and Clive would have appreciated that particular Edward Bond observation. Nor, for that matter, would Tony Blair, a leader fond of the flag, displays of righteous military force and of the consoling judgement of history. In the present case of another self-serving British politician aspiring to put the world to rights through a rebirth of the long arm of moral imperialism, the jury may still be out. Were the judge to be Gladstone, it would probably not be for very long.

Whatever the wait, salutary thoughts might be provided by a more astute American from an earlier age. In a letter to a New York paper in 1900, Mark Twain denounced the Anglo-American rush for China through 'A Greeting from the Nineteenth to the Twentieth Century', presenting:

> the princely state named Christendom, returning bedraggled, besmirched and dishonest, from pirate raids in Kiao-Chou, Manchuria, South Africa and the Philippines, with her soul full of meanness, her pocket full of boodle and her mouth full of hypocrisies. Give her soap and towel, but hide the looking-glass.

Arabia's Lawrence might well have felt some sympathy with such sentiment. He might have even hidden the bathroom basics as well.

Maps

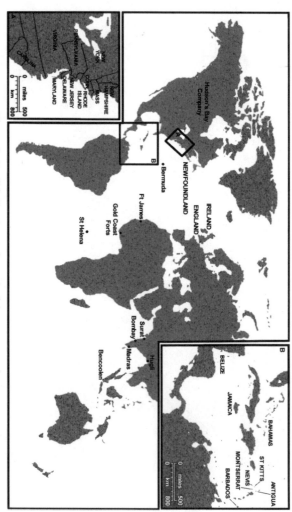

1 The early English Empire at the end of the seventeenth century

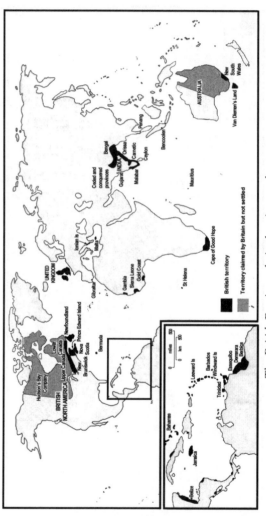

2 The British Empire early in the nineteenth century

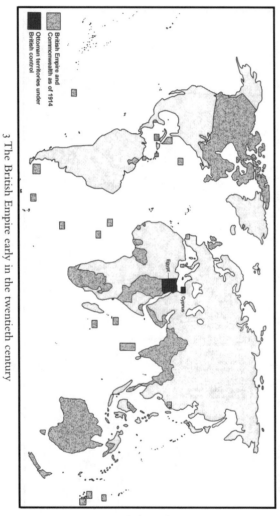

3 The British Empire early in the twentieth century

Legend:
British Empire and Commonwealth as of 1914
Ottoman territories under British control

Egypt

Cyprus

Chronology

1768	First voyage of Captain James Cook
1775	Start of War of American Independence (1775–83)
1776	Declaration of American Independence
1784	Loyalist settlement in Canada; India Act brings British government control in South Asia
1786	Malay coastal settlement at Penang
1787	Founding of Sierra Leone as free-slave settlement
1788	Establishment of New South Wales penal colony
1791	Upper and Lower Canada colonies established by Canada Act
1795	Occupation of Cape of Good Hope
1799	Conquest of Mysore
1807	Slave trade abolition
1813	Opening of East India Company India trade
1819	Acquisition of Singapore
1824	Recognition of Latin American republican independence
1829	Australia declared as British territory
1833	Abolition of slavery; seizure of Falkland Islands
1837	Abolition of East India Company China trade monopoly
1839	Start of Opium Wars with China
1840	Declaration of New Zealand as a British colony
1844	Colonial rule established in Gold Coast
1849	Repeal of Navigation Acts
1857	Outbreak of Indian Rebellion
1858	End of Indian Rebellion and assumption of overall British government rule
1860	Beginning of Maori Wars
1867	Creation of Canadian Confederation
1874	Opening of Suez Canal; annexation of Fiji
1876	Queen Victoria proclaimed as empress of India
1881	British North Borneo Company Charter
1882	Occupation of Egypt
1884	Publication of John Seeley's *The Expansion of England*
1884–85	Berlin Conference outlines spheres of influence for European scramble and partition of Africa
1885	Formation of Colonial Defence Committee; establishment of Indian National Congress
1886	Outlining of Anglo-German spheres of influence in East Africa; annexation of Burma
1888	British East Africa Company Charter; consolidation of

North Borneo, Brunei and Sarawak as protectorates
1889 British South Africa Company Charter
1895 Jameson Raid against Transvaal; establishment of East
      African protectorate
1899 Start of Anglo-Boer/South African War (1899–1902)
1901 Creation of Federal Commonwealth of Australia
1902 Establishment of preferential trade tariffs with Australia,
      New Zealand and Canada; final completion of British
      global telegraph network
1906 Formation of India Muslim League
1907 Definition of self-governing settler colonies as empire
      Dominions and formation of Dominions Department
      within Colonial Office
1910 Completion of post-war unification of South Africa
      through establishment of Union of South Africa
1912 Founding of South African Natives National Congress (ANC)
1914 Outbreak of First World War with universal empire
      involvement; unification of Northern and Southern
      Nigeria; Egypt turned into a protectorate
1917 Balfour Declaration pledges national homeland for Zionist
      Judaism
1919 Treaty of Versailles, League of Nations, imperial Mandate
      system; Amritsar massacre
1922 Formation of National Congress of British West Africa;
      qualified recognition of Egyptian independence (retention
      of Suez Canal control)
1929 Passing of Colonial Development Act
1930 Mahatma Gandhi leads civil disobedience campaign
1931 Dominion independence granted by Statute of Westminster
1932 Establishment of Imperial Preference tariff system at
      Ottowa Conference
1936 Palestinian Arab rebellion
1939 Outbreak of Second World War with independent
      Dominions backing imperial war effort
1942 Fall of Singapore to Japan
1947 Indian partition and independence of India and Pakistan
1948 Transition to apartheid in South Africa; Gandhi
      assassinated; commencement of Malayan emergency;
      withdrawal from Palestine

1952	Mau Mau rebellion in Kenya
1956	Suez Crisis
1957	Ghana and Malaya independence
1960	Nigeria and Cyprus independence; Prime Minister Harold Macmillan's 'Wind of Change' tour of Africa
1961	Tanganyika (Tanzania) and Sierra Leone independence; South Africa becomes a republic and leaves the Commonwealth
1962	Uganda, Jamaica, Trinidad and Tobago independence; Western Samoa independence
1963	Zanzibar (joined Tanganyika to form Tanzania) and Kenya independence; Sarawak and North Borneo (joined Malaya to form Malaysia) and Singapore independence
1964	Nyasaland (Malawi), Northern Rhodesia (Zambia) and Malta independence
1965	Gambia and Cook Islands independence; creation of Commonwealth Secretariat in London; formation of British Indian Ocean Territory
1966	British Guiana (Guyana), Barbados, Basutoland (Lesotho) and Bechuanaland (Botswana) independence
1967	Leeward Islands, Windward Islands and Aden (South Yemen) independence
1968	Swaziland and Mauritius independence
1970	Fiji independence
1973	Britain joins European Economic Community (EEC)
1979	Gilbert Islands (Kiribati) independence
1980	Rhodesia (Zimbabwe) independence
1982	Falklands War with Argentina
1994	South Africa rejoins Commonwealth after transition to majority rule
1997	Hong Kong relinquished to Chinese rule
2002	Death of Queen Elizabeth, The Queen Mother (former empress of India)
2003	American-Anglo invasion of Iraq
2004	Continuing dependent territories of the British crown consist of around 200 small named islands, rocks and scattered ocean outcrops. Besides Gibraltar and the Falklands, residual possessions include Isle Parasole, and Inaccessible, Barren, Candlemas, Junk and Coronation Islands

Further Reading

Usually, few things go without saying, and nowhere can this be truer than of the state of literature on British imperialism. The list of available secondary texts is longer even than the pocket of Robert Clive, and it would consume a lifetime (quite possibly, several) to wade through the mind-boggling range of books, essays, chapters and reviews, which are useful for any study of the British Empire. These encompass not only general histories of empire, but, obviously, also specialist research studies of its ideological, cultural and other dimensions, and a profusion of modern national histories which might start with Australia and end with Zimbabwe, and include Britain itself. And that is to say nothing of the richness of the imaginative literature of empire, and of colonial and post-colonial fiction, poetry and other creative writing.

As a proper bibliography would require an additional volume or two, the following small sample of general studies is restricted to more modern, lengthier books which are either of general relevance, covering the full span or a large portion of the period tackled by this volume, or which are particularly stimulating or essential. Virtually all carry their own lists of reading to open up further vistas of knowledge.

COMPLETE GENERAL HISTORIES

Stephen Howe, *Empire: A Very Short Introduction* (Oxford University Press, 2002) is a slim and digestible general introduction to global empires in world history. Few single-author texts hazard the whole story of centuries of British overseas expansion and decline. T.O. Lloyd, *The*

British Empire 1558–1983 (Oxford University Press, 1984) is detailed and accessible, while Martin Kitchen, *The British Empire and Commonwealth: A Short History* (Macmillan, 1996) is concise and squarely political in focus. Another diverting, if rather rosy, one-volume guide is Lawrence James, *The Rise and Fall of the British Empire* (Abacus, 1995). Altogether more scholarly and heavyweight is the thumping great multi-authored series, W.M. Roger Louis (ed.), *The Oxford History of the British Empire*, 5 vols (Oxford University Press, 1998–2001). The most powerful and sustained examination of the economic imperatives for empire is still P.J. Cain and A.G. Hopkins, *British Imperialism, vol.1: Innovation and Expansion 1688–1914* (Longman, 1993) and *British Imperialism, vol.2: Crisis and Deconstruction 1914–1990* (Longman, 1993). E.J. Hobsbawm, *Industry and Empire* (Weidenfeld & Nicholson, 1968) maintains its value as a classic survey of the Mother Country and the economic impact of its world power. David Cannadine's *Ornamentalism: How the British Saw Their Empire* (Allen Lane Penguin, 2001) is a stylish exploration of the empire's scaffolding of race, class, status and hierarchy. Volume III of Simon Schama's deluxe history, *A History of Britain: The Fate of Empire 1776–2001* (BBC, 2002), turns on the deep transformation of national character, from conceited assumptions of a civilising imperialism to knuckling down as a multicultural society, now dangling uneasily between continental Europe and the United States of America. Niall Ferguson, *Empire: How Britain made the Modern World* (Penguin, 2003) offers a strong emphasis on nineteenth-century economic forces, especially large British migration, and presents an essentially optimistic view of the orderly impact of empire on the world order. Explicitly encouraging the United States to learn from Britain's imperial past, it assumes the need for the world to have its top-dog nation, now the age of the wolf rather than that of the Corgi.

SUBSTANTIAL PARTIAL OVERVIEWS

An absorbing study of early English conquest and colonisation of the British Isles is provided by R.R. Davies, *The First British Empire: Power and Identities in the British Isles 1093–1343* (Oxford University Press, 2002). Angus Calder, *Revolutionary Empire: The Rise of the English-Speaking Empires from the Fifteenth Century to the 1780s* (Jonathan Cape, 1991) provides much well-organised detail and breadth of vision in its account of unfolding transatlantic developments. Linda Colley, *Captives:*

Britain, Empire and the World 1600–1850 (Jonathan Cape, 2002) underlines the essential vulnerability of earlier imperial power, and explores the careless tendency for many of its servants to fall captive to wily native opponents. P.J. Marshall (ed.), *The Cambridge Illustrated History of the British Empire* (Cambridge University Press, 1996) is a stylishly constructed and sumptuously illustrated thematic treatment of the topic from the late eighteenth century onwards. C.A. Bayly, *Imperial Meridian: The British Empire and the World 1780–1830* (Longman, 1989) is a shorter study, but provides deft and comprehensive illumination. G.C. Eldredge, *Victorian Imperialism* (Hodder, 1978) is fairly dated, yet is a fair enough reminder of an epoch when even God was an Englishman. Also dated, but unsurpassed for its evocative prose and grasp of the ironies of empire is the classic James Morris trilogy, *Pax Britannica*, consisting of *Heaven's Command: An Imperial Progress* (Faber, 1973); *Pax Britannica: The Climax of an Empire* (Faber, 1968); *Farewell the Trumpets: An Imperial Retreat* (Faber, 1978). Ronald Hyam, *Britain's Imperial Century 1815–1914: A Study of Empire and Expansion* (2nd edn, Macmillan, 1993) is mostly an argument for the role of empire in exporting and mopping up sexual energies and frustrations. Erudite and thorough in its narrative coverage, Denis Judd, *Empire: The British Imperial Experience from 1765 to the Present* (Harper Collins, 1996) is both discriminating and pungent on what it has all added up to. Bernard Porter, *The Lion's Share: A Short History of British Imperialism 1850–1995* (Longman, 1996) contends that the empire shored up British weakness in the world rather than reflecting its actual strength, and is elegant, incisive and witty. Although more about overseas policy since the 1890s than the imperial experience itself, David Reynolds, *Britannia Overruled: British Policy and World Power in the Twentieth Century* (Longman, 1991) is a clear and careful assessment of the crab-like nature of British decline.

SPECIAL THEMES

Nowadays, typical research topic subjects can be both conventional (emigration, slavery, decolonisation) and innovative (colonial masculinities, visual representations of empire, sports). The following are singled out merely as distinguished examples of a very large range of stimulating works on particular subjects. David Armitage, *The Ideological Origins of the British Empire* (Cambridge University Press, 2000) is engaging on the intellectual ways in which early imperialist impulses became bound up with domestic British history. The linkages between imperial expansion and scientific knowledge are analysed authoritatively by Richard Drayton, *Nature's Government: Science, British Imperialism and the 'Improvement' of the World* (Yale University Press, 2000). Martin Daunton and Rick Halpern (eds), *Empire and Others: British Encounters with Indigenous Peoples, 1600–1850* (University of Pennsylvania Press, 1999) opens up perspectives on the early creation of complex new social identities by imperial expansion into a vast range of societies. For a penetrating exploration of the ways in which the pale British body with its pith helmet came to serve as a symbolic instrument of imperial authority, there is E.M. Collingham, *Imperial Bodies: The Physical Experience of the Raj, c. 1800–1947* (Polity, Oxford, 2001). Prem Chowdry, *Colonial India and the Making of Empire Cinema* (Manchester University Press, 2000) is a fascinating study of the impact of imperial cinema upon Indian audiences. For a crisp and synoptic account of decolonisation and the dismantling of empire, there is John Darwin, *Britain and Decolonisation: The Retreat from Empire in the Post-War World* (Macmillan, 1988). Simon Winchester, *Outposts: Journeys to the Surviving Relics of the British Empire* (Penguin, 2003) is a wry, nostalgic and entertaining guide to the tiny oceanic remains of imperial territory, a dozen or so moribund crown islands propped up by brandy, barracks and beaches. More can be said of the continuing importance of tea, which remains one of the empire's great world conquests. Its ugly conditions of cultivation and production are not spared in a telling and highly personal investigation, Alan Macfarlane and Iris Macfarlane, *Green Gold: The Empire of Tea* (Ebury, 2003). Christopher Hitchens, *Blood, Class and Nostalgia: Anglo-American Ironies* (Chatto & Windus, London, 1990) is a rich and acerbic guide to the mutual deceptions, and self-deceptions, of the lengthy modern Anglo-American 'special relationship'. For myths about the British as a nation of homely male shopkeepers, Michael Parris, *Warrior Nation: Images of War in British Popular Culture, 1850–2000* (Reaktion, 2000) is a compelling antidote. A lively argument for metropolitan British uninterest in empire is provided by Bernard Porter, *The Absent-Minded Imperialists: Empire, Society and Culture in Britain* (Oxford University Press, 2005).

MAPS, GUIDES, CHRONOLOGY AND DOCUMENTS

A.N. Porter (ed.), *Atlas of British Overseas Expansion* (Routledge, 1991) does a fine job of charting the global growth of imperialism. A useful and highly varied collection of readings on the growth and nature of the empire is provided by Janet Samson (ed.), *The British Empire* (Oxford University Press, 2001). Alan Palmer, *Dictionary of the British Empire and Commonwealth* (John Murray, 1996) is a diverting guide to imperial personalities and institutions, and much else besides. A prodigious bibliographical guide to wide-ranging historical writings is supplied by Andrew Porter (ed.), *Bibliography of Imperial, Colonial, and Commonwealth History since 1600* (Oxford University Press, 2002).

HISTORICAL FICTION

John M. Mackenzie (ed.), *Imperialism and Popular Culture* (Manchester University Press, 1986) provides a usefully broad view on aspects of literary culture. For an accessible survey of significant historical events and associated literary texts, there is David Johnson and Prem Poddar (eds), *A Historical Companion to Postcolonial Literatures in English* (Edinburgh University Press, 2004). As to literary works themselves, after the inevitable agonising over what or whom to list here, I have decided to restrict it to volumes by a single modern author which seem to me to carry the best British historical consciousness of novels on the imperial past. Meticulously researched, they illuminate the contradictions and extremes of colonial experience with an acerbic eye and a persuasively credible evocation of varied colonial worlds. By the late J.G. Farrell, these are *Troubles* (NYRB Books, 2002) on early twentieth-century Ireland; *The Siege of Krishnapur* (Orion, 1996) and *The Hill Station* (Orion, 1993) on nineteenth-century India; and *The Singapore Grip* (Orion, 1996) on the Malayan peninsula during the Second World War. As for the large number of other creative writers on Britannia and its colonial outposts, perhaps all that is needed is a nudge to readers. Who, after all, could ask for more than an empire of stories and poems which has Rudyard Kipling, Joseph Conrad, E.M. Forster, George Orwell and Joyce Cary at one end; and Chinua Achebe, Derek Walcott, Salman Rushdie, Vikram Seth and Thomas Kenneally at the other? If your taste runs to playscripts, it should include John Arden, *Sergeant Musgrave's Dance* (Methuen, 1959).

List of Illustrations

17   Gilbey's caricature of a disaffected and bloody-minded Irish
     chieftain at Wexford in the 1790s. A 1798 secessionist rebellion
     against the Protestant governing elite at a jittery time of war
     with revolutionary France was stamped down ferociously
     by an imperial army of nearly 100,000 soldiers under Lord
     Cornwallis, determined that Sligo would not become another
     Yorktown. Courtesy of Jonathan Reeve.

18   In its pacification of upstart Catholics in the wars of the 1640s,
     Oliver Cromwell's army was not short of bloodlust: depiction
     of atrocities carried out by English forces in Ireland, 1641.
     Courtesy of Jonathan Reeve.

19   English soldiers swing through Ireland, 'that barbarous land', no
     Gaelic on their lips or bog in their breeches. The deployment
     of large expeditionary forces there was a major cost for the
     Elizabethan state. Courtesy of Jonathan Reeve.

20   The detested pennies and shillings that started it all: royal
     stamps for the American colonies, 1760s. Courtesy of Jonathan
     Reeve.

21   Those rebellious American colonists broke more than just
     George III's heart. Tempus Archive.

22   An early indication of terms for the later Anglo-American
     alliance: Lord Cornwallis with nothing left to lay down but
     his sword after defeat at Yorktown, Virginia, 1781. Courtesy of
     Jonathan Reeve.

23   English medal awarded to Indian chiefs for loyal service in the
     imperial war effort. Courtesy of Jonathan Reeve.

24   Colonel Robert Clive does his bit alongside East India
     Company troops to batter Mughal Bengal in the 1750s, soon
     netting it as a valuable commercial prize for the British. Not
     one to be left behind in the scramble, the adventurous Clive
     amassed an enormous personal fortune before he left India.
     H.E. Marshall, *Our Empire Story* (Thomas Nelson, London,
     1908).

25   An eighteenth-century country-house world in the heat of the
     East: Company officials and their families resident in pleasant
     parts of towns like Calcutta and Bombay yielded little in
     matching the swagger of the Indian gentry. Expatriates spilled
     out onto imposing greens and parklands in public displays of
     wealth and authority, turning these into a customary part of

the Anglo-Indian scene, here displayed at Bombay Green, 1767. Courtesy of Jonathan Reeve.

26 In 1799 Colonel Arthur Wellesley (the future duke of Wellington) restored the ancient rights and liberties of Hindu people by disposing of an implacable foe, Tipu Sultan, the legendary ruler of Mysore. A stiff opponent of East India Company expansion, the state of Mysore fought several eighteenth-century wars of resistance, with 'Tipoo' being demonised by the British as a cruel, satanic tyrant. His character even made it onto the London popular stage as a classic Oriental ogre. H.E. Marshall, *Our Empire Story* (Thomas Nelson, London, 1908).

27 Mughal emperor, Shah Alam, casts an expert eye over some of Robert Clive's more persuasive assets: the sovereign reviews East India Company troops in Bengal, 1760s. Courtesy of Jonathan Reeve.

28 Imperial glory and a grave for General James Wolfe in North America: in his victorious 1759 assault on Quebec, the stronghold of New France, Wolfe perished on the cliffs of the St Lawrence. Courtesy of Jonathan Reeve.

29 The sentimental pieties of European imperial fighting: Admiral Mazareddo surrenders the Spanish fleet to Admiral Nelson at Cape St Vincent in the late 1790s, with conspicuous good grace. Courtesy of Jonathan Reeve.

30 Heroes of the lawns of India: East India Company militiamen parading in Calcutta, 1802. Courtesy of Jonathan Reeve.

31 Napoleon making it difficult to rule the waves: battle engagement between a French fleet and East India Company vessels, 1804. Courtesy of Jonathan Reeve.

32 On one of his encounters with the Maori along the coasts of New Zealand in 1770, Captain James Cook explains the value of market relations and the benefits of a Westminster connection with the Pacific islands. H.E. Marshall, *Our Empire Story* (Thomas Nelson, London, 1908).

33 In the Pacific, Captain James Cook finds peace, fraternity and flowery artistry of an almost classical kind. On all of his later eighteenth-century voyages he was accompanied by artists and illustrators who portrayed a pure realm of native nobility, a benign world of nature. Courtesy of Jonathan Reeve.

34 In a land often depicted as well tamed and highly agreeable for
    European settlement in the nineteenth century, some free white
    colonists found that Australian Aboriginals were not all melting
    away. *The Boys' Own Paper*, 1909.

35 Disembarking from *The Investigator* in the early years of the
    nineteenth century, maritime explorer Matthew Flinders
    decides upon Australia as a land title, and invites its Aboriginals
    to open bidding on an attractive ship's cask. H.E. Marshall, *Our
    Empire Story* (Thomas Nelson, London, 1908).

36 The value of the bayonet in pressing home commercial
    advantage: rollicking local caricatures mocking British soldiers
    and sailors on the China coast in the 1840s, invading to
    clear trading ground for ambitious eastern firms like Jardine
    Matheson. *Narrative of the Voyages and Services of The Nemesis from
    1840 to 1843* (Henry Colburn, London, 1845).

37 A 'foreign devil' pecking at the Chinese economy: Chinese
    caricature of an English sailor in the 1839–42 Opium War.
    Courtesy of Jonathan Reeve.

38 Prince Kung, relative of the emperor and leading Chinese
    statesman of the 1850s and 1860s. Lt. G. Allgood, *China War
    1860: Letters and Journal* (Longmans Green, London, 1901).

39 A diplomat who shared Lord Palmerston's partiality to gunboats
    in dealing with those frustrating Chinese: Lord Elgin, British
    high commissioner and envoy to China. Lt. G. Allgood, *China
    War 1860: Letters and Journal* (Longmans Green, London, 1901).

40 He fell in with Sir Stamford Raffles, ceded Singapore to
    Britain, received a leg up from the East India Company in his
    contested bid for dynastic power and was proud of the baubles
    bestowed on him by the English throne: Sultan Hussein of
    Johore, a nineteenth-century Malayan ruler. *Illustrated London
    News*, March 1895.

41 Victims of the battle for peaceful commerce: Chinese fort at
    Taku on the approach to Peking, captured in 1858 by British
    forces of an Anglo-French expedition despatched to enforce
    liberal foreign trade treaties upon the Chinese empire. Lt. G.
    Allgood, *China War 1860: Letters and Journal* (Longmans Green,
    London, 1901).

42 Nothing like the tropics for those who had had enough of drab
    Victorian rituals: depiction of 'Miss Bird' at a Malayan wedding

Hot Lakes. With Maori fortunes at a low ebb by the 1890s after the loss of land and control, what their chieftainship retained was dignity of a distinctly doleful kind. *The Strand Magazine*, vol.19, 1895.

53   Plucky redcoats were indispensable to the martial cult of Victorian valour, rarely more so than here: greatly outnumbered, a small British garrison at Rorke's Drift mission station held out against a sustained onslaught by Zulu regiments in 1879, forcing attackers to withdraw. Despite, or perhaps because of, their fighting power, the Zulu came off well in the imperial imagination, respected as a fearsome but manly warrior society. H.E. Marshall, *Our Empire Story* (Thomas Nelson, London, 1908).

54   British official ready to dispense justice, enforce treaty obligations and keep an eye on customs revenues: as always, the flag had not only to be sold but also underwritten by local agents. *Illustrated London News*, June 1895.

55   The rosy African empire of water, energy, machinery, communications, technology and porters. Early twentieth-century advertisement. Courtesy of University of Cape Town Libraries.

56   Even the most juvenile of colonial Africans absorbing those essential qualities of English cricket: honesty and fair play to the other side. *Illustrated London News*, May 1906.

57   Late nineteenth-century 'railway imperialism' in tropical Africa saw the laying down of the Uganda railway from 1895, designed to develop colonial infrastructure by linking the East African hinterland to the port of Mombasa. It also went on to be a service to the Edwardian shooting aristocracy, enabling big hunters to adorn their country houses with stuffed lions or elephant tusks. Courtesy of University of Cape Town Libraries.

58   Provision for white settlers, speculators and syndicates to move through Southern Africa at an optimistic pace: Rhodesia and Mashonaland Railways supplies the pretty side of colonialism. Courtesy of University of Cape Town Libraries.

59   Late Victorian colonial preference: if British agriculture needed protection, so did the British liver. A popular pint for those imperial subjects addicted to sandals and vegetarianism. *The Graphic Queen's Diamond Jubilee Number*, June 1897.

and gorgeously clothed English commandant of the 18th
Bengal Lancers. *Navy and Army Illustrated*, March 1897.

70 One thoroughbred meeting another: an Asian elephant
obligingly accepts sugar cane from the prince of Wales on his
later nineteenth-century tour of Ceylon, relieved that it has
escaped being added to his collection of sporting trophies. *Girls'
Own Paper Annual*, 1889.

71 Thanks to British investors, merchants, entrepreneurs and
technologically minded contractors, by the end of the
nineteenth century the Indian elephant had the enviable travel
option of some 25,000 miles of railway track at its disposal.
Navy and Army Illustrated, February 1897.

72 For the Englishman prepared to travel far afield and willing to
rough it, there were few rewards greater than a tiger rug for the
drawing room. *The Boys' Own Paper*, 1909.

73 Local colonist and labour agent for the British army in the
South African War 1899–1902 holds one of the keys to imperial
victory – African camp and transport labour, however young. In
its war against the Boer Republics, British forces used roughly
100,000 black volunteers and conscripts for labouring duties.
Courtesy of the South African Library, Cape Town.

74 Earning his keep and keeping the flag: Cecil Rhodes (front,
centre) displays his knack for choosing financial associates
whose business ethics and moustaches were always above
reproach. Courtesy of Manuscripts and Archives, University of
Cape Town Libraries.

75 Scott of the Antarctic. Initially offering little other than crisp
snow, penguins and frostbite, Antarctica's frozen wastes suddenly
provided a new imperial dividend after the outbreak of the
First World War. This was whale oil, a valuable source of
glycerine for use in explosives. *The Voyages of Captain R.F. Scott,
R.N.* (Wm Green, Edinburgh, 1913).

76 Sir Herbert Baker, the grandiose architect and master of
Edwardian conceit. With Sir Edward Lutyens he designed
imperial New Delhi in the earlier twentieth century. His
worldwide buildings continue to outlive the British dominion
that they once serenaded. Courtesy of Manuscripts and
Archives, University of Cape Town Libraries.

77 Cecil Rhodes at the site of his eventual grave in 1902, the

All maps have been provided courtesy of Andrea Court.

For their expert assistance in the provision of illustrations, thanks are due to Tanya Barben of the Special Collections and Rare Books division of the University of Cape Town Libraries, Lesley Hart of the Manuscripts and Archives holdings of the University of Cape Town, Irene Staunton of Harare, Zimbabwe, Robert McKend, and the South African National Library, Cape Town.

Index

TEMPUS – REVEALING HISTORY

D-Day
The First 72 Hours
WILLIAM F. BUCKINGHAM
'A compelling narrative'
The Observer
£9.99
0 7524 2842 X

The London Monster
Terror on the Streets in 1790
JAN BONDESON
'Gripping'
The Guardian
£9.99
0 7524 3327 X

London
A Historical Companion
KENNETH PANTON
'A readable and reliable work of reference that deserves a place on every Londoner's bookshelf'
Stephen Inwood
£20
0 7524 3434 9

M: MI5's First Spymaster
ANDREW COOK
'Well-researched, penetrating and engagingly written'
Andrew Roberts
£20
0 7524 2896 9

Agincourt
A New History
ANNE CURRY
'A highly distinguished and convincing account of one of the decisive battles of the Western world'
Christopher Hibbert
£25
0 7524 2828 4

Battle of the Atlantic
MARC MILNER
'The most comprehensive short survey of the U-boat battles'
Sir John Keegan
£12.99
0 7524 3332 6

The English Resistance
The Underground War Against the Normans
PETER REX
'An invaluable rehabilitation of an ignored resistance movement'
The Sunday Times
£12.99
0 7524 3733 X

Elizabeth Wydeville: The Slandered Queen
ARLENE OKERLUND
'A penetrating, thorough and wholly convincing vindication of this unlucky queen'
Sarah Gristwood
£18.99
0 7524 3384 9

If you are interested in purchasing other books published by Tempus, or in case you have difficulty finding any Tempus books in your local bookshop, you can also place orders directly through our website

www.tempus-publishing.com

TEMPUS – REVEALING HISTORY

Quacks
Fakers and Charlatans in Medicine
ROY PORTER

'A delightful book'
The Daily Telegraph

£12.99

0 7524 2590 0

The Kings & Queens of England
MARK ORMROD

'Of the numerous books on the kings and queens of England, this is the best'
Alison Weir

£9.99

0 7524 2598 6

The Tudors
RICHARD REX

'Up-to-date, readable and reliable. The best introduction to England's most important dynasty'
David Starkey

£9.99

0 7524 3333 4

The Covent Garden Ladies
Pimp General Jack & the Extraordinary Story of Harris's List
HALLIE RUBENHOLD

'Marvellous' *Leonie Frieda*
'Compelling' *Independent on Sunday*
'Lewd' *The Daily Telegraph*

£9.99

0 7524 3739 9

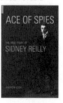
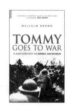

Okinawa 1945
GEORGE FEIFER

'A great book... Feifer's account of the three sides and their experiences far surpasses most books about war'
Stephen Ambrose

£17.99

0 7524 3324 5

Ace of Spies The True Story of Sidney Reilly
ANDREW COOK

'The most definitive biography of the spying ace yet written... both a compelling narrative and a myth-shattering *tour de force*'
Simon Sebag Montefiore

£12.99

0 7524 2959 0

Sex Crimes
From Renaissance to Enlightenment
W.M. NAPHY

'Wonderfully scandalous'
Diarmaid MacCulloch

£10.99

0 7524 2977 9

Tommy Goes To War
MALCOLM BROWN

'A remarkably vivid and frank account of the British soldier in the trenches'
Max Arthur

£12.99

0 7524 2980 4

If you are interested in purchasing other books published by Tempus, or in case you have difficulty finding any Tempus books in your local bookshop, you can also place orders directly through our website

www.tempus-publishing.com